W9-BRI-487

Friendship with God

• an uncommon dialogue •

BOOKS BY NEALE DONALD WALSCH

Conversations with God, book 1

Conversations with God, book 2

Conversations with God, book 3

Conversations with God, book 1 Guidebook

Meditations from Conversations with God, book 1

Meditations from Conversations with God, book 2: A Personal Journal

The Little Soul and the Sun

Questions and Answers on Conversations with God

Neale Donald Walsch on Relationships

Neale Donald Walsch on Abundance and Right Livelihood

Neale Donald Walsch on Holistic Living

Friendship with God

• an uncommon dialogue •

Neale Donald Walsch

G. P. PUTNAM'S SONS

NEW YORK

G. P. Putnam's Sons
Publishers Since 1838
a member of
Penguin Putnam Inc.
375 Hudson Street
New York, NY 10014

Copyright © 1999 by Neale Donald Walsch

All rights reserved. This book, or parts thereof, may not
be reproduced in any form without permission.
Published simultaneously in Canada

An application to register this book for cataloging has
been submitted to the Library of Congress.

ISBN 0-399-14541-9

Printed in the United States of America
1 3 5 7 9 10 8 6 4 2

This book is printed on acid-free paper. ∞

Acknowledgments

I want to again acknowledge, first and foremost, my best friend, God. I am deeply grateful to have found God in my life, deeply grateful to have made *friends* with God at last, and deeply grateful for all that God has given me—and has given me a chance to give.

On a somewhat different plane, though no less heavenly, is my friendship with my partner and wife, Nancy, who is a living definition of the word "blessing." I have been blessed from the moment we met, and in every moment since.

Nancy is an astonishing person. She radiates, from the heart of her being, a quiet wisdom, endless patience, deep compassion, and the purest love I have ever known. In a world of sometimes darkness, she is a bringer of the Light. To know her is to be reunited again with every thought I've ever had about all that is good and kind and beautiful; with every hope I've ever held about gentle and supporting companionship; and with every fantasy I've ever entertained about lovers truly in love.

I am indebted to all the wonderful people who have impacted

my life and helped me in my work, modeling behaviors and attributes and ways of *being* that have inspired and instructed me. Oh, what a priceless gift to have such teachers who show the way! Among them, I am so grateful to . . .

Kirsten Bakke, for defining absolute dependability, and showing me that spectacular, take-charge leadership never has to leave compassion, sensitivity, or caring behind.

Rita Curtis, for demonstrating stunningly that personal power does not subtract from femininity one bit but adds to it.

Ellen DeGeneres, for modeling human courage that most people do not think is possible, and for thus making it possible for every one of us.

Bob Friedman, for showing me that integrity exists, indeed.

Bill Griswold and Dan Higgs, for modeling what life-long friendship was meant to be.

Jeff Golden, for showing me that searing brilliance, passionate conviction, and gentle persuasion can go hand in hand.

Patty Hammett, for demonstrating what love, loyalty, and unwavering commitment are all about.

Anne Heche, for modeling absolute authenticity, and how not to give it up for anything.

Jerry Jampolsky and Diane Cirincione, for showing me that when humans are willing to love, there is no limit to what can be compassionately created—and gently overlooked.

Elisabeth Kübler-Ross, for showing me that it is possible to make a staggering contribution to an entire planet without being staggered, yourself, by it.

Kaela Marshall, for always modeling forgiveness when faced with the unforgiveable, allowing me to believe God's promise that there is redemption for us all.

Scott McGuire, for demonstrating stunningly that sensitivity does not subtract from masculinity one bit but adds to it.

Will Richardson, for showing me that you don't have to have had the same mother to be a brother.

Bryan L. Walsch, for role modeling steadfastness, and the importance of family.

Dennis Weaver, for showing me everything there could be to know about male grace, and about using one's gifts and celebrity to enhance the lives of others.

Marianne Williamson, for demonstrating that spiritual and temporal leadership are not mutually exclusive.

Oprah Winfrey, for modeling uncommon personal determination and bravery, and what it means to put it all on the line for what you believe.

Gary Zukav, for modeling soft wisdom, and how to find Center, and the importance of staying there.

These teachers, and many more, have I had, and from them have I learned. I know, then, that any good thing that may proceed from me has come in some degree from them, for they have taught it to me, and I have merely passed it on.

We are here to do that for each other, of course. We are all each other's teachers. Are we not truly blessed?

For

DR. ELISABETH KÜBLER-ROSS

who has changed the world's understanding
of death and life, and who first dared to speak
of a God of unconditional love with
whom we might be friends.

and for

LYMAN W. ("BILL") GRISWOLD

whose friendship of thirty years
has taught me acceptance and patience
and generosity of spirit and so many
things that names cannot name,
but souls can never forget.

Introduction

Try telling someone that you've just had a conversation with God and see what happens.

Never mind. I can tell you what happens.

Your whole life changes.

First, because you've *had* the conversation, second, because you've *told* someone about it.

To be fair, I should say that I did more than have a conversation. I've had a six-year dialogue. And I did more than "tell" someone. I kept a written record of what was said and sent it to a publisher.

Things have been very interesting ever since. And a little surprising.

The first surprise was that the publisher actually read the material and even made it into a book. The second surprise was that people actually bought the book, and even recommended it to their friends. The third surprise is that their friends recommended it to *their* friends, and even made it into a bestseller. The fourth surprise is that it is now sold in twenty-seven countries. The fifth surprise is that any of this was surprising, given who the coauthor was.

When God tells you He's going to do something, you can count on it. God always gets Her way.

God told me, in the middle of what I thought was a private dialogue, that "this will one day become a book." I didn't believe Him. Of course, I haven't believed two-thirds of what God has been telling me since the day I was born. That's been the problem. Not just with me, but with the whole human race.

If we would just listen . . .

The book that was published was called, unoriginally enough, *Conversations with God.* Now you may not believe that I've had such a conversation, and I have no need for you to believe it. It doesn't change the fact that I did. It simply makes it easier, if you choose to do so, to dismiss out of hand what I was told in that conversation—which some people have done. On the other hand, there have been many people who have not only agreed that such a conversation is possible, but have also made communicating with God a regular part of their own lives. Not just one-way communicating, but communicating *two ways.* Those people have learned to be careful about who is told of this, however. It turns out that when people say they talk to God every day, they're called devout, but when people say that God talks to *them* every day, they're called crazy.

In my case, that's perfectly okay. As I've said, I have no need for anyone to believe anything that I say. In fact, I'd rather that people listen to their own hearts, find their own truths, seek their own counsel, access their own wisdom, and, if they wish, have their own conversations with God.

If something I say *leads* them to do that—causes them to question how they've been living, and what they've believed in the past, brings them to a place of larger exploration of their own experience, moves them to make a deeper commitment to their own truth—then the sharing of my experience will have been a pretty good idea.

I think this was the idea all along. In fact, I'm convinced of it. That's why *Conversations with God* became a bestseller, as did books 2 and 3, which followed. And I think the book you are *now* reading has found its way into your hands to once again cause you to wonder, to explore, and to search for your own truth—but this time on an even larger topic: Is it possible to have more than a conversation with God? Is it possible that you can have an actual *friendship* with God?

This book says yes, and it tells you *how.* In God's own words. For in this book, happily, our dialogue continues, taking us to new places, and powerfully reiterating some of what has been told to me earlier.

I am learning that this is how my conversations with God proceed. They are circular, reviewing what has already been given, then dazzlingly spiraling into new territory. This two-steps-forward, one-step-back approach allows me to keep in mind previously shared wisdom, planting it firmly in my consciousness in order to form a solid basis for further understanding.

That is the process here. It is not without design. And while at first this process is a bit frustrating, I have come to deeply appreciate its workings. For by planting God's wisdom firmly into our consciousness, we *affect* our consciousness. We awaken it. We elevate it. And as we do so, we understand more; we come to remember more of Who We Really Are, and we begin to demonstrate that.

In these pages I am going to share a little about my past, and about how my life has changed since the publication of the *Conversations with God* trilogy. A lot of folks have asked me about all that, and that's understandable. They want to know something about this person who says he's having casual chats with the One Upstairs. Yet that's not why I'm including these anecdotes. Snippets of my "personal story" are part of this book not to satisfy people's curiosity, but to show how my life demonstrates what it's like to have a friendship with God—and how *all of our lives demonstrate the same thing.*

That's the message, of course. All of us have a friendship with God, whether we know it or not.

I was one of those who didn't know. Nor did I know where that friendship could take me. That is the great surprise here; that is the wonder. Not so much that we can and do have a friendship with God, but what that friendship was designed to bring us—and where it can take us.

We are on a journey here. There is a purpose for this friendship we're being invited to develop, a reason for its being. Until recently, I did not know the reason. I was not remembering. Now that I am, I no longer fear God, and that has changed my life.

On these pages (and in my life) I still ask plenty of questions. But now I also provide answers. That's the difference here. That's the change. I am now speaking *with* God, not merely *to* God. I am walking *alongside* God, not simply following God.

It is my deepest wish that your life will be changed in the same way as mine; that you, too, with the help and guidance of this book, will develop a very real friendship with God, and that as a result, you also will speak your word and live your life with a new authority.

It is my hope that you will no longer be a seeker, but a bringer, of the Light. For what you bring is what you will find.

God, it seems, is not looking for followers so much as leaders. We can follow God, or we can lead others *to* God. The first course will change us, the second course will change the world.

—Neale Donald Walsch
Ashland, Oregon
July 1999

One

I remember exactly when I decided I should be afraid of God. It was when He said that my mother was going to hell.

Okay, *He* didn't say it, exactly, but somebody said it on His behalf.

I was about six years old, and my mother, who considered herself somewhat of a mystic, was "reading the cards" at our kitchen table for a friend. People came to the house all the time to see what sort of divinations my mother could extract from an ordinary deck of playing cards. She was good at it, they said, and word of her abilities quietly spread.

As Mom was reading the cards on this particular day, her sister paid a surprise visit. I remember that my aunt was not very happy with the scene that she encountered, when, knocking once, she came bursting in through the back screen door. Mom acted as if she'd been caught red-handed doing something she wasn't supposed to be doing. She made an awkward introduction of her lady friend and gathered up the cards quickly, stuffing them into her apron pocket.

Nothing was said about it in that moment, but later my aunt came to say good-bye in the backyard, where I had gone to play.

"You know," she said as I walked with her to her car, "your mom shouldn't be telling people their future with that deck of hers. God is going to punish her."

"Why?" I asked.

"Because she is trafficking with the devil"—I remember that shivering phrase because of its peculiar sound to my ear—"and God will send her to straight to hell." She said this as blithely as if she were announcing that it was going to rain tomorrow. To this day I remember quaking with fear as she backed out of the driveway. I was scared to death that my mom had angered God so badly. Then and there the fear of God was deeply embedded inside me.

How could God, who is supposed to be the most benevolent creator in the universe, want to punish my mother, who was the most benevolent creature in my life, with everlasting damnation? This, my six-year-old mind begged to know. And so I came to a six-year-old's conclusion: if God was cruel enough to do something like that to my mother, who, in the eyes of everyone who knew her, was practically a saint, then it must be very easy to make Him mad—easier than *my father*—so we had all better mind our p's and q's.

I was scared of God for many years, because my fear was continually reinforced.

I remember being told in second-grade Catechism that unless a baby was baptized, it would not go to heaven. This seemed so improbable, even to second-graders, that we used to try to trip up the nun by asking pin-her-in-the-corner questions like, "Sister, Sister, what if the parents are actually taking the baby to be baptized, and the whole family dies in a terrible car crash? Wouldn't that baby get to go with her parents to heaven?"

Our nun must have come from the Old School. "No," she sighed heavily, "I'm afraid not." For her, doctrine was doctrine, there were no exceptions.

"But where would the baby go?" one of my schoolmates asked earnestly. "To hell or to purgatory?" (In good Catholic households, nine is old enough to know exactly what "hell" is.)

"The baby would go neither to hell *nor* purgatory," Sister told us. "The baby would go to limbo."

Limbo?

Limbo, Sister explained, was where God sent babies and other people who, through no fault of their own, died without being baptized into the one true faith. They weren't being punished, exactly, but they would never get to see God.

This is the God I grew up with. You may think I'm making this all up, but I'm not.

Fear of God is created by many religions and is, in fact, *encouraged* by many religions.

No one had to encourage me, I'll tell you that. If you thought I was frightened by the limbo thing, wait until you hear about the End of the World thing.

Somewhere in the early fifties I heard the story of the children of Fatima. This is a village in central Portugal, north of Lisbon, where the Blessed Virgin was said to have appeared on repeated occasions to a young girl and her two cousins. Here's what I was told about that:

The Blessed Virgin gave the children a Letter to the World, which was to be hand delivered to the Pope. He, in turn, was to open it and read its contents, but then reseal the letter, revealing its message to the public years later, if necessary.

The Pope was said to have cried for three days after reading this letter, which was said to contain terrible news of God's deep disappointment in us, and details of how He was going to have to punish the world if we didn't heed this final warning and change our ways. It would be the end of the world, and there would be moaning and gnashing of teeth and unbelievable torment.

God, we were told in catechism, was angry enough to inflict the punishment right then and there, but was having mercy on us and giving us this one last chance, because of the intercession of the Holy Mother.

The story of Our Lady of Fatima filled my heart with terror. I ran home to ask my mother if it was true. Mom said that if the priests and nuns were telling us this, it must be so. Nervous and anxious, the kids in our class pelted Sister with questions about what we could do.

"Go to Mass every day," she advised. "Say your rosary nightly and do the Stations of the Cross often. Go to confession once a week. Do penance, and offer your suffering up to God as evidence that you have turned from sin. Receive Holy Communion. And say a Perfect Act of Contrition before going to sleep each night, so that if you are taken before you wake, you'll be worthy of joining the saints in heaven."

Actually, it never occurred to me that I might *not* live 'til morning until I was taught the childhood prayer . . .

Now I lay me down to sleep,
I pray the Lord my soul to keep.

And if I die before I wake,
I pray the Lord my soul to take.

A few weeks of that and I was afraid to go to bed. I cried every night, and nobody could figure out what was wrong. To this day, I have a fixation with sudden death. Often when I leave the house for a flight out of town—or sometimes when I go to the *grocery store*—I'll say to my wife Nancy, "If I don't come back, remember that the last words I said to you were 'I love you.' " It's become a running joke, but there's a tiny piece of me that's dead serious.

My next brush with the fear of God came when I was thirteen. My childhood babysitter, Frankie Schultz, who lived across the street from us, was getting married. And he invited me—*me*—to be an usher in his wedding party! Whoa, was I proud. Until I got to school and told the nun.

"Where is the wedding taking place?" she asked suspiciously.

I gave her the name of the place.

Her voice turned to ice. "That's a Lutheran church, isn't it?"

"Well, I don't know. I didn't ask. I guess I . . ."

"It *is* a Lutheran church, and you are not to go."

"How come?" I asked.

"You are *forbidden,"* she declared, and something felt very final about that.

"But *why?"* I persisted nonetheless.

Sister looked at me as if she couldn't believe I was questioning her further. Then, clearly pulling from some deep inner source of infinite patience, she blinked twice and smiled.

"God does not want you in a heathen church, my child," the nun explained. "The people who go there do not believe as we believe. They do not teach the truth. It is a sin to attend church anywhere other than a Catholic church. I'm sorry that your friend Frankie has chosen to be married there. God will not consecrate the marriage."

"Sister," I pressed, way, *way* past the toleration point, "what if I usher at the wedding anyway?"

"Well, then," she said with genuine concern, "woe be unto you."

Whew. Heavy stuff. God was one tough hombre. There would no stepping out of line here.

Well, I stepped out of line. I wish I could report that I based my protest on higher moral grounds, but the truth is I couldn't stand the thought of not getting to wear my white sport coat (with a pink carnation—just like Pat Boone was singing about!). I decided not to tell anyone what the nun had said, and I went to that wedding as an usher. Boy, was I scared! You may think I'm exaggerating, but all day long I actually waited for God to strike me down. And during the ceremony I remained watchful for the Lutheran lies that I had been warned about, but all that the minister said were warm and wonderful things that made everyone in the church cry. Still, by the end of the service I was sopping wet.

That night I begged God on hands and knees to forgive me my transgression. I said the most Perfect Act of Contrition you've ever heard. (O my God, I am heartily sorry for having offended Thee. . . .) I lay in bed for hours, afraid to fall asleep, repeating over and over again, *and if I die before I wake, I pray the Lord my soul to take . . .*

Now, I've told you these childhood stories—and I could tell you many more—for a reason. I want to impress on you how real my fear of God was. *Because my story is not unique.*

And, as I've said, it isn't just Roman Catholics who stand in frightened pose before the Lord. Far from it. Half the world's people believe God is going to "get them" if they are not good. Fundamentalists of many religions strike fear into the hearts of their followers. You can't do this. Don't do that. Stop it, or God will punish you. And we're not talking about major prohibitions here, like Thou Shalt Not Kill. We're talking about God being upset if you eat meat on Friday (He's changed His mind on that, though), or pork *any* day of the week, or get a divorce. This is a God you will anger by failing to cover your female face with a veil, by not visiting Mecca in your lifetime, by failing to stop all activities, roll out your carpet, and prostrate yourself five times a day, by not marrying in the temple, by failing to go to confession or attending church every Sunday, *whatever.*

We have to be careful with God. The only problem is that it's hard to know the rules, because there are so many. And the most difficult thing is that everyone's rules are *right.* Or so they say. Yet they can't *all* be right. So how to choose, how to know? It's a nagging question, and not an unimportant one, given God's apparently small margin for error here.

Now along comes a book called *Friendship with God.* What can this mean? How can it be? Is it possible that God is not the Holy Desperado after all? Could it be that unbaptized babies do go to heaven? That wearing a veil or bowing to the East, remaining celibate or abstaining from pork have nothing to do with anything? That Allah loves us without condition? That Jehovah will select *all* of us to be with Him when the days of glory are at hand?

More fundamentally earthshaking, is it possible that we shouldn't be referring to God as "Him" at all? Could God be a *woman?* Or, even more unbelievably, without gender?

For a person raised as I was, even *thinking such thoughts* can be considered a sin.

Yet we have to think them. We have to challenge them. Our blind faith has led us down a blind alley. The human race has not progressed very far in the past two thousand years in terms of its spiritual evolution. We've heard teacher after teacher, master after master, lesson after lesson, and we're still exhibiting the same behaviors that have produced misery for our species since the beginning of time.

We're still killing our own kind, running our world on power and greed, sexually repressing our society, mistreating and maleducating our children, ignoring suffering, and, indeed, creating it.

It has been two thousand years since the birth of Christ, twenty-five hundred since the time of the Buddha, and more since we first heard the words of Confucius, or the wisdom of the Tao, and we still haven't gotten the Main Questions figured out. Will there ever be a way to turn the answers we have already received into something workable, something that can function in our day-to-day lives?

I think there is. And I feel pretty certain about it, because I've discussed it a lot in my conversations with God.

Two

The question I have been most frequently asked is: "How do you know you've really been talking to God? How do you know it's not your imagination? Or, worse yet, the *devil,* trying to trick you?"

The second-most asked question: "Why you? Why did God pick you?"

And the third: "What's life been like since all this happened? How have things changed?"

You would think that the most frequently asked questions would have to do with *God's words,* with the extraordinary insights and the breathtaking revelations and the challenging constructs of our dialogue—and there have been many of those inquiries, to be sure—but the most frequently asked questions have had to do with the human side of this story.

In the end, what we all want to know about is each other. We have an insatiable curiosity about our fellow human beings, more than just about anything else in the world. It's as if we somehow know that if we can learn more about one another, we can learn more about ourselves. And the yearning to know more about ourselves—about Who We Really Are—is the deepest yearning of all.

And so we ask more questions about each other's experiences than about each other's understandings. What was that like for you? How do you know that's true? What are you thinking right now? Why do you do those things? How come you feel that way?

We're constantly trying to get into each other's skin. There's an internal guidance system that directs us intuitively and compellingly toward *each other.* I believe that there is a natural mechanism, at the level of our genetic code, which contains universal intelligence. This intelligence informs our most basic responses as sentient beings. It takes eternal wisdom to the cellular level, creating what some have called the Law of Attraction.

I believe we are attracted to each other *inherently,* out of a deep knowing that in each other we will find our Selves. We may not be aware of this consciously, we may not articulate this specifically, but I think we understand this cellularly. And I believe that this microcosmic understanding derives from a macrocosmic one. I believe we know at the highest level that We Are All One.

It is this supreme awareness that pulls us toward each other, and it is the ignoring of it that creates the deepest loneliness of the human heart, and every misery of the human condition.

This is what my conversation with God has shown me: that every sadness of the human heart, every indignity of the human condition, every tragedy of the human experience, can be attributed to one human decision—the decision to withdraw from each other. The decision to ignore our supreme awareness. The decision to call the natural attraction that we have for each other "bad," and our Oneness a fiction.

In this we have denied our True Selves. And it is from this self-denial that all our negativity has sprung. All of our rage, all of our disappointment, all of our bitterness has found its birth in the death of our greatest joy. The joy of being One.

And the conflict of the human encounter is that even as we seek at the cellular level to experience our Oneness, we insist at the mental level on denying it. Thus, our thoughts about life and how it is are out of alignment with our deepest inner knowing. In essence, we are acting every day against our instincts. And this has led to our present madness, in which we persist in acting out the insanity of separateness, all the while yearning to know the joy of Oneness once again.

Can the conflict ever be resolved? Yes. It will end when we resolve our conflict with God. And that is the reason for this book.

This is a book I had no idea I was going to write. Like *Conversations with God,* it was *given* to me to share. I thought that when the *CWG* trilogy was finished, so, too, would be my "career" as an "author by accident." Then I sat down to write the Acknowledgments Page for the *Guidebook* to book 1, and I had what felt to me like a mystical experience.

I'm telling you what happened then so that you can better understand why this book is being written now. When they heard that I was writing this book, some people said to me, "I thought there was only supposed to be a trilogy?" It was as if producing more material somehow violated the integrity of the original process. So I want you to know how this book happened; how it became clear to me that I had to write it—even though now, as I sit here, I have no idea where it's going, or what it has to say.

It was spring 1997, and I had completed work on the *Guidebook.* I was nervously awaiting reaction from my publisher, Hampton Roads. Finally, the call came.

"Hey, Neale, great book!" Bob Friedman said.

"You mean it? You're not kidding?" There's always a part of me that can't believe the best and is expecting to hear the worst. So I was ready for him to say, "I'm sorry. We can't accept this. You'll have to do a complete rewrite."

"Of course I mean it," Bob chuckled. "Why would I lie to you about a thing like that? You think I want to publish a bad book?"

"Well, I just thought you might be trying to make me feel good."

"Trust me, Neale. I'm not going to try to make you feel good by telling you you've got a great book if what you've got is a stinker."

"Okay," I said warily.

Bob chuckled again. "Man, you authors are the most insecure people I know. You can't even believe someone whose livelihood depends on telling you the truth. I'm telling you, it's a great book. It's going to help a lot of people."

I let out my breath. "Okay, I believe you."

"There's only one thing."

"I knew it! I *knew* it. What's wrong?"

"Nothing's wrong. You just didn't send any acknowledgments. We just wanted to know whether you had any acknowledgments, and just forgot that page, or if you want to run without any. That's all."

"That's all?"

"That's all."

"Thank God."

Bob laughed. "Are those your acknowledgments?"

"They might as well be." I told Bob I'd e-mail him something right away. When I hung up, I let out a yelp.

"What's that about?" my wife Nancy called from the next room. I marched in triumphantly.

"Bob says the book is great."

"Oh, good," she beamed.

"Do you think he really means it?"

Nancy rolled her eyes and smiled. "I'm sure Bob's not going to lie to you about that."

"That's just what he said. There's one thing, though."

"What?"

"I've got to go write the acknowledgments."

"Well, that's no problem. You can knock something out in fifteen minutes."

Obviously, my wife should have been a publisher.

So I sat down on a Saturday morning and began my task by asking myself, "Whom do I want to acknowledge in the front of this Guidebook?" Immediately my mind said, "Well, God, of course." Yes, I argued with myself, but I thank God for everything, not just this book. "Then *do* it," my mind argued back. So I picked up a pen and wrote, *For the entirety of my life, and anything good or decent or creative or wonderful I may have done with it, I thank my dearest friend and closest companion, God.*

I remember surprising myself with the way I put that. I had never described God in quite that way, and I became consciously aware that this was exactly the way I felt. Sometimes it is only as I am writing that I come to know exactly how I feel. Have you ever had that experience? There I was, writing this, and I suddenly realized . . . you know, I *do* have a friendship with God. That's just how it feels. And my mind said, "So, write that *down.* Go ahead and *say* that." I began the second paragraph of the acknowledgments:

I have never known such a wonderful friendship—that's exactly what it feels I have going here—and I want never to miss an opportunity to acknowledge it.

Then I wrote something without having any idea why.

Someday I hope to explain to everyone in minute detail just how to develop such a friendship, and how to use *it. For God wants most of all to be used. And that's what we want as well. We want a* friendship with God. *One that's* functional *and* useful.

At precisely that point, my hand froze. A chill went up my back. I felt a major rush inside my body. I sat quietly for a moment, stunned into a complete awareness of something that a moment before I had no thought of, but which now seemed perfectly obvious.

That particular experience was not new. I'd had it often while writing *Conversations with God.* A few words, a few sentences, would fly out of my mind. And when I saw them on paper in front of me, I would suddenly be clear that this is what is so, even though a few minutes beforehand I'd had no idea about "this." The experience was usually followed by some kind of physical sensation—a sudden tingling, or what I call a happy trembling, or, sometimes, tears of joy. And, on occasion, all three.

This time it was all three. The triple whammy. So I knew that what I had written was absolute truth.

Then I received an important personal revelation—and this, too, has happened before. The feeling is one of abruptly being "aware" of something in its totality. You know it "all at once."

What I was caused to know (that is the only way I can describe it) is that I was not going to be finished with my writing at the end of the trilogy. It was suddenly clear that there were going to be at least two more books. And then a knowingness about these books, and what they would have to say, swept over me. I heard God's voice whisper . . .

Neale, your relationship with Me is no different from your relationship with each other. You begin your interactions with each other with a conversation. If that goes well, you form a friendship. And if that goes well, you experience a sense of Oneness—communion—with the other person. *It is exactly the same way with Me.*

First, we have a conversation.

Each of you experiences your conversations with God in your own way—and in different ways at different times. It will always be a two-way conversation, such as the one we are having right now. It could be a conversation "in your head," or on paper, or with My responses taking just a little more time, and reaching you in the form of the next song that you hear, or the next movie you see, or the next lecture you attend, or the next magazine article you read, or in the chance utterance of a friend whom you "just happen" to run into on the street.

Once you have become clear that we are always in conversation, then we can move into friendship. Ultimately, we will experience communion.

You are, therefore, to write two more books: *Friendship with God* and *Communion with God.* The first will deal with how to take the principles shared in your conversations with God and turn your new relationship into a fully functioning friendship. The second will reveal how to elevate that friendship into the experience of communion, and what will happen when you do. It will provide a blueprint for every seeker of truth, and will contain a breath-taking message for all humankind.

You and I *are* One right now. You simply don't know it. You do not choose to experience it—any more than you know or choose to experience your Oneness with each other.

Your books, Neale, will end that division for all those who read them. They will destroy the illusion of separation.

This is your assignment. This is your work. You are to destroy the illusion of separation.

This was always the mission. It was never anything less. Your conversations with God were always, and only, the beginning.

I was stunned. Another chill went up my back. I began to feel an inner tremble, the kind that no one can detect, but that you feel in every cell of your body. And that's what's happening, of course. Every cell of your body is vibrating at a faster rate. Oscillating at a higher frequency. Dancing with the energy of God.

That's a very good way of putting it. That's a wonderful metaphor.

Whoa, hold it! I didn't know You were going to show up so soon. I was just relating what You had said before, in 1997.

I know. I couldn't help it. I was going to wait until somewhere in the middle of the book, but you started writing very poetically, and I couldn't stay away.

Nice. That's nice.

Well, it's almost automatic, really. Whenever you write lyrically, speak poetically, smile lovingly, sing a song or dance a dance, I have to show up.

You do?

Let Me put it this way. I'm *always* there, in your life. All Ways. But you become much more *conscious* of My presence when you do these things; when you smile or love or sing or dance or write from your heart. This is the highest version of Who I Am, and when you are expressing these qualities, you are expressing Me. I mean that literally. You are *expressing* Me. That is, *pushing Me out.*

You are taking Me from the inside of you, where I always reside, and showing Me on the outside of you. And so, I seem to be "just showing up." The truth is, I am always there, and you are only in these moments aware of Me.

Yes, well, I had a lot more I was going to say here before I got into another dialogue with You.

Go ahead and say it.

Excuse me, but it's sort of hard to ignore You. Once You're here, it's difficult to pretend that You're not. It's like that stockbroker who speaks and everybody listens. Now that You've opened up the dialogue, who wants to hear from me?

A lot of people do. Probably everybody does. They want to hear how it's been for you. They want to know what you've learned. Don't retreat just because I've shown up. That's the problem with so *many* people. God shows up and they think they have to get smaller. They think they have to humble themselves.

We aren't supposed to humble ourselves in the presence of God?

I have not come to humble you, but to exalt you.

You have?

When you are exalted, so, too, am I. And when you are humbled, so, too, am I.

There is only One of Us. You and I are One.

Yes, that's what I was getting to. I was going there.

So go. Don't let Me stop you. Tell the people reading this all about your experience. They *do* want to know about that. You *were* right about that. As people get to know you, they get to know themselves.

They'll see themselves in you, and if they see that in you is Me, then they'll see that I am in them as well. And this will be a great gift. So go ahead with your story.

Well, I was saying that every cell in my body seemed to be shaking, vibrating, oscillating. I was trembling a wonderful tremble of excitement. And a tear dropped out of one eye, made its way down my cheek, and salted my tongue as I licked it from my beard. I was having that feeling again. I thought I would overflow from the inside out . . . with love.

I couldn't write another word for the acknowledgments. I had to do something with what I was just given. I wanted to begin writing *Friendship with God* right then and there.

"Hey, hey, you can't do that," my mind admonished. "You haven't even written book 3 yet." (Book 3, of course, refers to the third installment in the *Conversations with God* trilogy.)

I knew that I had to finish the trilogy before I dared start on another project. Still, I wanted to do *something* with the energy that was coursing through my veins. So I decided to call my editor at my other publishers, the Putnam Publishing Group in New York.

"You're not going to believe this," I blurted when she answered the phone, "but I've just been given the subject of *two more books* and a command to write them."

I never command anyone to do anything.

Well, I think I used the word "command" with my editor. Maybe I should have said, "And the *inspiration* to write them."

That would have been a better word, a more accurate word.

I was so excited, I wasn't watching every word I used, measuring them for accuracy.

I understand, and yet this is precisely the kind of thing that has, through the years, created a false impression about Me.

I've come here now to correct that impression. I've come to tell you what it's like to have a true *friendship with God*—and *how* you can have one.

I'm excited all over again! Begin, *begin!*

Finish your story.

Who wants to hear about that? I want to hear about *this.*

Finish your story. It has relevance. And it will bring us to the present day.

Well, I told my editor just what You told me about the next two books, and she flipped. I asked her if she thought Putnam would be interested in publishing them.

"Are you kidding? Of course we would," she said, adding that she'd like to have me write up a little summary of what I'd just told her.

I faxed something the next day, and the company very kindly gave me a two-book contract.

Why didn't you just put the books on the Internet?

What?

Why didn't you just make them available for free?

Why are You asking me this?

Because it's what many people want to know. Did the publishers offer you a lot of money?

Well, yes.

Why did you agree to take it? "If you were a man of God, you would agree to share this information with the world at no charge. You wouldn't run around signing multi-book contracts." Isn't that what some people are saying?

Exactly. They *are* saying that. They're saying I'm in it for the money.

Well?

I'm not in it for the money, but that's no reason not to take it.

A man of God would not do it.

He wouldn't? Don't priests take salaries? Don't rabbis eat?

Yes, but not very *much.* Teachers of God live in poverty, they don't demand a fortune for sharing simple truth.

I didn't demand a fortune. I didn't demand anything. I was offered it.

You should have turned it down.

Why? Who says that money is bad? If I have a chance to earn a great deal of money by sharing eternal truth, why shouldn't I?

Besides, what if I had dreams of doing extraordinary things with some of it? What if I had dreams of setting up and funding a non-profit foundation that would carry Your message around the world? What if I had dreams of making the lives of others better?

That might help a bit. That might make Me not so mad.

And what if I simply gave a great deal of it away? What if I helped others in need?

That would also help. We could understand. We could begin to accept. But you, yourself, should live very modestly. You should not spend it on yourself.

I shouldn't? I shouldn't celebrate who I am? I shouldn't live in magnificence? Have a beautiful home? Drive a new car?

No. Neither should you have fancy clothes nor eat in expensive restaurants nor buy luxurious things. You should give all the money to the poor, live as if it doesn't matter.

But that's how I *do* live! I live as if money *doesn't matter.* I spend it freely and give it away easily and share it generously and act, actually, *just that way*—as if it *doesn't matter.*

When I see something expensive that I'd like to have or do, I act as if the money doesn't matter. And when my heart calls out to me to assist another, or to do something magnificent in the world, I also act as if the money doesn't matter.

You keep acting *that* way with your money, and you're going to lose it all.

You mean *use* it all! You can't *lose* money. You can only *use* it. Money that is used is not lost. Somebody *has it!* It hasn't disappeared. The question is, who has it? If it went to people who sold me things, or did things for me that I wanted done, how did I "lose" anything? And if it goes to doing good works, or meeting the needs of others, where is the loss in that?

But if you don't hold onto it, you won't have any left.

I don't "hold onto" anything that I have! I've learned that it's when I hold onto something that I lose it. If I "hold onto" love, I may as well not have any. If I hold onto money, it is worthless. The only way to have the experience of "having" anything is to *give it away.* Then—and *only* then—can you know that you have it.

You've escaped My larger point. With your neat verbal gymnastics, you've side-stepped the issue entirely. But I'm not going to let you get away with it. I'm going to drag you back.

The point is that people who teach the *real* word of God do not, and should not, do it for the money.

Who told You that?

You did.

I did?

Yes, you did. All your life you've told Me that. Until you wrote these books and made lots of money. What made you change?

You did.

I did?

You did. You told me that money was not the root of all evil, though I might decide that the *misuse* of it was. You told me that life was created for us to *enjoy*, and that it was okay to do that. *More* than okay. You told me that money was no different from anything *else* in life—that it was all God's energy. You told me that there was nowhere that You are not, that You are expressed in, around, and through everything—indeed, that You *are* everything, the All in All—and that includes money.

You told me that all my life I have held an inaccurate view about money. That I'd made it wrong. Dirty. Unworthy. And that when I did this I was making *God* wrong, dirty, and unworthy, because money is part of Who You Are.

You told me that I had created an interesting life philosophy in which money was "bad" and love was "good." Therefore, the more loving or important to society a thing was, the less money I or anyone else should make from it.

In this, You told me, *half the world has it backwards.*

We pay our strippers and our first-basemen unfathomable sums to do what they do, while our scientists who search for a cure for AIDS, and the teachers in the classrooms with our children, and the ministers and rabbis and priests who look after our souls, live on bread and water.

You told me that this created an upside-down world in which the things we value *most* receive the least reward. And you told me that not only did this not work (if we really want to create the world we say we want to create), but it was not even necessary, because it was *not Your will at all.*

You told me that Your will was that every human being live luxuriously, and that there was nothing wrong with luxury, and that our only problem here on Earth is that we haven't yet learned how to *share* it—even after all these thousands of years.

You also made it clear that I don't teach the world anything about the real truth of money by shunning it. I only encourage the world's dysfunction by modeling that dysfunction myself.

You said it would be a far more powerful teaching if I joyfully *accepted* money—and, indeed, *all* good things in life, and joyfully shared these things as well.

I told you these things?

Yes. Without equivocation.

And you believed Me?

I sure did. In fact, these new beliefs changed my life.

Good. That's very good. You've learned well, My son. You have heard well, and you have learned well.

I *knew* it! You were just testing me. I knew that You just wanted to see how I would answer those questions.

Yes. But now I have more questions for you.

Oh, boy.

Why should people have to pay for this message? Forget about why you think it's okay for you to receive money for it. Why should people have to *give* money for it? Shouldn't the Word of God be free for all? Why not just *put it on the Internet?*

Because people are jamming the Internet night and day with thousands of words telling people about their beliefs, and why others should adopt them. Have you surfed the Web lately? There's no *end* to it. We've opened a Pandora's box.

Can you imagine how many people would have paid attention had I jumped on the Internet when this all began, to announce that I was having conversations with God? Do you really think that would have been *news* on the Internet? Excuse me.

Okay, but now your books have become very popular.

Everyone knows about them. Why not put them on the Internet now?

The reason people know that the *CWG* books have value is because other people have given something they value *for* them. It is the value that people have placed *in* them which causes them to have the value they have. All of life is people doing good things for another. That's all any of us are doing here. We're all just offering the world our "goods." When the world *agrees* that what we offer is worthwhile—whether it's fixing plumbing, baking bread, healing others, or teaching truth—the world says it is "value-able," that is, able to have value. And if we *give* a thing value by offering in exchange something of value which is ours, we not only receive the value we give—we make that thing at once more valuable for others to have as well.

And so, others are drawn to it, for people will always seek to bring value to their lives. Our system of commerce allows us to determine what is valuable and what is not.

It's not a perfect system, nor are our decisions about what to value. But this imperfect system is what we've got now. I'm working within the system to change it.

What about poor people who can't afford your books?

There are books in nearly every home in this country. It is not a question of *whether* there are books, but of *which books are there.*

Conversations with God may be found, furthermore, at virtually every library. And it is made available through a Books for Friends program to people who are in prisons, and others in need.

So I'm not getting here that the material is not available. It's been translated into many languages, and people are finding their way to it throughout the world. From Hong Kong to Tel Aviv, from Poland to Japan, from Berlin to Boston, people are reading it, studying it in groups, and sharing it with others.

I will acknowledge, however, that these have been tough questions for me. This whole issue of money in my life, and of what is appropriate to have and to do, has plagued me for decades. As You've said, in this I am no different from most of the human race.

Even today there is a part of me that thinks I should denounce the fame, denounce the financial abundance, and every other reward the *Conversations with God* trilogy has brought me. There's a huge part of me that wants to wear a hair shirt, live in a hovel, and accept nothing of the world's goods for whatever good I've given the world. My idea is that this would somehow render it worthy.

Do You see how insidious this is? I've set up a construction in which *I ask other people to value that for which I would take nothing of value.*

Yet how can I expect others to value what I do not? That is not a question I ask myself. It is too deep for me, too close to the core issue. And what value do I place on myself if I believe I must suffer for others to see my value? Another core issue. Another topic to ignore.

But, since You've raised the issue, I ask: Is Ted Turner less valuable than Mother Teresa? Is George Soros less of a good person than Ché Rivera? Are the politics of Jesse Jackson, who appears to have plenty of the good things in life, less worthy than the politics of Václav Havel, who may have less? Should the Pope, whose very garments cost more than it would take to feed a poor child for a year, have his words called blasphemy because he lives like a king as the head of a church which owns billions?

Ted Turner and George Soros have given away millions of dollars. They've empowered the dreams of humanity with the rewards of their own dreams, lived.

To empower the dreams of humanity with the living of our *own* dreams. What a magnificent idea!

Jesse Jackson has brought hope to millions with the hope that brought *him* to a place of great influence. The Pope has inspired people throughout the world and would be no more inspirational to the world's Catholics (indeed, conceivably, a great deal less) were he to appear in rags.

So I have come to terms with the fact that the *CWG* experience has brought me more of the good things in life—and given me more of the good things to share.

I want to point out here, however, that the publication of these books was not the *cause* of this happening. *You* put the cause into place *before* the books were published. In fact, that is *why* they were published and why they became so popular.

Yes, I see that this is true.

You can be *sure* that it is. Your life, and your reality around money—and *all* good things—changed when *you* changed.

They changed for *you* when you changed your mind about *them.*

Well, now, you see, I thought that You did that. I keep telling people that these books became popular because You wanted them to be. In fact, I'm kind of attracted to the idea that this was all the will of God.

Of course, you are. That relieves you of responsibility for it, and, furthermore, gives the whole thing higher credential. So I hate to burst your bubble here, but this was *not* My idea.

It wasn't?

No. It was *yours.*

Oh, great. So now I can't even say that I was inspired by God. But what about this very book I'm writing? *You came to me and told me to do this!*

Okay, this is as good a place as any to start our discussion on how to have a *friendship with God.*

Three

If you and I are to have a true friendship—a *working* friendship, and not just a friendship in theory . . .

That's important. Let's stop here and make that distinction, because that's an important distinction. Many people think that God is their friend, but they don't know how to use that friendship. They see it as a distant relationship, not a close one.

Many more people do not even think of Me as a friend at all. That's the sad part of it. Many people think of Me as a *parent,* not a friend—and a harsh, cruel, demanding, angry parent at that. A Father who will tolerate absolutely no failure in certain areas—such as, for instance, how to worship Me.

In the minds of these people, I not only demand your worship, I demand it in a specific way. It is not enough that you come to Me. You must come to Me by a particular path. Should you come to Me by another path—*any* other path—I will reject your love, ignore your entreaties, and, indeed, condemn you to hell.

Even though my search for You was sincere, my intent pure, and my understandings the best I could reach?

Even though. Yes, even though. In the minds of these people, I am a stringent parent who will accept nothing less than absolute correctness in your understandings of Who I Am.

If you are not correct in the understandings at which you have arrived, I will punish you. You can be as pure in your intent as possible; you can be so filled with love for Me that you overflow. I will cast you into the fires of hell nonetheless, and you will suffer there forever if you come to Me with the wrong name on your lips, the wrong ideas in your head.

It *is* sad that so many people see You that way. This is not how a friend would behave at all.

No, it is not. And so the very idea of having a friendship with God, the kind of relationship you have with your *best friend,* who will accept anything given in love, forgive everything done in error—*that* kind of friendship—is unfathomable to them.

Then, among those who *do* see Me as their friend, you are right; most of them hold Me at a great distance. They do not have a working friendship with Me. It is, rather, a very distant relationship that they hope they can count on if they should ever have to. But it is not the day-to-day, hour-to-hour, minute-to-minute friendship that it could be.

And You were starting to tell me what it would take to have *that* kind of friendship with You.

A change of mind and a change of heart. That is what it would take. A change of mind and a change of heart.

And courage.

Courage?

Yes. The courage to reject every notion, every idea, every teaching of a God who would reject you.

This will take enormous bravery, because the world has contrived to fill your head with those notions, ideas, and teachings. You will have to adopt a new thought about all of this, a thought that runs counter to virtually everything you've ever been told or heard about Me.

That'll be tough. For some, that'll be very tough. But it will be necessary, because you can't have a friendship—not a real, not a close, not a working, give-and-take friendship—with someone you fear.

So a big part of forging a friendship with God is forgetting our "fearship" with God.

Oh, I like that. That's not an actual word in your language, but I like it.

That's exactly what you've had with Me all these years—a *fearship with God.*

I know. I was explaining that at the outset. From the time I was a little boy I was taught to be afraid of God. And afraid of God I was. Even when I slipped out of it, I'd get talked back into it.

Finally, when I was nineteen years old, I'd rejected the God of Anger of my youth. Yet I did it not by replacing that God with a God of Love, but by rejecting God altogether. You were simply not part of my life.

This was in stark contrast to where I was just five years earlier. At fourteen, all I could think about was God. I thought the best way to avoid the wrath of God was to make God love me. I had dreams of going into the priesthood.

Everyone thought I was going to be a priest. The Sisters at school were sure of it. "He has the calling," they said. My mom was sure, too. She watched me set up an altar in our kitchen and don my "vestments" to play at saying Mass. Other kids were wearing towels as Superman capes and jumping off of chairs. I imagined the towel as my priestly garment.

Then, as I entered my last year of parochial elementary school, my father suddenly put a stop to the whole thing. We were talking about it one day, Mom and I, when Dad happened into the kitchen.

"You're not going into the seminary," he interrupted, "so don't get any ideas."

"I'm not?" I blurted. I was astonished. I'd thought it was a foregone conclusion.

"No," Dad said evenly.

"Why not?" My mom sat silently.

"Because you're not old enough to make that decision," my father declared. "You don't know what you're deciding."

"Yes, I do! I'm deciding to be a priest," I cried. "I *want* to be a priest."

"Ah, you don't know what you want," Dad growled. "You're too young to know what you want."

Mom finally said something. "Oh, Alex, let the boy have his dreams."

Dad was having none of it. "Don't encourage him," he ordered, then shot one of his "This discussion is over" looks at me. "You're not going to seminary. Get it out of your head."

I ran out of the kitchen, down the back stairs, and into the backyard. I sought refuge under my beloved lilac tree, the one that anchored the far corner of the yard, the one that bloomed not nearly often enough, not nearly long enough. But it was in bloom then. I remember smelling the incredible sweetness of the purple flowers. I buried my nose in it like Ferdinand the Bull. Then I cried.

It wasn't the first time my father had snuffed out the light of joy in my life.

At one point I thought I was going to be a pianist. I mean a professional one, like Liberace, my childhood idol. I watched him every week on television.

He was from Milwaukee, and everyone in town was agog that a local boy had made it big. There still was not a TV in every home—at least not on Milwaukee's working-class South Side—but, by golly, Dad had managed to buy a 12-inch Emerson with a black-and-white picture tube that looked like a set of parentheses. There I'd sit each week, mesmerized by Liberace's smile, his candelabra, and those ring-laden fingers flying across the keyboard.

I had perfect pitch, someone once said. I don't know if that's true or not, but I do know I could sit down at a piano and pick out a simple melody by ear as easily as I could sing it. Every time Mom took us to Grandma's house, I'd bee-line it to the upright that hugged one wall of the living room and start plunking out *Mary Had a Little Lamb,* or *Twinkle, Twinkle, Little Star.* It took me exactly two minutes to find the right notes to any new song I wanted to try, then I'd play it over and over again, excited at the deepest part of my being with the music I could make.

At this time in my life (and for many years thereafter), I also worshipped my oldest brother, Wayne, who could play the piano without reading music, too.

My mom's son from a previous relationship, Wayne was not very much in favor with my dad. In fact, that would be putting it mildly. Anything Wayne liked, Dad hated, anything Wayne did, Dad put down. Playing piano was, therefore, "for bums."

I couldn't understand why he kept saying that. I *loved* playing piano—what little I could do of it at my Grandma's—and Mom and everyone else saw that I had obvious talent.

Then one day Mom did something incredibly daring. She went out somewhere, or called someone out of the classifieds, or something, and bought an old upright player piano. I remember she'd spent twenty-five dollars on it (a lot of money in the early fifties), because Dad was upset and Mom said he had no right to be, because she'd scrimped on the grocery money for months and saved up for it. She said she hadn't hurt the family budget at all.

She must have had it delivered by the seller, because one day

I came home from school and there it was. I was out of my mind with happiness and immediately sat down to play. It didn't take long for that piano to become my best friend. I had to be the only ten-year-old on the South Side who didn't have to be browbeaten into practicing the piano. You couldn't get me *away* from the thing. Not only was I picking out familiar melodies right and left, I was making them up!

The exhilaration of finding songs inside my soul and splashing them across the keyboard was electrifying to me. The most exciting part of my day was when I came home from school or back from the playground and flew to the piano.

My father was not nearly as enthusiastic. "Stop pounding on that damned piano" was the way I believe he put it. But I was falling in love with music and my ability to make it. My fantasies of one day becoming a great pianist shifted into high gear.

Then I awoke one summer day to a terrible racket. Jumping into my clothes, I scampered downstairs to see what in the heck was going on.

Dad was taking the piano apart.

Not taking it apart, *tearing* it apart. Banging on it from the inside with a sledge hammer, then ripping it with a crowbar until the wood heaved and split with a terrible screech.

I stood transfixed, utterly shocked. Tears streamed down my cheeks. My brother saw me shaking with silent sobs and couldn't resist, "Neale is a cry baby." Dad turned from what he was doing. "Don't be an eepsie-peepsie," he said. "It was taking up too much room in here. It was time to get rid of it."

I turned on my heels and ran to my room, slammed the door (a very dangerous thing for a child to do in my house), and threw myself on the bed. I remember wailing—literally, wailing—*"No, noooo . . ."* as if my wretched pleas could save my best friend. But the pounding and ripping continued, and I buried my head in my pillow, heaving with bitterness.

I feel the pain of that experience to this day.

To this very moment.

When I refused to come out of my room for the rest of the day, my father ignored me. But when I would not leave my bed for three days more, he grew increasingly aggravated. I could hear him arguing with Mom about her bringing me food. If I wanted to eat, I could come down to the table like everyone else. And if I did come down, I was not to sulk. There was no sulking or pouting allowed in our house, at least not over a decision Dad had made. He considered such a display an open repudiation, and he would not put up with that. In our house, you not only accepted my father's domination, you accepted it with a smile.

"You keep up that crying and I'll come up there and give you something to cry *about,"* he'd bellow from the bottom floor, and he meant it.

When, even after my father's prohibition of meals, I still would not come out, he must have known he'd crossed a line with me that was larger than even he wanted to cross. Dad was not, I should say here, a heartless man, just one very much used to getting his way. He was used to not being questioned, and to not using many niceties in announcing and implementing his decisions. He grew up in an era when being the father meant being the "boss," and he didn't suffer gladly any signs of disloyalty.

It wasn't easy for him, then, to come to my room, finally, and actually knock on my door—an implied request for permission to enter. I could only guess that my mother must have worked on him pretty hard.

"It's Dad," he announced, as if I didn't know, and as if he didn't *know* that I knew. "I'd like to talk with you." It was as close as he would ever come in his life to an apology to me for anything.

"Okay," I managed, and he came in.

We talked for a long time, him sitting on the side of the bed, me propped up against the headboard. It was one of the best talks I ever had with my dad. He said that while he knew I liked playing the piano, he hadn't realized it meant so much to me. He said that all he was trying to do was make space in the family room to put our couch along the wall, because we were getting some new furniture for the living room. Then he said something I'll never forget.

"We'll get you a new piano, a spinet, which will be small enough for you to have up here, in your bedroom."

I was so excited I could hardly breathe. He said he'd start putting money aside, and that I'd have the piano in no time.

I hugged my dad long and hard. He understood me. It was going to be all right.

I went downstairs for dinner.

Weeks passed and nothing happened. I thought, "Oh, he's waiting for my birthday."

September tenth arrived, and there was no piano. I said nothing. I thought, "He's waiting 'til Christmas."

As December approached, I began holding my breath. The anticipation was almost unbearable. So was the incredible letdown when my spinet didn't arrive.

More weeks went by, more months. I don't know when it was, exactly, that I realized my father was not going to keep his promise. I do know that it wasn't until I was thirty that I realized he probably never intended to.

I had just made a promise to my oldest daughter that I knew I wasn't going to keep. It was to stop her from crying. It was to put her out of some childhood misery that I now can't remember. I don't even remember now what the promise was. I only remember saying something to mollify her. It worked. She threw her little arms around me and cried, "You're the best Daddy in the whole wide world!"

And the sins of the father were visited upon the son . . .

You took a lot of time telling that story . . .

I'm sorry. I . . .

No, no, no—that wasn't a complaint; that was an observation. I merely meant to point out that this episode has obviously become very important to you.

It is. It was.

And what have you learned from it?

Never to make a promise I can't keep. Especially with my children.

Is that all?

Never to use my knowledge of what someone else wants as a manipulative tool to get something that *I* want.

But people "trade" with each other all the time. Such trades are the basis of your entire economy, and most of your social interactions.

Yes, but there is such a thing as a "fair trade" and there is such a thing as manipulation.

What is the difference?

A fair trade is a straightforward transaction. You have something I want, I have something you want, we agree they are of more or less equal value, and so we trade. That's a clean transaction.

Then there's exploitation. That's when you have something I want and I have something you want but, they are *not* of equal value. But we do the trade anyway—one of us desperately—because he needs what the other has and will pay any price. This is what some multi-national corporations are doing when they offer seventy-four cents for an hour's work in Malaysia, Indonesia, or Taiwan. They call it economic opportunity, but it's exploitation, pure and simple.

Finally, there's manipulation. That's when I don't even have any intention of *giving* you what I am offering. In some cases, this is unconscious. That's bad enough. But in the worst cases, it's done with full awareness that what's being made is a promise one has no intention of keeping. It is a stall, a technique, designed to shut the other person up, to appease them in the here-and-now. It's a lie, and it's the worst kind of lie, because it soothes a wound that is going to be reopened, deeper, later on.

That is very good. You are growing in your understanding of what it is to have *integrity.* Integrity is important to all systems. If the integrity of any system is faulty, the system itself will collapse. No matter how sophisticated the construction, it cannot hold anything up if its integrity is compromised. Given where you say you wish to go in your life, this is good.

Yet what else have you learned?

Uh, I don't know. Is there something in particular that you're driving at?

I was hoping you had also learned something about victimhood. I was hoping you'd remembered the truth—that there are no victims and there are no villains.

Oh, that.

Yes, that. Why don't you tell Me all you know about that? You are the teacher now, you are the messenger.

There is no such thing as a victim or a villain. There are no such things as the "good guys" and the "bad guys." God created nothing but Perfection. Every soul is perfect, pure, and beautiful. In the state of forgetfulness in which they reside here on Earth, God's perfect beings may do imperfect things—or what we would *call* imperfect things—yet everything that occurs in life occurs for a perfect reason. There is no such thing as a mistake in God's world, and nothing happens by chance. Nor does any person come to You without a gift for You in his hands.

Excellent. That is very good.

Yet that's a hard one for many people. I know You made it all very clear in the *Conversations with God* trilogy, but some people are still having a hard time with that.

All things become clear in time. Those who seek a deeper understanding of this truth will find it.

Reading *The Little Soul and the Sun* will definitely help, as will rereading the trilogy.

Yes, and a number of people would do well to do that, judging from your mail.

Wait a minute! You've seen my mail?

Please.

Oh.

Do you imagine there is anything that happens in your life that I don't know about?

I suppose not. I just don't like to think about that.

Why not?

I guess because some of the stuff that's happened is stuff I'm not so proud of.

So?

So the idea that You know all about it is a bit discomforting.

Help Me understand why. You've told your best friends about some of these things through the years. You've had lengthy conversations deep into the night in which you've told your lovers some of these things.

That's different.

What's different about it?

A lover or a friend is not God. A lover or a friend knowing these things is not the same as God knowing these things.

Why not?

Because a lover or friend is not going to judge you or punish you.

I'll tell you something you may not want to hear. Your lovers and friends have judged you *and* punished through the years a lot more than I ever have. In fact, I *never* have.

Well, no, not *yet.* But on Judgment Day . . .

Here we go again.

Okay, okay, but tell it to me once more. I've got to keep hearing it.

There is no such thing as Judgment Day.

And no condemnation or punishment, ever.

None, except that which you inflict upon yourself.

Still, the idea that You know everything I've ever said or done . . .

. . . you forgot everything you've ever thought.

Okay, everything I've ever *thought,* said or done . . . is not comfortable for me.

I wish it were.

I know You do.

That's what this book is about—how to have a friendship with God.

I know. And I *do* think I now have a friendship with You. I've felt that way for a long time now. It's just that . . .

What? It's just that—what?

It's just that once in a while I revert to old patterns, and I sometimes have a hard time thinking of You that way. I still keep thinking of You as God.

Good, because I *am* God.

I know. That's the whole point. Sometimes I can't seem to think of You as "God" and "Friend" in the same breath. I can't seem to put those words in the same sentence.

That's very sad, because they belong in the same sentence.

I know, I know. You keep telling me.

What would it take for you to have a real friendship with Me, and not just some kind of artificial one?

I don't know. I'm not sure.

I know you're not, but if you thought you were, what would your answer be?

I guess I'd have to trust You.

Good. That's a good start.

And I guess I'd have to love You.

Excellent. Keep going.

Keep going?

Keep going.

I don't know what else to say.

What else do you do with your friends, besides trusting them and loving them?

Well, I try to be around them a lot.

Good. What else?

I guess I try to do things for them.

To earn their friendship?

No, because I *am* their friend.

Excellent. What else?

Um . . . I'm not sure.

Do you let them do things for you?

I try to ask as little of my friends as possible.

Why?

Because I want to keep them my friends.

You think keeping friends means asking nothing of them?

I think so, yes. At least, that's what I've been taught. The fastest way to lose friends is to impose on them.

No, that's the fastest way to find out *who your friends are.*

Perhaps . . .

Not perhaps. *Precisely.* A friend is somebody who *can't be imposed upon.* Everybody else is an acquaintance.

Wow, You draw up tough ground rules.

Those aren't My rules. Those are your own definitions. You've simply forgotten them. And so you've been mixed up about friendship. A true friendship is something to be *used.*

It's not like the expensive china that never gets used because you're afraid you'll break it. A true friendship is like Corel Ware. You can't break it no matter how many times you use it.

I have a hard time going there.

I know you do, and that's the problem. That's why you've not had a functioning friendship with Me.

So how can I get over that?

You've got to see the truth about all interactions. You've got to understand how things really work, and why people do the things they do. You've got to come to clarity about some basic principles in Life.

That's what this book is about. I'm going to help you.

But we've completely lost track of where we were. You were talking about there being no victims and no villains.

We haven't lost track of anything. It's all the same discussion.

I don't get it.

Hang on a minute, you will.

Okay. So how can I have a friendship with God?

Do the same things you would do if you had a friendship with another.

Trust You.

Trust Me.

Love You.

Love Me.

Be around You a lot.

Yes, invite Me over. Maybe even for a long stay.

Do things for You . . . although I don't have the faintest idea what *I* could do for *You.*

There's plenty. Believe Me, there is plenty.

Okay. And the last thing . . . let You do things for me.

Not only "let" Me. *Ask* Me. *Require* Me. *Command* Me.

Command You?

Command Me.

I have a hard time with that one, too. I can't even imagine doing that.

That's the whole problem, My friend. That's the whole problem.

Four

I should think it would take a lot of nerve for people to start demanding things of God.

I prefer the word "courage." Yes, I've already told you that having a true, working friendship with God will take a change of mind, a change of heart, and courage.

How can I rearrange my entire understanding of my right relationship with God to the point where I get that it's okay for me to demand things of God?

Not simply okay, but the best way to get results.

Okay, but how do I get this? How do I reach that understanding?

As I've said, you've got to understand, first, how things really work. That is, how *life* works. But we'll get into that in a minute. First, let's lay down the Seven Steps to Friendship with God.

Good, I'm ready.

One: Know God.
Two: Trust God.
Three: Love God.
Four: Embrace God.
Five: Use God.
Six: Help God.
Seven: Thank God.

You may use these same Seven Steps with anyone of whom you choose to make a friend.

You really could, couldn't you?

Yes. In fact, you probably do use them, unconsciously. If you used these steps consciously, you'd make friends with everyone you meet.

It would have been nice to have been given those steps when I was young. I was so socially inept then. My brother always made friends easily, and I never did. So I tried to make his friends my friends. It was tough on him, because I always wanted to go where he wanted to go, do what he wanted to do.

By the time I got to high school, I'd developed my own interests. I still loved music, so I joined the marching band, the choir, and the orchestra. I was also in the photography club, on the yearbook staff, and a reporter for our school newspaper. I was in the drama club, the chess club, and, perhaps most notably, on the debating team—the championship debating team, I might add.

And high school was when I got my start in broadcasting. One of the local radio stations got the idea to do a high school sports report every night, using student announcers. I was already the student public-address announcer at all of our football and basketball games, so I was a natural to be selected as the representative from our school. It was my first exposure to radio, and it launched a thirty-five-year career.

Still, with all that I was doing (or perhaps because of it), I wasn't making many friends. I'm sure that most of this had to do with the fact that I had developed an enormous ego. Partly as a compensation for my younger years when I was constantly being told by my father that I was to be "seen and not heard," and partly because I'd always been a bit of a show-off. I'm afraid that I became unbearable; not many kids in high school could stand me.

I know what that was about now. It was about seeking the approval from others that I did not feel I was getting from my father. My dad was very stingy with praise. I remember the time I won a debating tournament and came home with the trophy. My father's only comment: "I didn't expect anything less."

It's tough to feel good about yourself when a championship isn't enough to get even a little praise from your father. (The saddest part about his comment was that I know he thought it was praise.)

So I developed the habit of telling my father everything that I was doing, and about all of my accomplishments, hoping to one day hear him say, "That's incredible, son. Congratulations. I'm proud of you." I never heard it—so I began looking for it from others.

I haven't shaken the habit to this very day. I've tried to mute it, but I haven't shaken it. What's worse, my own children would probably tell you that I've been equally blasé about their achievements. And the sins of the father are visited upon the son . . .

You really *do* have a "father issue," don't you?

Do I? I hadn't thought about it in those terms.

No wonder you've had a difficult time thinking of Me as somebody who knows everything about you. No wonder you've had a problem with the concept of God at all.

Who said I've had a problem with the concept of God?

C'mon, it's okay. You can acknowledge it. Half the population of your planet has that problem, and for largely the same reason: they see God as a kind of "parent." They imagine I'm going to be like their mother or father.

Well, You *are* called "God the Father."

Yes, and whoever came up with that should be ashamed.

I believe it was Jesus.

No. Jesus merely used the idioms and the language of his day—just as you are doing here. He didn't invent the idea of God as a father.

He didn't?

The patriarchy, with its patriarchal religions, had established itself long before Jesus.

Then You are not "Our Father, who art in heaven?"

No, I am not. Anymore than I am your Mother in heaven.

Well, then, who *are You?* We've been trying to figure this out for thousands of years. Why don't You give us a break and just *tell* us!

The problem is that you insist on personifying Me, and *I am not a person.*

I know that. And I think most people know that. But it sometimes helps us to think of You as a person. We can relate to You better.

But *can* you? That's the question. Can you? I'm not so sure you can.

One thing I will say: keep thinking of Me as a *parent,* and you'll have a devil of a time.

I'm sure that was just a turn-of-phrase.

Of course.

Well, if we aren't supposed to think of You as a parent, how should we think of You?

As a friend.

"Our Friend, who art in heaven"?

Exactly.

Boy, would *that* turn some heads around on Sunday morning.

Yes, and it might also turn some *thinking* around.

Yet, if we *could* all think of You as a friend rather than a parent, it might make it possible for some people to really relate to You at last.

You mean they might one day become comfortable with Me knowing what their friends and lovers know?

Touché.

So what do you say—do you want a friendship with God?

I thought I already had one.

You did. You do. But you haven't been acting like it. You've been acting as if I'm your parent.

Okay, I'm ready to get off that. I'm ready to have a fully functioning friendship with You.

Great. So here's how to do that. Here's how the whole human race can have a friendship with God . . .

Five

First, you have to know Me.

I thought I did know You.

Only casually. You don't know Me intimately yet. We've had a good conversation—at last—but it's going to take more than that.

Fine. So how can I get to know You better?

Willingness.

Willingness?

You have to have a real willingness. You have to be willing to see Me where you find Me, not only where you expect to find Me.

You have to see Me where you find Me—and find Me where you see Me.

I don't understand what that means.

A lot of people see Me but don't find Me. It's like a cosmic game of *Where's Waldo?* They're looking right at Me, but they don't find Me.

But how can we make sure we recognize You?

That's a great word you chose to use there. To "recognize" is to "know again." That is, to re-*cognize.*

You have to come to know Me again.

How do we do that?

First, you must believe that I exist. Belief precedes willingness as a tool with which to know God. You must believe that there is a God to know.

Most people do believe in God. Surveys show that in recent years belief in God has actually increased on our planet.

Yes, I'm happy to say that the largest number of you *do* believe in Me. So it's not your belief *in* Me that creates problems, it's your belief *about* Me.

One of the things you believe about Me is that I do not want you to know Me. Some of you even believe that you dare not so much as utter My name. Others feel that you should not write the word "God," but, out of respect, should write "G-D." Still others of you say that it's all right to speak My name, but that it must be My *correct* name, and that if it's an incorrect name, you will have committed a blasphemy.

But whether you call Me Jehovah, Yaweh, God, Allah, or Charlie, I am still Who I am, What I am, Where I am, and I will not stop loving you because you got my name wrong, for heaven sake.

So you can stop quarreling over what to call Me.

It's pitiful, isn't it?

That's your word, reflecting a judgment. I'm merely observing what's so.

Even many of those religions which are *not* arguing about My name are teaching that for you to seek too much knowledge of God is unwise, and for you to say that God has actually *talked* to you is heresy.

So, while a belief IN God is necessary, your belief ABOUT God is also important.

That's where willingness comes in. You must not only *believe* in God to know Me, you must also be willing to *really know Me*—not simply know what you *think* you know about Me.

If your beliefs about Me make it impossible to know Me as I really am, then all the belief in the world won't work. You'll continue to know what you think you know, instead of what is really so.

You must be willing to suspend what you imagine you

already know about God in order to know God as you never imagined.

That is the key here, because you have many imaginings about God which bear no resemblance to reality.

How can I get to this place of willingness?

You are already there, or you wouldn't be spending time with this book. Now, expand on this experience. Open yourself to new ideas, new possibilities about Me. If I was your best friend, and not your "father," think of what you could tell Me, what you could ask of Me!

In order to know God, you have to be "ready, willing, and able." Belief in God is the beginning. Your belief in *some* sort of higher power, in *some* kind of Deity, makes you "ready."

Next, your openness to some new thoughts about God—thoughts you've never had before, thoughts that may even shake you up a bit, like "Our Friend, who art in heaven"—signals that you are "willing."

Finally, you must be "able." If you are simply unable to see God in any of the new ways to which you have opened yourself, you will have completely dis-*abled* the mechanism by which you would come to know God in truth.

You must be able to embrace a God who loves and embraces *you,* without condition; be able to welcome into your life a God who welcomes you into the kingdom, no questions asked; be able to stop punishing yourself for acknowledging a God who will not be punishing you; and be able to talk with a God who has never stopped talking to you.

All of these are radical ideas. The churches do indeed call these heresies. And so, in the irony of all ironies, you may have to abandon the church in order *to* know God. Without a doubt, you will have to at least abandon some of the church's teachings. For churches teach of a God whom you are told you cannot know, and whom you would not choose as a friend. For what friend would you have who would punish you for your every misdeed? And what kind of friend considers it a misdeed to simply be called by the wrong name?

In my *Conversations with God* I was told many things which contradicted everything I thought I knew about You.

I know that you believe in God, or you could never have had conversations with God to begin with. So you were "ready" to have a friendship with Me, but were you "willing"? I see that you were—because willingness takes great courage, and you've demonstrated that courage, not only by exploring other, non-traditional, points of view, but by doing so publicly. Thus, your conversation not only allowed *you* to undertake these explorations, but millions of others along with you. They did so vicariously, through your three published books, which have been eagerly read worldwide—a huge signal that the general public is willing now, too.

Are you "able" now to know Me, and thus have more than just a conversation, but also a friendship, with God?

Yes, because I have had no trouble moving from my old beliefs about You to an acceptance of the new ideas about You which were given me in the *Conversations.* In fact, to be truthful, many of those ideas were ideas I already had.

In this sense, the *CWG* trilogy was not so much a revelation as it was a confirmation.

My mail over the past five years tells me it was that way for thousands of others as well. And this is as good a place as any to tell the story of how the book was written.

The *Conversations with God* dialogue was not written *as* a book. Unlike the material I am now writing. I had no idea, when the dialogue began, that it was ever going to see print. As far as I knew, I was having a private process, to which no one else would ever be privy.

That process began on a night in February of 1992 when I was on the verge of falling into chronic depression. Nothing had been going right in my life. My relationship with my significant other was kaput, my career had hit a dead end, and even my health was failing.

Usually in my life it had been one thing or another, but now it was everything at once. The whole construction was collapsing, and I couldn't seem to do anything to stop it.

It wasn't the first time that I'd stood by helplessly, watching what I had thought would be a permanent relationship dissolve right before my eyes.

Nor was it the second, or third, or fourth.

I was becoming very angry about my inability to hold a relationship together, my apparent total lack of understanding about what it takes to do that, and the fact that nothing I tried seemed to work.

I was coming to feel that I had simply not been given the equipment to play the game of Life, and I was furious.

My career wasn't going any better. Things had pretty much dwindled to nothing, my over thirty years of hovering around the broadcasting and journalism businesses reaping pitifully meager rewards. I was forty-eight years old with nothing much to show for a half century on the planet.

Not surprisingly, my health had taken a downhill turn as well. I'd suffered a broken neck in a car accident a few years before and hadn't ever fully recovered. Prior to that in my life, I'd had a collapsed lung and suffered from ulcers, arthritis, and severe allergies. I felt at forty-eight as if my body was falling apart. And so it was that on a February night in 1992, I awoke with anger in my heart.

Tossing and turning as I tried to go back to sleep, I was a mountain of frustration. Finally, I threw back the covers and stomped out of the bedroom. I went where I always go in the middle of the night when I'm seeking wisdom—but there was nothing decent in the refrigerator, so I found myself on the couch instead.

There I sat, stewing in my own juice.

Finally, in the moonlight streaming through the window, I saw a yellow legal pad on the coffee table in front of me. I picked it up, found a pen, flicked on a lamp, and began writing an angry letter to God.

What does it take to make life WORK????? What have I done to deserve a life of such continuing struggle? And what are the rules here? Somebody tell me the RULES! I'll play, but first somebody has to tell me the rules. And after you tell me, don't change them!!!

On and on like that I wrote, scribbling madly all over the pad—writing very large, as I do when I am angry, pressing down so hard that a person could hold a sheet five pages lower up to the light and see what I had written.

Finally, I'd emptied myself out. The anger, frustration, and near-hysteria had dissipated, and I remember thinking, I've got to tell my friends about this. A yellow legal pad in the middle of the night might be the best therapy, after all.

I held out my arm to put down the pen, but it wouldn't leave my hand. That's amazing, I thought to myself. A few minutes of intensive writing and your hand cramps so badly, you can't even let go of the pen.

I waited for my muscles to relax but was struck instead with a feeling that there was something more I needed to write. I watched as I brought pen back to paper, fascinating myself even as I did it, because I knew of nothing more that I wanted to write. Yet here I was acting as if there was more to be written.

No sooner had the pen reached the pad than my mind filled with a thought. The thought was *said* to me, by a *voice*. It was the softest, kindest, most gentle voice I had ever heard. Except that it wasn't a voice. It was a . . . what I could only call a voiceless voice . . . or maybe, more like . . . like a feeling that had words all over it.

The words that I "heard" in this way were:

> **Neale, do you really want answers to all of these questions, or are you just venting?**

I remember thinking, *I AM venting, but if you've got answers, I'd sure as hell like to know what they are.* To which I received the reply:

You ARE "sure as hell"—about a lot of things. But wouldn't you rather be "sure as heaven"?

And I found myself answering, *What in the hell is that supposed to mean?*

Thereafter came the most extraordinary thoughts, ideas, communications, call them what you will, that I've ever experienced. The thoughts were so stunning that I found myself writing them down—*and responding to them.* The ideas being given to me (through me?) were answering my questions, but they were also bringing up other questions I'd never had before. So here I was, having a pen-and-paper "dialogue."

It went on for three hours, and then suddenly it was 7:30 in the morning and the house was starting to come alive, so I put the pen and pad away. It was an interesting experience, but I didn't make much more of it—until the next night when I was awakened out of a sound sleep, at 4:20 in the morning, as abruptly as if someone had come into the room and flipped the light switch. I sat up in bed, wondering what *that* was all about, when I felt an urgent pull to get out of bed and back to the yellow legal pad.

Still wondering what was going on, and why, I stumbled around the house, found the pad, and returned to my nesting place on the living room sofa. I began writing again—picking up right where I had left off, asking questions and receiving answers.

I don't think I know to this day what made me begin to write it all down, or save the stuff I'd written. I guess I thought I was going to be keeping a journal, or a special little diary. I had no idea that it would one day be published, let alone read from Tokyo to Toronto, San Francisco to São Paulo.

It is true that at one point in the dialogue the voice said, "This will one day become a book." But I thought to myself, *Yeah, you and a hundred other people are going to send your middle-of-the-night mental meanderings to a publisher, who is going to say, "Of course! Why, we'll publish this AT ONCE."* And that first dialogue went on for a year—me being awakened in the darkness at least three nights a week.

One of the questions I am most frequently asked is, When did I decide, when did I know, that it was God I was talking to? During the first several weeks of the experience I didn't know what to think about what was happening. At first a part of me thought I was just talking to myself. Then somewhere along the way I wondered if it couldn't be my so-called "higher self" I'd heard about from which I was drawing the answers to my questions. But finally, I had to let go of my self-judgments and fear of ridicule and call it exactly what it seemed to be: a conversation with God.

This occurred the night I heard the statement, "There is no such thing as the Ten Commandments."

Nearly half of what ultimately became book 1 had been written when this spectacular assertion was made. I'd been exploring the question of the path to God, and which was the "right" one. Do we earn our way to heaven by "being good," I wanted to know, or are we free to act as we wish without being punished by God?

"Which is it," I asked, "traditional values, or make-it-up-as-you-go-along? Which is it? The Ten Commandments or the Seven Steps to Enlightenment?"

When the reply was that the Ten Commandments don't exist, I was flabbergasted. Even more flabbergasting, though, was the explanation.

Oh, there had been ten statements all right, and they'd been given to Moses for sure, but they were not "commandments." They were, I was told, "commitments" made by God to the human race; ways that we could know that we were on the path back to God.

This was unlike anything else in the dialogue to that point. This was breakthrough information. Some of what I'd heard in the conversation up until that moment I knew I had heard before, from other teachers or other sources, or perhaps read somewhere. But such astonishing statements about the Ten Commandments I knew I'd *never* heard before. Furthermore, these ideas violated everything I'd ever been taught, or thought, about the subject.

Years later I received a letter from a theology professor at a major East Coast university saying this was the most original new perspective on the Ten Commandments to be published in three hundred years, and that while he wasn't sure he agreed with *CWG*'s statements, they would provide his theology classes with rich material for serious debate and discussion for many terms to come. At the time, though, I didn't need any letters from theology professors to know that what I'd heard was very special—and came from a very special source.

I began to experience that source as God. Nothing has changed my mind about it since. In fact, the information which came through in the rest of the eight-hundred-page dialogue—including the extraordinary information about life among Highly Evolved Beings in the Universe in book 3, and the outline for building a new society on Planet Earth in book 2—has only made me more convinced than ever.

I'm very glad to hear that. And it's interesting that you should point to this portion of our dialogue, because this was also the section where I last talked about knowing God.

It was there that I said, "In order to truly know God, you have to be out of your mind."

Come to Me, I said, along the path of your heart, not through a journey of your mind. You will never find Me in your mind.

In other words, you can't really know Me if you think about Me too much. That's because your thoughts contain nothing more than your previous ideas about God. Yet the reality of Me will not be found in your previous ideas, but in your present moment *experience.*

Think of it this way: your mind holds the past, your body holds the present, your soul holds the future.

Put another way, the mind analyses and remembers, the body experiences and feels, the soul observes and knows.

If you want to access what you remember about God, look to your mind. If you want to access what you feel about God, look to your body. If you want to access what you know about God, look to your soul.

I'm confused. I thought that feelings were the language of the soul.

They are. Yet your soul talks through your body, which gives you a here-and-now experience of your truth. If you want to know your truth on any subject, look to your feelings. Checking in with your body is the fastest way of doing this.

I see. I call that giving it the "Tummy Test." There's an old saying, "The tummy knows."

And it's true. Your stomach actually provides you with a very good barometer. So if you want to get in touch with what your soul knows about the future—including the possibilities surrounding your future experience of God, listen to your body—listen to what your body is telling you right now.

Your soul knows everything—past, present, *and* future. It knows Who You Are, and Who You Seek to Be. It knows Me, intimately, because it is the part of Me that is closest to you.

Oh, wow, I *like* that. "The soul is the part of God that is closest to you." What a great statement!

And it's true. So to know Me, all you have to do is truly know your own soul.

To have a friendship with God, all I really have to do is have a friendship with my Self.

Exactly.

That sounds so *simple.* It's almost too good to be true.

It's true. Trust Me. But it's not simple. If knowing your Self, much less having a friendship with your Self, was simple, you would have done it a long time ago.

Can You help me?

That's what we're doing here. I'm going to lead you back to your Self . . . and thus, lead you back to Me. And this you will one day do for others. You will give people back to themselves—and thus, back to Me. For when you find your Self, you find Me. There I have always been, and there I will always be.

How can I have a friendship with my Self?

By coming to know Who You Really Are. And by becoming clear about who you are not.

I thought I *have* had a friendship with my Self. I like me a lot! Maybe a bit *too* much. As I said, if I've had any personality problem in my life, it's been my ego.

A big ego is not a sign that one likes oneself, but just the opposite.

If people "brag" and "show off" a lot, it raises the question, what do they dislike about themselves so much that they feel they have to get others to like them to compensate?

Whoa. That almost hurts.

A painful observation is almost always a truthful one. You are having growing pains, My son. It's all right.

So you mean I really *don't* like myself that much, and I'm trying to compensate for lack of self-love by substituting the love of others?

Only you can know that. Yet you're the one who said you had an ego problem. I observe that true self-love disappears the ego, it does not enlarge it. Put another way, the larger your understanding of Who You Really Are, the smaller your ego.

When you know Who You Really Are fully, your ego is fully gone.

But my ego is my sense of myself, no?

No. Your ego is who you *think* that you are. It has nothing to do with Who You Really Are.

Doesn't this contradict an earlier teaching that it's okay to have an ego?

It is okay to have an ego. In fact, it's *very* okay, because an "ego" is necessary in order for you to have the experience you are now having, as what you imagine to be a separate entity in a relative world.

Okay, now I'm thoroughly confused.

That's okay. Confusion is the first step toward wisdom. Folly is thinking you have all the answers.

Can You help me here? Is it good to have an ego, or not?

That's a big question.

You've entered the relative world—what I call the Realm of the Relative—in order to experience what you cannot experience in the Realm of the Absolute. What you seek to experience is Who You Really Are. In the Realm of the Absolute, you can know this, but you cannot experience it. The desire of your soul is to know itself *experientially.* The reason that you cannot experience any aspect of Who You Are in the Realm of the Absolute is that in this realm, there is no aspect you are *not.*

The Absolute is just that—the *absolute.* The All of Everything. The Alpha *and* the Omega, with nothing in between. There are no degrees of "Absoluteness." Degrees of things can only exist in the Relative.

The Realm of the Relative was created so that you can know your Self as magnificent, experientially. In the Realm of the Absolute, there is nothing but magnificence, and so magnificence "is not." That is, it cannot be experienced, it cannot be known experientially, because there is no way to experience magnificence in the absence of that which is not magnificent. In truth, you are One with everything. That is your magnificence! Yet you cannot know the magnificence of being One with everything while you are One with everything, because there is nothing else, and so, being One with everything means nothing. In your experience, you are simply "you," and you have no experience of the magnificence of that.

The only way for you to experience the magnificence of

being One with everything is for there to be some state or condition in which *not* being One with everything is possible. Yet since everything is One in the Realm of the Absolute—which is the ultimate reality—something not being One with everything is impossible.

What is not impossible, however, is the *illusion* of not being One with everything. It was for the purpose of creating this illusion, then, that the Realm of the Relative was created. It is like an Alice-in-Wonderland world, in which things are not what they seem to be, and in which things seem to be what they are not.

Your ego is your chief tool in creating this illusion. It is that device which allows you to imagine your Self as separate from All the Rest of You. It is the part of you that thinks of you as being an individual.

You are *not* an individual, yet you must be individualized in order to comprehend and appreciate the experience of the whole. And so in this sense, it is "good" to have an ego. Given what you are trying to do, it is "good."

Yet too *much* ego is—given what you are trying to do—"not good." That's because what you are trying to do is use the illusion of separateness to better comprehend and appreciate the experience of Oneness, which is Who You Really Are.

When the ego becomes so enlarged that all you can see is the separate Self, all chance of experiencing the unified Self is gone, and you are lost. You have literally become lost in the world of your illusion, and you may remain lost in that illusion for many lifetimes, until you finally bring your Self out of it, or until somebody else—another soul—

pulls you out. This is what is meant by "giving you back to yourself." This is what the Christian churches meant by their concept of a "savior." The only mistake those churches made was in declaring themselves and their religions to be the *only* way to be "saved," thus reinforcing once again the illusion of separateness—the very illusion from which they would seek to save you!

So, you ask if it is good to have an ego, and that is a very large question. It all depends on what you are trying to do.

If you are using the ego as a tool with which to ultimately experience the Only Reality, it is good. If the ego is using *you* to *stop* you from experiencing that reality, then it is *not* good. To the degree that it is stopping you from doing what you came here to do, it is "not good."

Yet you are always at free choice about what you remain here to do. If you find it enjoyable to *not* experience your Self as part of the One, you will be given the choice of not having that experience just now. Only when you've had enough of the separateness, enough of the illusion, enough of the loneliness and the painfulness, will you seek to find your way home, and then you will find that I will be there—that I have *always* been there.

All ways.

Whoa. Ask a question, get an answer.

Especially when you're asking God.

Yes, I see. I mean, it's not as if You have to stop and think about these things.

No, the answer is right there, on the tip of My tongue. It's right on the tip of your tongue, too, I might add.

What does that mean?

I mean I'm not keeping these answers to Myself. I never have been. All the answers to all of life's questions are, quite literally, on the tip of your tongue.

That's another way of saying, "As you speak it, so will it be."

Well, according to that, if I say that everything You say is hogwash, then all that You've just told me is not true.

That's true.

No, it's *not* true.

I mean, it's true that it's not true.

But if I say that everything You say is not true, then *it's not true* that it's not true.

That's true.

Unless it's not.

Unless it's not.

You see, you are creating your own reality.

That's what You say.

That's right.

But if I don't believe what You say . . .

. . . then you will not experience it as your reality. But catch the closed circle here—because if you do not believe that you create your own reality, then you will experience your reality as something you did not create . . . *proving that you create your own reality.*

Oh, boy, I feel like I'm in the Hall of Mirrors.

You are, My wonderful one. In more ways than you could know. For everything that you see is a reflection of you. And if the mirrors of life show you distortions, it is a reflection of your distorted thoughts about you.

That gets me back to where I was before we got off on this tangent.

There are no tangents, My son, only different routes to the same destination.

I was asking you how I can have a friendship with myself. You said I can know God when I know my own soul; that I can have a friendship with God when I have a friendship with myself. And I asked You how I can do that. I thought I had a friendship with myself already.

Some people do, some people don't. For some people, at best what they have is a truce.

Maybe what You said about a large ego being a sign that I do not like myself is true. I'm going to think about that.

It's not that people don't like themselves completely. It's just that there's a *part* of themselves they don't like, and so the ego compensates by trying to get other people to like them. Of course, they don't *show* the part of themselves they don't like to others until this growing intimacy of a relationship makes it impossible not to. When they finally do, and when the other person acts surprised, and maybe even negatively, then they can assure themselves that they were right about this aspect of themselves being unlikable—and the whole circle continues.

It's a very complex process, and you move through it every day.

You should have been a psychologist.

I *invented* psychology.

I know. I was just kidding.

I know. You see, "kidding" is a thing people do when they—

Enough!

You're right. Enough. I was just kidding.

You make me laugh, You know that?

I make *you* laugh? You make Me laugh.

That's what I like, a God with a sense of humor.

Laughter is good for the soul.

Couldn't agree more, but could we get back to the question? How can I have a friendship with myself?

By coming to clarity on Who You Really Are—and who you are not.

Once you know Who You Really Are, you'll fall in love with your Self.

Once you fall in love with your Self, you'll fall in love with Me.

How can I come to clarity about who I am and who I am not?

Let's start with who you are not first, because this is where the biggest problem is.

Okay, Who am I not?

You are not—first and foremost I want to tell you that you are not—your past. You are not your yesterdays.

You are not what you did yesterday, what you said yesterday, what you thought yesterday.

A lot of people are going to want you to *think* that you are your yesterdays. In fact, some others are going to *insist that you be.* They will do this because they have a big investment in your continuing to show up that way. For one thing, they can then be "right" about you. For another, they can then "depend" on you.

When other people see you as "bad," they don't want you to change, because they want to continue being "right" about you. This allows them to *justify* how they are treating you.

When other people see you as "good," they don't want you to change, because they want to continue being able to "depend" on you. This allows them to justify how they expect you to treat them.

What you are invited to do is live in the moment. Create your Self anew in the present moment.

This allows you to separate your Self from your former ideas about you—a remarkable percentage of which are foundationed in *other* people's ideas about *you.*

How can I forget my past? Other people's ideas about me are based, in part at least, on their experience of me—on my behaviors—in the past. What do I do, just forget that I did those things? Pretend they don't matter?

Neither.

Do not seek to forget your past, seek to change your future.

The *worst* thing you could do is forget your past. Forget your past and you forget all that it has to show you, all that it gave you as its gift.

Neither pretend that it doesn't matter. Rather, acknowledge that it *does* matter—and that, precisely *because* it does, you have decided not to repeat certain behaviors ever again.

Yet, once you have made that decision, *let go* of your past. Letting go of it does not mean forgetting it. It means stopping the holding on, ending the clinging to your past as if you are going to drown without it. You are drowning *because* of it.

Stop using your past to keep you afloat in your ideas of Who You Are. Let *go* of these old logs and swim to a new shore.

Even people with a wonderful past are not served by holding onto it as if that is Who They Are. This is called "resting on your laurels," and nothing stops growth faster.

Neither rest on your laurels nor dwell on your failures. Rather, start over; begin anew in each golden moment of Now.

But how can I change behaviors that have become habitual, or character traits that have become ingrained?

By asking yourself one simple question: Is this Who I Am?

It's the most important question you will ever ask yourself. You may ask it profitably before and after every decision in your life, from what clothes to wear, to what job to take, from whom to marry, to whether to marry at all. And certainly it is a key question to ask when you catch yourself in behaviors you say you want to discontinue.

And this will change long-held character traits or behaviors?

Try it.

Okay, I will.

Good.

After I decide who I am not, and after I free myself from the idea that I am my past, how do I discover Who I *Am?*

It is not a process of discovery, it is a process of creation. You cannot "discover" Who You Are, because you should be coming from ground zero when you decide this. You are not deciding this based on your discoveries, but rather, based on *preferences.*

Do not be who you thought you were, be who you *wish you were.*

That's a big difference.

It's the biggest difference of your life. Up to now you've been "being" who you thought you were. From now on you are going to be a product of your highest wishes.

Can I really change that much?

Of course you can. But remember: it's not about changing, and thus suddenly becoming acceptable. You're acceptable right now in the eyes of God. You are only changing because *you* choose to change, you choose a newer version of your Self.

The grandest version of the greatest vision I've ever had about who I am.

Precisely.

And a simple question like *Is this Who I Am?* will bring me to that?

It will, unless it won't. But it is a very, very powerful tool. It can be transformational.

It is powerful because it contextualizes what is happening. It makes it clear what you are doing. I observe that many people do not know what they are doing.

What do You mean? What *are* they doing?

They are creating themselves. Many people do not understand this. They do not see that this is what is happening, that this is what they are doing. They do not know that this is, in fact, *the purpose of all life.*

Because they do not know this, they do not realize how important, how impactful, every decision is.

Every decision you make—*every* decision—is not a decision about what to do. It's a decision about Who You *Are.*

When you see this, when you understand it, everything changes. You begin to see life a new way. All events, occurrences, and situations turn into opportunities to do what you came here to do.

We did come here with a mission, didn't we . . .

Oh, yes. Most assuredly. It is the purpose of your soul to announce and to declare, to be and to express, to experience and to fulfill Who You Really Are.

And who is that?

Whoever you *say* you are! Your life lived is your declaration. Your choices define you.

Every act is an act of self-definition.

So yes, a simple, five-word question like that can change your life. Because that question, if you can remember to ask it, places what's going on in a new context, a much larger context.

Especially if you ask the question at decision-making time.

There is no time that is *not* "decision-making time." You are *always* making decisions, all the time. There is no time when you are not making a decision. Even when you are sleeping, you are making decisions. (In fact, some of your *biggest* decisions are made while you're sleeping. And some people are sleeping even when it looks like they are awake.)

Someone once said, we are a planet of sleepwalkers.

They were not far from the truth.

So that's the magic question, eh?

That's the magic question. The five-word magic question.

Actually, there are two five-word magic questions. These questions, asked at the right moment, can propel you forward in your own evolution faster than you might ever imagine. The questions are:

Is this Who I Am?

What would love do now?

With your decision to ask and answer those questions at every juncture, you will move from student to teacher of The New Gospel.

The New Gospel? What is that?

In time, My friend. In due time. We have much to say before we get to that.

Then can I go back to guilt just one more time? What about people who have done such horrible things—killed people, for instance, or raped women, or abused children—that they just can't forgive themselves?

What they have done in the past, I am going to say again, is not who they are. It may be who *others* think they are, it may even be who *they* think they are, but it is not Who They Really Are.

But most of these people can't hear that. They are too consumed with their own guilt—or perhaps with bitterness at the cards life has dealt them. Some of them are even afraid that they'll do it again. So, they see their life as hopeless. Pointless.

No life is pointless! And I tell you that *no* life is hopeless.

Fear and guilt are the only enemies of man.

You've told me that before.

And I'll tell you again. Fear and guilt are your only enemies.

If you let go of fear, fear lets go of you. If you release guilt, guilt will release you.

How do we *do* that? How do we let go of fear and guilt?

By deciding to. It is an arbitrary decision, based on nothing but personal preference. You simply change your mind about yourself, and how you choose to feel.

It is as your Harry Palmer says: *Only a decision is required to change one's mind.*

Even a murderer can change his mind. Even a rapist can re-create himself anew. Even a child abuser can be redeemed. All it takes is a decision deep in the heart and soul and mind: This is not Who I Am.

That goes for any of us, whatever our misdeeds, large or small?

That goes for any of you.

Yet how can I forgive myself if I have done the unforgivable?

There is no such thing as the unforgivable. There is no offense so great that I would refuse to forgive it. Even the strictest of your religions teach that.

They may not agree on the *way* of atonement, they may not agree on the path, but they all agree that there *is* a way, there *is* a path.

What *is* the way? How can I achieve atonement if I, *myself,* consider my offenses unforgivable?

The opportunity for atonement comes to you automatically at what you call death.

You must realize that "atonement" is *just that*—it is "at-one-ment." It is the awareness that you and all others are One. It is the understanding that you are One with everything—including Me.

This experience you will have—you will remember this—immediately after death, after you depart from your body.

All souls experience their at-one-ment in a most interesting way. They are allowed to move through, once again, every moment of the life they've just completed—and to experience it not only from *their* viewpoint, but from the viewpoint of everyone else who was affected by that moment. They get to rethink every thought, resay every word, redo every deed, and to experience its effect on every person it affected, as if they were that other person—which they *are.*

They get to *know* that they are, *experientially.* At this moment the statement "We Are All One" will no longer be a concept, it will be an experience.

That could be a living hell. I thought You said in *Conversations with God* that there's no such thing as hell.

There is no place of everlasting torment and damnation, such as you have created in your theologies. But you will all—all of you—experience the impact, the outcome, and the results of your choices and decisions. Yet this is about growth, not "justice." It is the process of evolution, never God's "punishment."

And during your "life review," as some have called it, you will not be judged by anyone, but simply be allowed to experience what the Whole of You experienced, rather than what the localized version of You that resides with your present body experienced, at each moment of life.

Ouch. That still sounds like it could be painful.

It is not. You will not experience pain, only awareness. You will be deeply in tune with, deeply aware of, the totality of every moment and what it held. Yet this will not be painful, but, rather, enlightening.

Not an "ouch," but an "aha"?

Exactly.

But if there's no ouch, where is the "payback" for the hurt we've inflicted and the harm we've done?

God is not interested in getting you *back*. God is interested in moving you *forward.*

This is the path of evolution you are on, not the road to hell.

The goal is *awareness,* not retribution.

God is not interested in "getting us back." God just wants to "back us getting it!"

Say, not bad. Not bad at all.

Well, I think it's important that we stay light-hearted here. I've spent years mired in guilt, and some people seem to think you should hang onto guilt forever. But guilt and regret are not the same thing. Because I've stopped feeling guilty about something does not mean I no longer regret it. Regret can be instructive, while guilt is only debilitating.

You are exactly right. That is well said.

When we're free of guilt, we can move forward, as You put it, with our lives. We can make something worthwhile out of them.

Then we can make friends with ourselves again—and then we can make friends with You.

You can, indeed. You'll make friends with your Self again, you'll fall in *love* with your Self, when you know and at last acknowledge Who You Really Are.

And when you know your Self, you'll know Me.

And step one in having a real, a working, friendship with God is complete.

Yes.

I wish it were as simple as you make it sound.

It is. Trust Me.

Six

That's Step Two, isn't it?

That's Step Two, and it's huge.

It is huge, because I don't know if I *can* trust You.

Thank you for your honesty.

I'm really sorry.

Don't be sorry. Never be sorry for honesty.

I'm not sorry for what I said. I'm sorry if it hurt You.

You can't hurt Me. That's the point.

I can't hurt You?

No.

Even if I do something horrendous?

Even if you do something horrendous.

You won't become upset, and punish me?

I will not.

That means I can go out and do anything I want.

You've always been able to do that.

Yes, but I haven't wanted to. Fear of punishment in the hereafter has stopped me.

You need fear of God to stop you from being "bad"?

Sometimes, yes. Sometimes, when the temptation's very great, I do need fear of what will happen to me after I die—fear for my immortal soul—as a motivator, to stop me.

Really? You mean you've wanted to do such horrible things that you think you'd lose your immortal soul if you did them?

Well, I can think of one example of that in my life, yes.

What was it?

Right here? You want me to tell You right here, in front of God and everybody?

Cute.

Yes, go ahead. Confession's good for the soul.

Well, if You must know—suicide.

You've wanted to commit suicide?

I once thought about it very seriously. And don't act so surprised. You know all about it. You're the one who stopped me.

With love, not fear.

There was a bit of fear in there, too.

There was?

I was afraid of what would happen to me if I took my own life.

So we began our dialogue.

Yes.

And now, three *Conversations with God* books later, are you still afraid of Me?

No.

Good.

Except when I am.

And when is that?

When I don't trust You. When I don't trust that this is even You talking to me, much less trust the outlandish promises You make.

You still don't trust that God is talking to you? Boy, that'll be interesting to your readers.

What, that I'm human? I think they know that I'm human.

Yes, but I think that they imagine you to be clear about some things—and at least convinced that you *are* having a conversation with God.

I am convinced.

That's better.

Except when I'm not.

And when is that?

When I don't feel that I can trust what You're telling me.

And when is that?

When it's too good to be true.

I see.

I go into fear. What if it's *not* true? What if I'm making it all up? What if I'm creating a God who will say anything I want Him to say? What if You're saying just what I want to hear so that I can justify continuing my behavior? I mean, based on what You're telling me, I can do anything I want, with impunity. No worry, no muss, no fuss. No price to pay in the hereafter. Hell's bells, who wouldn't want *that* kind of a God?

You, apparently.

But I *do*—except when I don't.

And when is that?

When I'm afraid. When I think I can't trust You.

What are you afraid will happen to you?

You mean, if I believe the things You say, and it turns out that You're not really God?

Yes.

I'm afraid God will throw me in hell.

Why? For having, at worst, a fanciful conversation?

For denying the one and only true God, and for leading others to do so. For telling others that there are no consequences to their actions, and thereby causing some people to do things they might not otherwise do, because now they're not afraid of You.

You really think you're that powerful?

No, I think other people are that easily influenced.

Then why haven't they been influenced enough by those who say I'm to be feared to stop their self-destructive behaviors?

Huh?

Religion has been around for centuries, telling people I'll send them to hell if they don't believe in Me this way or that way, and if they don't stop certain behaviors.

I know. I know that.

Well, do you see those behaviors being stopped?

No, not really. The human race is killing itself, just as it always has.

Faster, actually, than it ever has, because now you have weapons of mass destruction.

And we're being no less cruel to each other now than we ever were.

That's My observation as well. So what makes you think that if after centuries—millennia, really—of religion not having easily influenced people, that somehow *you're* going to easily influence them, and also then be personally accountable for their actions?

I don't know. I guess I just need to think that once in a while, in order to temper my actions.

Why? What are you afraid you would do if you didn't temper your actions?

I'd shout from the highest rooftop that I have found, at last, a God I could love! I'd invite everyone else to meet my God, and to know Him as I do! I'd share everything I know about You with everyone whose life I touch! I'd free people of their fear of You, and therefore their fear of each other! I'd free them of their fear of death!

And for this you think God is going to punish you?

Well, if I have it *wrong* about You, You will. Or He will. Or It will—whatever.

I will not. Oh, Neale, Neale, Neale . . . if your biggest crime is that you've painted a picture of a God too loving,

I think you'll be forgiven for that—if you *have* to continue to believe in a God of Reward and Punishment.

And if other people do bad things, like kill, or rape, or lie, because of me?

Then every philosopher from the beginning of time who has ever spoken or written against the then-current belief system must likewise be guilty of all the deeds of man.

Perhaps they are.

Is that the kind of God you want to believe in? Is that the God you choose?

This isn't a question of *choice.* We're not in a God-supermarket. We don't get to make a choice about this. God is God, and we'd better have our understanding about that right, or we could be going straight to hell.

Do you believe that?

No. Except when I do.

And when is that?

When I don't trust You. When I don't trust in the goodness of God, and in the unconditional love of God. When I see us, all of us here on Earth, as children of a lesser God.

Is that often? Do you feel that way often?

No. I have to say, no, not very often. I used to. Man, did I ever used to! But not since our conversations. I've changed my mind about a lot of things. Well, not *changed* my mind, really. What actually happened is that I allowed myself to believe what I always knew in my heart, and wanted to believe, about God.

And has that been so bad for you?

Bad? No, it's been *good.* My whole life has changed. I've been able to believe in Your goodness again, and so, I've been able to believe in *my* goodness again. Because I've been able to believe that You forgive me for all I've done, I've been able to forgive *myself.* Because I've stopped believing that someday, somehow, someplace, I'm going to be punished by God, I've stopped punishing myself.

Now, there are those who say that failing to believe in a punishing God *is bad.* Yet I see nothing but good coming from this, because if I'm ever going to do *anything* worthwhile—even if I'm in prison, just talking another prisoner out of hurting someone, or continuing to hurt himself—I'm going to have to forgive, and stop punishing, myself.

Excellent. You understand.

I do understand. I really do. And I *haven't* abandoned everything I've been told in our conversations. I just need a tool now. A tool with which I can create a real friendship with You at last.

I'm giving you those tools, right here.

Yes, You are. Even before I've asked, You've answered.

As always.

As always. So tell me, how can I learn to trust?

By not having to.

I can learn to trust by not having to trust?

That's right.

Help me here.

If I don't want or need anything from you, do I have to trust you for anything?

I suppose not.

You are correct.

So the highest level of trust is not *having* to trust?

You are correct again.

But how can I get to a place of not wanting or needing anything from You?

By realizing that it's already yours. That whatever you need is already yours. That even before you ask, I will have answered. Therefore, asking is not necessary.

Because I don't have to ask for what I already have.

Exactly.

But if I already have it, why would I even *think* I needed it?

Because you don't *know* you already have it. It is a matter of perception.

Do You mean that if I perceive that I need something, I do?

You will *think* that you do.

But if I think that God will meet all my needs, then I will *not* "think that I do."

That is correct. That is why faith is so powerful. If you have faith that all your needs will always be met, then, technically, you have no needs at all. And this is the *truth,* of course, and it will become your experience, and so your faith will be "justified." Yet all you will have done is change your perception.

What I expect is what I get?

Something like that, yes. Yet the true Master lives outside the space of expectation. He expects nothing and desires nothing more than what "shows up."

Why?

Because he already knows he has everything. And so he happily accepts whatever part of Everything it is that shows up in any particular moment.

He knows that it is all perfect, that life is perfection, playing itself out.

Under these circumstances, trust is not required.

Or, to put it another way, "trust" becomes "knowing."

Yes. There are three levels of awareness around everything. These are: hope, belief, and knowing.

When you have a "hope" about something, you are wishing that it is true, or that it will happen. You are not certain, in any sense of the word.

When you have a "belief" about something, you are thinking that it is true, or that it will happen. You are not certain, but you *think* you are certain, and you continue to think so unless something to the contrary appears in your reality.

When you have a "knowing" about something, you are clear that it is true, or that it will happen. You are certain, in every sense of the word, and *you continue to be certain* even if something to the contrary appears in your reality.

You judge not by appearances, because you *know* what is so.

So I can learn to trust You by knowing that I don't *have* to trust You!

That is correct. You have come to a knowingness that the perfect thing is going to occur.

Not that a particular thing is going to occur, but that the perfect thing is going to occur. Not that what *you* prefer is going to occur, but that which is *perfect* is going to occur. And, as you move toward mastery, these two become one. Something occurs, and you prefer no occurrence other than what is occurring. It is your very preferring of whatever is occurring that renders that occurrence perfect. This is called "letting go and letting God."

A Master always prefers what occurs. You, too, will have reached mastery when you are always preferring what is occurring.

But . . . but . . . that is the same as having no preferences at all! I thought that You've always said, "Your life proceeds out of your intentions for it." If you have no preferences, how can this be true?

Have intentions, but don't have expectations, and certainly don't have requirements. Do not become addicted to a particular result. Do not even prefer one. Elevate your Addictions to Preferences, and your Preferences to Acceptances.

That is the way to peace. That is the way to mastery.

A wonderful teacher and writer, Ken Keyes, Jr., talked about just this idea in an exceptional book called *A Handbook to Higher Consciousness.*

Indeed. His formulations in that book were very important, and for many people, ground-breaking.

He spoke of changing addictions to preferences. He had to learn how to do that in his own life, because for most of it he was in a wheelchair, immobile from the chest down. Had he been "addicted" to greater mobility, he could never have found a way to be happy. But he came to realize that it was not outer circumstances that were the source of happiness, but rather our inner decisions about how we choose to experience them.

This formed the core of his writing, though most of his books didn't mention his physical challenges. So when he was asked to give lectures, people were often shocked to see him virtually immobile, in his wheelchair. He wrote with such joy of love and life that they imagined him to have everything he ever wanted.

He *did* have everything he ever wanted! But those last three words contain an enormous secret. The secret of life is not to have everything you want, but to *want everything you have.*

To borrow from another wonderful writer, John Gray.

John is a wonderful writer, that is true, but who do you think is "borrowing" from whom? I *gave* him those ideas, just as I inspired Ken Keyes.

Who is there with You now.

Who is, indeed—and free of his wheelchair, I might add.

I'm so glad! It's a shame he had to spend so much of his life in one.

It is not a shame! It is a blessing! Ken Keyes changed millions of lives because he was in that wheelchair. *Millions* of lives. Let's make no mistake about this. Ken's life was a blessing, as was every circumstance in it. It provided the exact and perfect people, places, and events to produce for the soul then calling itself Ken, the experience and the expression for which it yearned, and which it had intended.

This is true of *everyone's* life. There is no such thing as bad luck, nothing happens by accident, there are no coincidences, and God doesn't make mistakes.

In other words, everything is perfect, just the way it is.

That's right.

Even if things don't look perfect.

Especially if they don't look perfect. That's a sure sign that there's something huge for you to remember here.

So You're saying we should be *grateful* for the worst things that happen to us?

Gratitude is the fastest form of healing.

What you resist, persists. What you are grateful for can then serve you, as it was meant to do.

I have told you:

I have sent you nothing but angels.

Now I will add:

I have given you nothing but miracles.

Wars are miracles? Crimes are miracles? Diseases and illnesses are miracles?

What do you think? If you were beginning to give answers rather than ask all the questions, what would you say?

You mean, what would I say if I were You?

Yes.

I would say. . . . Every event of life is a miracle, as is life itself. Life is designed to provide your soul with the perfect tools, the perfect circumstances, the perfect conditions with which to realize and experience, announce and declare, fulfill and become Who You Really Are. Therefore, judge not, and neither condemn. Love your enemies, pray for your persecutors, and embrace every moment and circumstance of life as a treasure; a perfect gift from a perfect Creator.

I would say . . . seek results and outcomes, but do not require them.

You would have spoken well, My friend. You are becoming a messenger, as Ken Keyes was. Yet now let us take

Ken Keyes' teachings one step further, for Ken taught: elevate your Addictions to the level of Preferences. Now *you* will teach: do not even have Preferences.

I will?

Yes.

When?

Now. Go ahead and teach it. What would you say if you were to teach this?

You mean, what would I say if I were You?

Yes.

I would say . . . if you require a certain result in order to be happy, you have an Addiction. If you simply desire a certain result, you have a Preference. If you have no Preference whatsoever, you have Acceptance. You have achieved mastery.

Good. That is very good.

But I have a question. Isn't setting one's intentions the same as announcing one's Preferences?

Not at all. You can intend for something to happen without preferring it to. In fact, holding a Preference is an announcement to the universe that alternative outcomes are possible. God doesn't imagine such things, so God never has Preferences.

Do you mean that God actually intended everything that has happened on Earth to happen?

How else could it have happened? Is it your imagining that *anything* can happen that is against God's will?

When You put it that way, it feels like the answer must be no. Yet when I look at all the awful things that have occurred in the history of the world, I find it hard to believe that God could have *intended* for those things to occur.

My intention is to allow you to choose your own outcomes, to create and experience your own reality. Your history is a record of what you have intended, and what *you* have intended, *I* have intended, since there is no separation between us.

It does not feel to me as though everything that has happened in human history—or even all that has happened in my own life—is in every case what was intended. It feels as if there have been what I would call unintended results many times along the way.

No results are unintended, although many are unanticipated.

How can a thing be unanticipated if it is intended? And, conversely, how can a thing that is intended be unanticipated?

What you always intend at the soul level is to produce the outcome that is perfectly reflective of your current state of evolution so that you can experience Who You Are.

This is also the outcome that is perfectly suited to facilitate your movement to the next highest state, so that you can become Who You Seek to Be.

Remember that the purpose of life is to re-create yourself anew in the next grandest version of the greatest vision ever you held about Who You Are.

I bet I could repeat that in my sleep.

Which is interesting, because when you can repeat that in your sleep, it is a sure sign that you are *awake at last.*

That's clever. That's a neat twist.

All of life is, My friend. All of life is.

So, what have we learned here? What have you been caused to remember?

That what I intend is always what is happening, but what is happening may not always be what I anticipated. But how can this be possible?

It occurs when you are not very clear about what you are intending.

You mean I *think* I'm intending one thing, and I'm actually intending another?

Exactly. At the physical level you believe you are calling forth a particular result, but at the soul level you are calling forth another.

Man, that's crazy-making! How can I possibly know what to expect if I'm creating my reality at levels of consciousness that I'm not even in touch with?

You can't. That's why it is said, "Live your life without expectations." That is also why you have been told, in every circumstance and situation, and in the face of any result or outcome, to "see the perfection."

You did say both of those things in *Conversations with God.*

And now, so that you may understand more fully, let us talk briefly about the Three Levels of Experience—superconscious, conscious, and subconscious.

The superconscious level is the place of experience at which you know about, and create, your reality with full awareness of what you are doing. This is the soul level. Most of you are not aware at a conscious level of your superconscious intentions—unless you are.

The conscious level is the place of experience at which you know about, and create, your reality with some awareness of what you are doing. How much of what you are aware of depends upon your "level of consciousness." This is the physical level. When you are committed to the spiritual path, you move through life ever seeking to elevate your consciousness, or to enlarge the experience of your physical reality to include and encompass a larger reality that you know exists.

The subconscious level is the place of experience at which you do not know about, or consciously create, your reality. You do so subconsciously—that is, with very little awareness that you are even doing this, much less why. This is not a bad level of experience, so do not judge it. It is a gift, because it allows you to do things automatically, such as grow your hair, or blink your eyes, or beat your heart—or create an instant solution to a problem. Yet if you are unaware of what parts of your life you have chosen to create automatically, you might imagine yourself to be at the "effect" of life, rather than at cause in the matter. You could even see yourself as a victim. Therefore, it is important to be aware of what you have chosen to be unaware of.

Later, toward the end of this dialogue, I will speak to you again of awareness, and the differing levels of awareness which produce the experience that some of you call enlightenment.

Is there a way to set the same intentions on the conscious, superconscious, and subconscious levels at the same time?

Yes. This three-in-one level of consciousness might be called *supra*-consciousness. Some of you also call it "Christ consciousness," or "elevated consciousness." It is Fully Integrated Consciousness.

When you are in this place, you are fully creative. All three levels of consciousness have become one. You are said to "have it all together." But it is really more than that, because in this, as in all things, the whole is greater than the sum of the parts.

Supra-consciousness is not simply a mixture of the superconscious, the conscious, and the subconscious. It is what happens when all are mixed, *and then transcended.* You then move into pure *beingness.* This *beingness* is the ultimate source of creation within you.

And so, for a person of "elevated consciousness," outcomes and results are *always* intended and *never* unanticipated?

Indeed, that is true.

And the degree to which a result appears unanticipated is a direct indication of the level of consciousness at which an experience is being perceived.

That is precisely correct.

Therefore, the Master is one who always agrees with results, even if they do not appear favorable, because he knows that at some level he must have intended them.

You understand now. You are beginning to comprehend something that is very complex.

And that is why the Master sees everything as perfect!

Wonderful! You've got it!

What the Master may not always see is the level at which the outcome was intended. Yet she has no doubt that at *some level* she is *responsible for the result.*

Exactly.

And that is why the Master never sits in judgment of another person, place, or thing. The Master knows that *he put it there.* He's aware that at some level he created what he is experiencing.

Yes.

And that if he doesn't like what he's created, it's up to him to change it.

Yes.

And that condemnation has no part in that process. Indeed, that which you condemn, you keep in place.

This is also very deep, very complex. Your understanding of it is perfect.

Just as it would be perfect if I did *not* understand it.

Indeed.

We are, all of us, exactly where it is perfect for us to be, all the time.

Exactly—or you wouldn't be there.

And we need nothing more for our evolution than exactly what we have, and are experiencing, right now.

Once more, you are correct.

And if we don't *need* anything, we don't have to trust God.

That is what I have been saying, yes.

And when we don't *have* to trust God, then we actually *can.* Because trust then means not having to have a particular result, but rather, knowing that whatever results is for our highest good.

You have brought it full circle. Bravo!

The beauty of this is that not *needing* a particular result frees the subconscious mind from all thoughts about why you can't *have* a particular result, which in turn opens the path to the particular result which was consciously intended.

Yes! You are able to put more things on automatic. When you face a challenge, you automatically assume that things will go well. When you face some difficulty, you automatically know that it will be handled. When you encounter a problem, you automatically understand that it has already been solved for you—*automatically.*

You have created these outcomes, *subconsciously.*

> Things start to happen automatically, seemingly without any effort on your part at all. Life starts working. Things start coming to you, rather than you having to chase after them.
>
> This change occurs without conscious effort. Just as negative, self-defeating, self-denying thoughts about Who You Really Are, and what you can be, do, and have, were *acquired* subconsciously, so, too, are they released subconsciously.
>
> You don't know how or when you picked up such ideas, and you won't know how or when you dropped them. Life will simply and suddenly change for you. The time between your thinking a thought consciously and it being made manifest in your reality will begin to shrink. Ultimately, it will disappear altogether, and you will create results instantly.

And, actually, I am not creating results at all, but simply realizing they are already there. Everything has already been created, and I am experiencing the outcome I am able to choose, given my understandings and my perception.

> I see that you are now a messenger. You are one who brings a message, rather than one who seeks it. You are able now to articulate the entire cosmology. You have even worked into your last statement the truth about time.

Yes. Time as we have understood it does not exist. There is only one moment, the Eternal Moment of Now. All things that have ever happened, are happening, and ever will happen, are occurring right now. As You explained in *Conversations with God, book 3,* it's like a giant CD-ROM. Every possible outcome has already been "programmed." We experience the outcome we produce by the choices we make—like playing games with a computer. All of the computer's moves already exist. Which outcome you experience depends on which move *you* make.

That is a very good example, because it allows for quick understanding. It has one drawback, however.

Which is?

It likens Life to a game. It makes it sound as if all I'm doing is playing with you.

Yes. I've received letters from people who were angry about that. They said that if what was said in *Conversations with God* about events and time were true, they were deeply disappointed. If, after all is said and done, we are all nothing more than pawns, being moved around on the chessboard of life by a God who does so for His own amusement. They were not very happy.

Is that the kind of God you think I am? Because, you know, if you do, that's what you'll see Me as. Humans have been having their thoughts about God, and then seeing Me as that, for thousands of years. This, then, is the greatest secret of all about God:

I will appear to you as you see Me.

Wow.

Yes, wow, indeed. God will seem to be what you seem to see. So how do *you* see Me?

I see You as a God Who empowers me to create whatever experience I choose, and gives me the tools with which to do that.

And one of the most powerful of those tools is your friendship with God. Trust Me on this.

I do. I trust You. Because I've learned that I don't have to. The process of life is what it is. Trust is not necessary, merely knowing.

Exactly.

Seven

It hasn't always been like this with me. I mean, I didn't always have to have things so exhaustively explained to me before I could trust. In fact, when I was younger, I always trusted that everything would go right.

I was a person of unbridled optimism. One might even call it reckless optimism. Given the fact that I'd grown up being afraid of God, this state of mind might seem to have been doubly reckless. Still, that's the way it was with me. As a child, I always "knew" I was going to get what I wanted—and I always did. Usually, I might add, without much effort. This really bothered my brother, who used to complain loudly that "Neale has all the luck." Once I overheard my dad responding to this complaint. "Neale," he said, "makes his own luck."

He was right. And part of the reason was my parents. My mother imbued me with a love of life, and all things creative, and my father blessed me with self-confidence. No matter what the challenge, he asked me over and over again, "How are you going to do it if you don't try?"

He also told me something when I was about fifteen years old that I have always remembered. "Son," he said, "there's no 'right way' to do something. There's only the way you're doing it. *Make* your way the right way."

"How do I do that?" I asked. And he answered, "By getting it done." Thirty-five years later the Nike Company put this neat little philosophy into a three-word slogan.

Just do it.

As I said earlier, as a freshman in high school I jumped right into things. All those extracurricular activities kept me wildly busy, and I did well in the classes I liked: English, speech, political science, music, foreign languages. I have to admit that I barely squeaked by in the subjects that bored me—biology, algebra, geometry—but the University of Wisconsin at Milwaukee accepted my enrollment anyway . . . on probation.

I didn't last very long. The dean of men asked me to give up my chair after just three semesters, but I wasn't too upset. I was impatient with life, and I wanted to get into radio, right then, right there.

After I flunked out of college, my father said to me, "Okay, son, you're on your own. I did what I could for you, but you want to do it your way."

Part of me was scared out of my mind and part of me was so excited I couldn't stand it. I'd already been logging some on-airtime working gratis for a tiny *fm* station that had just gone on the air. And when Dad cut me loose, I marched into the general manager's office at another *fm* station a little further up the dial, and boldly told him that he should hire me.

Larry LaRue threw his head back and cackled, "And why should I do that?"

I didn't miss a beat.

"Because I'm better than anyone you've got on the air."

Larry stopped laughing, but the smile never left his face.

"Kid," he said, "I like you. You got *chutzpah."* (I didn't know what the word meant then. I remember thinking, *This is good?*) "Tell you what." He squeaked toward me in his swivel chair. "You come back here at eight o'clock tonight and I'll have the night man show you the ropes. At nine o'clock, you go on. I'll be listening. If I don't call you by nine-thirty, get out of there, and don't ever let me see you again."

His grin became mischievous.

"Fair enough," I chirped, reaching out to shake his hand. Then I added, "Be hearing from you tonight." I walked out—and nearly lost my lunch in the parking lot.

I was still sick to my stomach when I took the mike that night. I gave a tentative station break and rolled right into music. A couple of songs later it was 9:28. There was no call, and I was pretty dejected as I prepared to let the regular night guy take over. He poked his head into the room just as I was gathering my things.

"The boss is on the back line," he said, and left. I picked up the phone.

"You're hired," Larry grunted. "Stay on 'til eleven. Be in my office tomorrow at nine."

I've never forgotten Larry LaRue for giving me that break. A different kind of person might have thrown me out of the place. Years later, when I was a program director at a radio station in Baltimore, I did my best to pass on the favor, using what I had come to call *La Rule LaRue:* always give the kid a chance.

I had plenty of kids wanting to break into the business knocking on my door. I couldn't just stick them into the studio and put 'em on the air the way Larry did—we were too important a station in too big a market to get away with that—but I always invited them into my office and gave their audition tape a fair listen. I gave 'em tips, too, on what I thought they needed to do to improve. I never hired any of them on the spot, though. I guess those days were over in radio. They certainly are today. There's no place where you can earn your spurs anymore. Today you've got to hit the ground running in any profession. My generation may have been the last to be able to sneak in through the side door. And that's too bad. We need more places where kids can serve their apprenticeships. The pressure to succeed that is placed on today's twenty- and twenty-five-year-olds is enormous.

To make matters worse, many are now more ill-equipped than ever. Which is something I'd like to talk about. The education I received at South Division High School in Milwaukee was equal to what a community college graduate would receive today—if he was lucky.

You must improve your education systems, reigniting the spirit of inquiry, and the joy of learning, in your schools. I gave you some wonderful clues on how you might do that in *Conversations with God, book 2.* I will not repeat them here. Rather, I will invite you to review them and to put them into practice.

Put them into practice?

Life is a process of re-creation. You are invited to empower the world to re-create the experience of "school" in the next grandest version of the greatest vision you ever held about what that is.

Re-creating school is not all we need to do. We need to make it clear that we are never going to ignite the thinking process and encourage independent inquiry if we allow our children to spend twenty hours a week watching television, then twenty hours more glued to video games. Children will not learn much that way.

On the contrary, they will learn a great deal. They will learn how to seek instant gratification, how to expect all life problems to resolve themselves in twenty-eight and a half minutes, and how to vent their frustrations over problems that don't instantly resolve themselves by using violence.

Entertainment industry executives deny that TV, movie, and video images, however violent, are responsible for young people's violent behavior.

Are these the same executives who sell Super Bowl commercials for a half-million dollars apiece, claiming that they can influence behaviors in sixty seconds?

Well, uh, yes.

I see.

But surely it can't be simply video games that are desensitizing kids to death and violence. Kids know it's "just a game."

Do you know what some police and military academies use to teach professionals quick hand-eye coordination, and to shoot to kill without emotion?

Video games?

I only asked a question. I'll leave you to discover the answer. But could you think of a faster, more effective teaching tool?

Oh, man, I probably shouldn't have put all this in here.

Why not?

People don't want social commentary from me, and they certainly don't want it from *You.* This is a book about God, and God isn't supposed to have opinions on social issues of the day.

You mean, real life?

I mean political and social issues. You're supposed to stick to spiritual matters, and so am I.

Is there any matter more spiritual than how to stop your children from killing each other? Do you need many more Columbine high schools to get you to understand that you've got a real problem here?

We know we've got a problem, we just don't know how to solve it.

You do know how to solve it. You simply have not gathered the will to do so.

First, spend more time with your children. Stop acting as if they're on their own from age eleven. Get involved, and stay involved, in their lives. Talk to their teachers. Make friends with their friends. Exert an influence. Have a real presence in their lives. Don't let them slip away from you.

Second, take an active stand against violence, and role models of violence, in their lives. Images *do* teach. Indeed, imagery teaches faster, and imprints deeper, than words.

Insist that those in charge of retelling your cultural story (moviemakers, TV producers, video game manufacturers, and other purveyors of imagery, from comic books to trading cards) create a *new* cultural story, with a new ethic—an ethic of *non-violence.*

Third, do what it takes to make sure that instruments of violence and tools of violence are unavailable to your children and your teenagers. Prevent easy access and effortless acquisition.

Most important, eliminate violence from *your* life. You are the greatest model for your children. If they see you using violence, they will use violence.

Does that mean we shouldn't spank our children?

Can you think of no other way to teach those that you say you deeply love? Is startling them, scaring them, or hurting them the only way you can think of to instruct them?

Yours is a culture that has long used physical pain as a

punishment for unwanted behavior not only in children, but in adults. You actually kill people to get people to stop killing people.

It is insanity to use the energy that created a problem to seek to solve the problem.

It is insanity to repeat the behaviors you want to stop in order to stop them.

It is insanity to model behaviors all over your society that you say you do not want your offspring to copy.

And the highest insanity is pretending that none of this is happening, then wondering *why your children are acting insane.*

Are You saying we are all insane?

I am defining insanity. It is up to you to decide who and what you are. You are deciding that every day.

Every act is an act of self-definition.

You've been using some pretty tough words here.

That's what friends are for. You want to know what it's like having a friendship with God? This is what it's like.

Friends tell you the truth. Friends say it like it is. Friends don't pander to you, or tell you only what they think you want to hear.

Yet friends don't tell you what is so and then leave you to deal with it. Friends are always there for you, offering constant support, a helping presence, and unconditional love.

That's what God does. That's what this on-going dialogue is all about.

How long will this dialogue be going on? I thought it would be over at the end of the *CWG* trilogy.

It will go on as long as you choose for it to on.

So there will be another book after this?

There will definitely be another book after this, as I indicated to you years ago—but it will not be a dialogue book.

It won't?

No.

What kind of book will it be?

A book that speaks with One Voice.

Your voice.

Our voice.

Our voice?

Your conversation with God has led to your friendship with God, and your friendship with God will lead to your communion with God.

We will speak with One Voice in *Communion with God,* and it will be an extraordinary document.

All of the *with God* books have been extraordinary.

Indeed.

Will there be any more dialogue books, where You and I just talk?

If you wish for there to be, there will be.

Well, I enjoy these conversations immensely, because they really make me think. I'm sometimes surprised, though, at how opinionated you are. For a God with no Preferences, You seem to express quite a few.

Giving directions is not the same as stating Preferences.

If you say you wish to go to Seattle and you are on the road to San Jose, and if you stop to ask directions, is it announcing a *Preference* to tell you that you are on the wrong road, that you have made a wrong turn? Is it being opinionated to tell you how you can get where you say you want to go?

You have used this analogy before. You have said this to me before.

And I will say it to you over and over again, so long as you keep trying to make me into a God who needs something from you.

I tell you this: I need nothing from you. Do you imagine Me to be such an impotent God that I would need something from you and not be able to get it? Do you think there is something that I want to have happen, but that I just don't know how to make it happen?

If I needed you to go to Seattle, do you think I'd be wholly unable to get you to do that?

It is not like that. It is like this. You tell Me where you seek to go, and I tell you how to get there.

Humans have been telling God for thousands of years what kind of life they'd like to have. You've declared to Me, and to each other, that you wish to live long lives of peace, harmony, health, and abundance. I, in turn, have been telling you for thousands of years how you can do that.

I am telling you once again, here. Therefore, let those who have ears to hear, listen.

Yes, but as I said, sometimes people don't want to hear that. Some people have not liked the parts of our dialogue when You've gotten political, or controversial on social issues. And it isn't just God we don't want to hear from. I learned that when I was in the media. I had to tone down a lot of my own opinions when I got on the radio. Larry LaRue was the first of many bosses to tell me that.

I worked for Larry for about eight months, and then I got another break. Though today, I wouldn't call such an event a break," because today I know that there is no such thing as "luck," and that life proceeds out of your intentions for it.

That is good. That is important. It is vital, if you're going to have a friendship with God—a real, *working* friendship—for you to understand *how God works.*

People are forever calling the good outcomes in life breaks, luck, coincidence, serendipity, fate, or whatever. The bad outcomes—the hurricanes, tornadoes, earthquakes, sudden deaths—they call "acts of God."

No *wonder* you had this idea that you have to be afraid of Me. Your whole culture supports the idea. It is reflected in everything you say, and how you say it. It is everywhere in your language.

Now I will tell you that what you call the *good* things that happen to you are *also* acts of God. No two people meet by chance, and nothing occurs by accident.

Do you imagine that Larry was sitting there—just the right person, at just the right time, with just the right attitude—by *a stroke of luck?*

Consider the possibility that you and Larry did not meet by chance at that time, on that date, but that, like a supporting player standing in the wings waiting for his cue, he marched on stage, said his lines, and made his exit. And the play, your play, went on, just as it always goes on—just as it is going on right now, with you writing the script through your every thought about tomorrow. With you directing the scenes with your every verbal command. With you acting them out with your every deed.

That's awesome. That could be a great depiction of how it really is.

Could be?

Like I said, that's a great depiction of how it really is. And now, of course, I know that. After my conversation with God, all of this became clear. But back then I thought it was just another break when one of our better on-air talents, a fellow named Johnny Walker, left the station two months after I arrived, to take a job in Richmond, Virginia. Soon after that, Johnny's boss in Richmond left to join a company that had purchased a small *am* outlet in Annapolis, Maryland. Johnny Walker didn't want to leave Richmond, but said that he knew of a new, young talent that Dean could use to help give the Annapolis station a new image and a good sound. That new, young talent was me.

Within a blink I was off to the East Coast, my mother wringing her hands, asking Dad to stop me. My father said, "Let the boy go. It's his time."

"But what if this is all a mistake?" Mom asked.

"Then it'll be a mistake," my father said simply. "He knows where we are."

I arrived in Annapolis in August 1963, with one month left in my nineteenth year. My starting salary was $50 a week, but, hey, I was on *real radio!* This was not *fm,* this was *am.* The kind of radio they had in *cars.* The kind they took in little portables to *beaches.* And by my twenty-first birthday I had become the production manager of the station, in charge of making all of its commercials.

I'm telling you these stories, and this one in particular, because I want you to see how God works in our lives; how we *do* have a "friendship with God" and don't even know it. I want to illustrate how God uses people, places, and events to help us on our way. Or, rather, how He allows *us* to, giving us the creative power to determine the reality of our lives—although I wouldn't have put it that way then.

By 1966, I'd worked my way into the production manager's job at a radio station in a city in the deep south, which I'm not going to name, because I do not wish to embarrass or anger its present residents. Things are different there now, I'm sure, but in 1966 I thought it was a mistake for me to go there. *There are no mistakes in God's world* was not a concept I had learned yet. I only see now that what happened was all part of my education, a preparation for the larger work that I was to do in the world.

What made me *think* it was a big mistake for me to be in southern city was the racial attitude that I found there. It was the mid-sixties, and the Civil Rights Act had just been signed by President Johnson. It had become law because it was needed (just as anti-hate crime legislation is needed today), and nowhere was that need more apparent than in some bastions of longstanding racial prejudice in certain corners of the deep south. I was in just such a corner—in more ways than one. I wanted out. I hated it.

When I first drove into town, I needed some gas. Pulling into a service station I was shocked to find a cardboard sign stuck to every gas pump that read: WHITES ONLY. "Coloreds" got their gas at a pump 'round back. Restaurants, bars, hotels, theatres, the bus station and other public places were similarly segregated.

Now, being from Milwaukee, I had never seen such things. Not that Milwaukee, or any other northern city, was free of racial prejudice. But I'd never been confronted with such blatant designation of a whole group of people as second-class citizens. I'd never lived in a place where the whole of society agreed that it was *okay* to do that.

Things went from bad to worse. I'd been invited to dinner at the home of some new acquaintances, and I made the mistake of asking about the racial attitudes I was encountering all over the place. I thought that my hosts, a genteel couple of obvious breeding, might be able to offer me some insight.

I got some insight, all right, but not the kind I'd expected.

Bristling as he held up his wine glass to be refilled by an elderly black servant named Thomas, my host drawled through a strained smile, "Well, now, my new fray-end, Ah hope y'all won't judge us too harshly. You see, we feel ree-all kindly toward our coloreds heah. Yessir, we do. Why, we treat them as regular members of the family." He turned to Thomas. "Now ain't that right, boy?"

I winced. The man didn't even know what he was doing.

Thomas, however, was not so unaware. He whispered, "That's a fact, Captain. That's a fact," and quietly left the room.

Now these days when I see blatant injustice, my first impulse is not to walk away from it, but to move toward it; to try to understand what sponsors it; to see if I can do anything to help heal it. But those were younger days when my heart was just deciding about its truth, not acting on it. And so, I simply wanted out. In the worst way. I had no tolerance for intolerance. I understood nothing about that level of prejudice, I understood nothing about what today we would call the Black Experience—and I just wanted to get away from the whole thing.

I cried out to God, "Get me *out of here.*" I couldn't imagine how I was going to actually leave very quickly, though. Broadcasting is a very specialized field, and jobs in the market of one's choice are not easy to find. I felt that I was lucky to be working anywhere.

Of course, I hadn't counted on God's friendship. In those days I still thought of God as Someone who would answer prayers sometimes, ignore prayers other times, and punish me severely for *all* time if I died with sins on my soul. These days I know that God answers prayers all the time—and I also know that everything we think, say, and do is a prayer, and produces a response from God. That's what a good friend He is! But in the sixties I didn't understand that, so I wasn't exactly expecting a miracle here.

Imagine my surprise when I got one.

It was a phone call, out of the blue, from a complete stranger. A man identifying himself as Tom Feldman called. "You don't know me, but I got your name from Marvin Mervis [the owner of the station I worked for] in Annapolis. I'm looking for a program director for our radio station in Baltimore. Marvin says you're a talented guy. Would you be interested in coming up here for an interview?"

I couldn't believe what I was hearing. *Are you kidding?* I shouted inside my head. "Yes, I think I could arrange that," I said to Tom Feldman.

"There's one thing you should know though." He continued, "This is an all-black radio station."

Ah, yes, I remember that. That was clever of Me, wasn't it?

Clever? It was downright conniving. Because when I was hired (surprise, surprise) at WEBB in Baltimore, I got to find out first-hand what prejudice was about and how *Blacks* experienced it, even in a so-called sophisticated larger city.

I learned a lot, too, about my own self-righteousness, and how I thought that we were somehow better in our big-city attitudes than the rural folks in the deep south. I found out that our racial attitudes were not much better at all—but I had to be deeply embedded in the Black Experience to be able to see that. Outside the deep south our prejudices were simply expressed differently—mainly, with much more hypocrisy.

I let go of a lot of my false and arrogant thoughts during my tenure at what was known in those days as a "Rhythm 'n' Blues" station, and I also learned a lot, first-hand, about black culture. Working side-by-side with a black staff and interacting daily within the black community brought me insights I could not have gained any other way.

When I'd learned what I'd come to the situation to learn, God stepped in again, giving me yet another incredible chance to prepare further for the work I was to eventually do in the world.

> Hold it. You realize, of course, that it was you doing this, not Me? You do understand, don't you, that I have no agenda for you, other than the agenda you set for yourself?

Yes, I know that now. But then I was still living in a paradigm which suggested that there was something God wanted me to do, and that suggested God controls and causes the circumstances and events of my life.

> Well, now, just for review, who does control and cause the circumstances of your life?

I do.

And how do you do that?

With everything that I think, say, and do.

Good. That needed clarifying here, otherwise someone could get the impression that I was the cause of your experience.

Yet You did chuckle just now at how clever it was of You to place me at that all-black radio station.

It was clever how I facilitated what *you* chose to call forth. This is how your friendship with God works. First, you decide what it is you choose, then I make it possible.

I decided that I wanted to work at an all-black radio station?

No. You decided that you wanted to understand more fully what racial prejudice—and righteousness—was all about. You decided this at a very high level. At the soul level. It was about giving your Self lessons. It was about bringing your Self reminders. It was about moving your Self toward awareness.

Your subconscious thought was to flee, to get out of there. Your superconscious thought was to find out more, at the conscious level, about racial attitudes and about intolerance, including your own. You obeyed *all of these impulses at once.*

And You, as my soul's friend, will always make it possible for me to do that?

Yes. I will place the tools in your hands with which you may fashion the experience of your choosing, that you might come to higher and higher levels of consciousness. You may choose to use those tools, or not to use them.

What would cause me to do one or the other?

How aware you are about why that which is occurring in your life right now is occurring.

Later, I will talk to you about levels of awareness, and levels within levels.

It seems that I was always a lot more conscious about things *after* they happened than while they were happening. I see now, clearly, why what happened next in my life occurred, but at the time, I was cursing You.

That is not uncommon.

I know, but now I feel bad about it, because I see two things that I couldn't see then. First, I see that what happened was something that *I called forth,* and second, I see that it was for my own highest good.

Given where you say you wanted to go in your experience.

Yes, given where I say I wanted to go. I see now that I have always been choosing to be a teacher, a raiser of consciousness among people, and that my whole life has been a preparation for that.

That is very true.

But I was angry with You about things that I, myself, created. I didn't understand that You were simply giving me the tools—the right and perfect people, places, and events—to prepare myself for the experience of my choosing.

That's all right, don't worry about it. As I said, it's common. Now you know. So now, just stop being angry about your life—about *anything* in your life. See it all as perfect.

Do you think I can?

Do *you* think you can?

I think I can.

Then you can.

But it would have been nice to know then what I know now.

You know now. Let that be enough.

My father used to say, "So old so soon, so smart so late."

I remember that.

Do you think I took that one in too deeply?

What do you think?

I think I did, but I'm tossing it out right now.

Good. So get back to where I "stepped in again," as you put it, allowing you to prepare your Self more and more for the work you'd already decided to do in the world.

Well, after I experienced what I came to the radio station to experience, I promptly got myself removed from there, too. It all happened very suddenly. One day I was asked by the station to leave the program director's job and become an on-the-road salesman of air time. I think the owners felt that I was not doing as well as they'd hoped as PD, but they didn't want to fire me outright, and so, gave me a chance to stay employed.

Now I don't think there's a tougher job in the world than that of a time salesman for a radio or television station. I was constantly begging for a moment of some businessman's day in order to make my "pitch," then trying as hard as I could to convince him to do something that he really didn't want to do. Then I had to work doubly hard to please him by writing snappy, effective ad copy once he did capitulate and spend a few dollars on a commercial. And, finally, I'd worry my head off that there would be results, so that he would continue advertising.

I was working on a draw against commission, as most time sales people do, and each week that I didn't earn my draw, I felt guilty for being paid for something I wasn't doing—and frantic that I was going to be fired. This didn't exactly produce an attitude of joy as I went off to work each morning.

I remember sitting in my car one day in the parking lot of a shopping center where I was to make a cold call. I hated cold calls, I hated my new job, and I hated myself for getting myself into it, even though it didn't seem that I had much choice. I'd married just before going down south, and my first child was now on the way. Sitting in that car, miserable and furious, I banged on the steering wheel with my fists, once again demanding of God (this time, actually screaming out loud), *"Get me out of this!"*

Someone walked by the car and looked at me strangely, then quickly opened the door. "What's the matter, lock yourself in?" I smiled sheepishly, pulled myself together, and trudged into the store. I asked if I could see the manager or owner, and was asked in return, "Are you a salesman?" When I said *yes,* I was told, "He can't see you now."

This happened a lot, and *I'm a salesman* were words I began to abhor. I dragged myself back to my car, driving straight home, rather than to the next prospect. I couldn't take it another day, yet I didn't have the courage to quit.

The next morning as the alarm buzzed its awful buzz, I turned over with a jerk, angrily reaching for the Off button. That's when the pain hit me. It felt as if someone had stabbed me in the back. I couldn't move another inch without absolute agony.

My wife called our family doctor and handed me the phone. The nurse asked if I could come into the office. "I don't think so,"

I winced. "I can't *move.*" So believe it or not, the doctor came to my house.

I had a collapsed disc, the doctor said, and it would take eight to twelve weeks to heal, during which time I was to stay off my feet as much as possible. I would probably have to be placed in traction. I called my boss and told him. The next day I was fired. "I'm sorry," Tom allowed, "but we just can't keep paying you a draw against future commissions for three months. It would take you a year to work that off. It's a tough break, but we're going to have to let you go."

"Yeah," I echoed, "tough break." I could hardly keep the smile off my face.

I'd been given a legitimate reason for leaving my job! It was a cruel world, but that's the way the ball bounces sometimes. That was my worldview, the myth I grew up with. It never occurred to me that I had created all this; that the "cruel world" was a world of my own construction. This realization—what some might call *self-realization*—came much later.

After only five weeks I found myself feeling much better (surprise, surprise). The doctor said my recovery was going faster than expected, and, cautioning against pushing myself, gave me the go-ahead for occasional trips out of the house. It wasn't a moment too soon. We were skimping by on my wife's salary as a physical therapist, and it was clear that before long I was going to have to find something to do for a living. But what could I do? There were no jobs in radio to be had, in Baltimore or back in good old Annapolis. And I'd never done anything else. . . .

Of course, there was that bit of writing for the high-school weekly back in Milwaukee, but surely that wasn't credential enough to get a real newspaper job.

But again I'm reminded of how God works as our best friend—supporting us in getting where we say we want to go, giving us the tools with which to create the experiences that will serve us in moving to greater and greater awareness, and, ultimately, prepare us to express Who We Really Are.

Taking a gamble, I went to the offices of *The Evening Capital,* Annapolis' daily newspaper. I asked to see Jay Jackson, then managing editor, and—unlike with Larry LaRue—begged him for a job.

Fortunately, I was not completely unknown to Jay, my days in Annapolis radio having brought me a bit of notoriety. I told him that I'd lost my job in Baltimore because of my health, let him know that my wife was pregnant, and said, "Mr. Jackson, the truth is, I need work. Any kind of work. I'll wash the floors. Be a copy boy. Anything."

Jay listened very quietly from behind his desk. When I finished, he said nothing. I imagined that he was trying to think of how he could get me out of there. Instead, he finally asked, "Do you know how to write?"

"I wrote for my high-school paper, and had some journalism in college, yes, sir," I answered hopefully. "I think I can put a few sentences together."

After another pause, Jay said, "All right, you can start tomorrow. I'm going to put you in the newsroom. You're going to be writing obituaries and church news and club notices—nothing you can screw up too badly. I'll be reading your stuff. We'll see how you work out for a couple of weeks. If it doesn't pan out, there'll be no harm done, and you'll have made yourself a few dollars. If you show me something, we'll have ourselves another staff writer. As it happens, we're one man short right now."

(Surprise, surprise.)

Now nothing can give you a liberal education faster than being a newspaper reporter, especially at the paper-of-record in a small town, because you cover everything. *Everything.* One day you're interviewing the governor, the next, you're doing a feature on the new Little League coach. Now catch the tie-in here. See the beauty of the design.

I've always wanted to be a communicator of God's love. At first I was confused, and later I became disaffected, by all the teachings about a God of fear. I knew that this couldn't be the real God, and my heart ached to bring people to an awareness of what I felt in my heart.

At some level I must have known that I was destined to do that, and also known exactly what it would *take* to do it. A part of me (my soul?) must have known that I would be dealing with people from all backgrounds and experiences, and interacting with them in deeply personal ways. To do this requires highly developed communication skills, and rich exposure to people from varied cultures and walks of life.

I'm not surprised—now—that I spent my early work-life honing exactly those skills—first in broadcasting, moving south where I exposed myself to racial attitudes foreign to me, then going to work in an environment in which I could understand that prejudice from the inside out, and finally creating a medical condition that allowed me to start a new career of delving into everything from the grisly police blotter, to what makes the town's new Presbyterian pastor tick.

When I was living these moments, I called some of them good luck and some of them bad luck. But now, from my present vantage point, I see that they were all part of the same process—the process of life itself, and of me, becoming.

I have learned to judge not, and neither condemn, but to accept with equanimity the experiences of my life, knowing that all things happen in their perfect way, at their perfect time.

I don't know when it was during my first month at the newspaper that I'd been officially "hired." I was too busy writing obituaries and church news and tidying up the press releases that came in from the Boy Scout troops and the community theaters and the Kiwanis and Lion's clubs. But one morning I found a note on my desk, handwritten in bold, red felt-tip strokes: *Please accept a $50 weekly increment—Jay.*

I was permanent! Everyone in the newsroom turned to look at me as I said, quite out loud, *All riiight!* A few of the old-timers smiled. They must have guessed, or maybe they'd been told already. I was one of them.

It hadn't taken me long to remember how much I'd loved newspaper writing from my high-school days. And now, here I was in a real newsroom, typewriters clacking (yes, manual typewriters), the smell of ink and newsprint everywhere. Five months after I'd started, I was given my first real "beat" covering the county government, which soon produced my first Page One byline. What an exciting, joyful experience! I think that only a newspaper reporter can appreciate what I was feeling in those days—a constant sense of exhilaration. Nothing has topped it since, save the moment I first saw my name on the cover of a book.

Now I've had some friends advise me not to include anything about that in these pages. They say that people will think less of me, and that it will invalidate what has come through me, if I admit that I am thrilled to see my name stamped on the binding of a published book.

I guess I'm supposed to pretend that I'm very blasé about these things, that none of it has affected me in the least, that I'm above it all—because as a spiritual messenger, I *should be.* But I don't believe that as a spiritual messenger I cannot be happy with what I'm doing, or thrilled to pieces that it is going so well. It seems to me that spiritual enlightenment is not measured by how unaffected we are by rewards of the ego, but by how *dependent* we are on them for peace and happiness.

Ego itself is not a bad thing—only ego run amok. We would do well to be wary of an ego that controls us, but we might welcome an ego that propels us.

In life, we are constantly propelling ourselves to our next greatest achievement. The ego is God's gift to us, just as is everything else in life. God has given us nothing that is not a treasure, and whether it shows up that way in our experience depends on how we use it.

I'm convinced that ego—like money—has gotten a bad name. It's been given a bad rap. It's not ego, or money, or power, or unbridled sexual pleasure that is bad. It is the *misuse* of these things which does not benefit us, which does not speak of Who We Really Are. If these things, in and of themselves, were bad, why would God have created them?

So I am very okay with admitting that I was thrilled to see my first byline on the front page of *The Evening Capital,* and with acknowledging that I am still thrilled today each time I see my name on the cover of a new book—even though I still find myself saying that these books were not written *by* me, but *through* me.

You have written these books, and it is very okay to say that you have. It is not necessary for you, or anyone else, to hide your light under a bushel. I have made that point before. Unless you learn to acknowledge Who You Are and what you have done, you can never acknowledge others for Who They Are and what they have done.

It is true that you have been inspired by Me to put these principles into print. It is true that I have given you the words to write. Does that make it any less your achievement? If it does, than you should not honor Thomas Jefferson for writing the Declaration of Independence, Albert Einstein for articulating the theory of relativity, Madam Curie, Mozart, Rembrandt, Martin Luther King, Mother Teresa, or anyone else who has done anything of note in the history of the human race—*because I inspired them all.*

My son, I cannot tell you how many people to whom I have given wonderful words to write, who have never written them. I cannot tell you how many people to whom I have given wonderful songs to sing, who have never sung them. Do you want the list of people to whom I have given gifts, who have never used them?

You have *used* the gifts I have given you, and if that isn't something to be thrilled about, I don't know what is.

You have a way of making people feel good about themselves, just when they're tempted to start feeling bad.

Only with those who listen, My friend. Only with those who listen. You'd be amazed at how many people are in the I-am-not-to-feel-good-about-myself trap, or the no-credit-is-to-come-to-me belief system.

The trick is not to do what you do for acknowledgment,

but rather, as an expression of Who You Are. Yet, to be acknowledged for Who You Are does not make you less of that, but only makes you want to experience more of it.

The true Master knows this, which is why the true Master acknowledges everyone for Who They Really Are, and encourages others to acknowledge themselves as well, and never to deny, in the name of modesty, the most magnificent aspects of the Self.

Jesus announced himself and declared himself unequivocally to all who could hear. So, too, has every Master who has walked your planet.

Therefore, announce yourself. Declare yourself. Then move fully into the beingness of that which you have declared.

Re-create your Self anew in every moment of Now in the grandest version of the greatest vision ever you held about Who You Are. In this will I be glorified, for the glory of God is the glory of *you,* expressed wondrously indeed.

Do you know what I like about You? You give people permission to feel the feelings they've always wanted to feel. *You give people back to themselves.*

That's what friends are for.

How could people not feel optimistic—about themselves and about the world—with someone like You around?

You'd be surprised.

Well, I've always been optimistic, even before I knew You as I know You now. Even when I thought that God was an angry, punishing God, it still seemed like He was on my side. I grew up *thinking* that, because I was *taught* that. After all, I was both Catholic and American. Who could beat that? We were told as children that the Catholic Church was the one true church. We were also told that God looked with special favor on the United States of America. We even stamped "In God We Trust" on our coins, and in the Pledge of Allegiance to our flag we declared ourselves to be ". . . one nation, under God . . ."

I considered myself very lucky—being born into the best faith, in the best country. How could anything I do go wrong?

Yet it is this very teaching of superiority that has caused so much pain in your world. The idea, deeply ingrained in a people, that they are somehow "better" than others may give them an extra measure of confidence, but it also too often translates "how can anything we do *go* wrong?" into "how can anything we do *be* wrong?"

This is not self-confidence, but a dangerous brand of hubris that allows an entire population to believe itself to be in the right, no matter what it says or does.

People of many faiths and nations have believed and taught this through the years, producing a righteousness so huge that it desensitized them to any other experience, including the abject suffering of others.

If there is one thing which it would benefit you to remove from your various cultural myths, it is this idea that, by means of some magic ingredient, you have been made better than some other humans; that yours is the superior race, or the superior faith, the better country or the better political system, the higher approach or the higher way.

I tell you this: the day that you cause cultures to do this is the day that you change the world.

The word better is one of the most dangerous words in your vocabulary, exceeded only by the word right. Both are connected, for it is because you think you *are* better that you think you are right. Yet I have made no ethnic or cultural group My chosen people, and I have made no path to Me the one true path. Neither have I singled out any nation or religion for special favor, nor given any gender or race superiority over another.

Oh, my God, *would you please repeat that?* Would You please *say that again?*

I have made no ethnic or cultural group My chosen people, and I have made no path to Me the one true path. Neither have I singled out any nation or religion for special favor, nor given any gender or race superiority over another.

I invite every minister, every priest, every rabbi, every teacher, every guru, every Master, every president, every prime minister, every king, every queen, every leader, every nation, every political party to issue one statement that would heal the world:

OURS IS NOT A BETTER WAY, OURS IS MERELY ANOTHER WAY.

Leaders could never say that. Parties could never announce that. The Pope, for heaven sake, *could never declare that.* That would destroy the whole basis of the Roman Catholic Church!

Not just that church, but many religions, My son. As I have already noted, most religions base their primary appeal on the idea that theirs is the one true path, and that to believe any other way is to risk eternal damnation. Thus, religions use fear, rather than love, to attract you. Yet that is the last reason I would have you come to Me.

Do You think that religions ever *could* affirm that? Do You think that nations ever *could* declare that? Do you think that political parties ever *could* make that statement part of their platform?

I say again: it would change the world overnight if they did.

Maybe then we could stop killing each other. Maybe then we could stop hating each other. Maybe then we could stop the Kosovos and the Auschwitzs, the endless religious wars in Ireland, the bitter racial strife in America, the ethnic and class and cultural prejudices around the world, which lead to so much cruelty and suffering.

Maybe then you could.

Maybe then we could ensure that there would never again be a Matthew Shepard, beaten unmercifully and left to die, tied to a cattle fence in Wyoming, because he was gay.

Can't You say something about gay people? I have been asked over and over again, at lectures and appearances and retreats all over the world: Won't You say something to end, once and for all, the violence and cruelty and discrimination against gay men and women? So much of it is done in Your name. So much of it is said to be justified by Your teaching, and Your law.

I have said before, and I will say again: *There is no form and there is no manner in which the expression of love that is pure and true is inappropriate.*

I cannot be more unequivocal than that.

But how do You define love which is pure and true?

It seeks to damage or hurt no one. It seeks to avoid the possibility of damage or hurt to anyone.

How can we hope to know if someone else might possibly be hurt by an expression of love?

You may not be able to know in every case. And when you cannot know, you cannot know. Your motives are pure. Your intentions are good. Your love is true.

Yet most times you can know, and most times you do.

It is clear to you at these times how an expression of love could cause another to experience hurt. At these times, you would do well to ask:

What would love do now?

Not just love for the current object of your affections, but love for all others as well.

But such a "ground rule" could stop us from loving practically everyone! There's always someone who can claim that they'll be hurt by something someone else does in the name of love.

Yes. Nothing has generated more hurt among your species than the very thing that was meant to heal it.

Why is that?

You do not understand what love is.

What is it?

It is that which is without condition, without limitation, and without need.

Because it is without condition, it requires nothing in order to be expressed. It asks nothing in return. It withdraws nothing in retaliation.

Because it is without limitation, it places no limitation on another. It knows no ending, but goes on forever. It experiences no boundary or barrier.

Because it is without need, it seeks to take nothing not freely given. It seeks to hold nothing not wishing to be held. It seeks to give nothing not joyously welcomed.

And it is free. Love is that which is free, for freedom is the essence of what God is, and love is God, expressed.

That is the most beautiful definition I have ever heard.

If people understood it, and lived it, everything would change. Your opportunity is to help them understand it and live it.

Then I'd better understand it myself. What do You mean when You say "love is freedom"? Freedom to do what?

Freedom to express the most joyous part of Who You Really Are.

What part is that?

The part that knows that you are One with everything and everyone.

This is the truth of your being, and it is the aspect of Self which you will most urgently and earnestly seek to experience.

We *do* seek to experience it, every time we connect with someone with whom we feel that sense of Oneness. And the difficulty is that we can feel that sense of Oneness with more than one person.

Indeed. A highly evolved being feels it for everyone, all of the time.

How do they get away with that?

Let Me see if I understand the question. How do they get away with feeling a sense of Oneness with everyone, all of the time?

Yes. How are they able to do that without getting into trouble?

What kind of trouble?

Every kind of trouble there is! Unrequited love, unfulfilled expectations, jealous partners—you name it.

You are bringing up a subject that will reveal the main reason there is pain and misery on your planet surrounding the experience called "love," the main reason you find it so difficult to love each other, and the main reason you find it so difficult to love God.

It is perfect that you should bring this up here, because Step Three in forming a true and lasting friendship with God is:

Love God.

Eight

So, to review, the first three steps to God are: Know God, Trust God, Love God.

Right.

Everybody loves God! That last one should be easy!

If it's so easy, why are so many of you having such a hard time doing it?

Because we don't know what it "looks like" to love You.

And that's because you don't know what it looks like to love *each other.*

The third step may not be easy on a planet where loving someone without need is unheard of, where loving another unconditionally is rarely practiced, and where loving everyone without limitation is actually thought of as "wrong."

Human beings have created a lifestyle in which feeling Oneness with everyone all of the time *does* get them "in trouble." And you've just named the chief causes of all this trouble. You might call these the three great love-enders.

1. Neediness
2. Expectation
3. Jealousy

You cannot truly love another when any of these three is present. And you certainly can't love a God who indulges in any one of these, much less all of them. Yet that is exactly the kind of God you believe in, and, since you've declared it to be good enough for your God, you've allowed it to be good enough for yourselves as well. So that is the environment within which you seek to create and sustain your love for each other.

You have been taught of a God who is jealous, who has enormous expectations, and who is so needy that if His love for you is unrequited, He'll punish you with everlasting damnation. These teachings are now a part of your cultural story. They are so imbedded in your psyche that it will be a major undertaking to root them out. And yet, until you do, you cannot ever hope to truly love each other, much less Me.

What can we do?

In order to solve a problem, you have to first understand it. Let's take a look at this particular problem one element at a time.

Neediness is the most potent love killer there ever was. Yet most members of your species do not know the difference between love and need, and so they have confused the two, and continue to do so daily.

"Need" is when you imagine that there is something outside of yourself that you do not now have, and that you require in order to be happy. Because you believe that you need this, you will do almost anything to get it.

You will seek to acquire what you think you require.

Most people acquire what they think they require by trading. They trade what they already have for what they seek to have.

It is this process they call "love."

Yes, we have had this discussion before.

Indeed, we have. But this time, let's take it one step further, because it is important to understand how you came to this idea about love.

You imagine that this is the way to show your love for each other because you have been taught that this is the way God shows love for you.

God has worked out a trade deal: if you love Me, I'll let you into heaven. If you don't love Me, I won't.

Someone has told you that this is the way God is, and so this is the way you have become.

It's as You've said: what's good enough for God ought to be good enough for me.

Precisely. Thus have you created in your human mythology a story that you live out every day: love is conditional. Yet this is not a truth, but a myth. It is part of your cultural story, but it is not a part of God's reality. In reality, God needs nothing, and thus requires nothing from you.

How can God need anything? God is the All-in-All, the Everything, the Unmoved Mover, the Source of anything that you could imagine that God needs.

Understanding that I have everything, am everything, and require nothing is part of knowing Me.

Step one in having a friendship with God.

Yes. Once you truly know Me, you begin to disassemble your myth about Me. You change your mind about who I am, and how I am. And once you change your mind about how I am, you begin to change your mind about how you have to be. That is the start of transformation. That is what a friendship with God does. It transforms you.

I am so excited about this! No one has ever explained things to me this simply, this clearly.

Then listen to this carefully, for here comes the greatest clarity of all.

You are made in the image and likeness of God. Now this you have always understood, for this, too, you have been taught. Yet you are mistaken about what My image and likeness *is.* Thus have you been mistaken about what your image and likeness can be.

You imagine that I am a God who has needs—among them, the need to have you love Me. (Now, some of your churches have sought to describe this as not having a *need* for your love, but merely a desire for it. It is simply, they say, My desire that you love Me, but I will never force you to. Yet is a "desire" not a "need" if I am willing to torture you for all eternity if I don't get it? What kind of a desire is that?)

And so, being made in My image and likeness, you have called it normal to experience the same kind of desire. Thus have you created your fatal attractions.

But now I am telling you that *I have no needs.* All that I am within My Self is all that I require in order to express all that I am outside of My Self. This is the true nature of God. This is the image and likeness in which you are made.

Do you understand the wonder of that? Do you see its implications?

You, *too,* are without needs. There is nothing that you need in order to be perfectly happy. You only think that there is. Your deepest, most perfect happiness will be found within, and once you find it, nothing exterior to your Self can match it, nor can anything destroy it.

Oh, boy, the old happiness is within sermon. Excuse me, but how come I don't experience that?

Because you do not seek to. You seek to experience the grandest part of your Self outside of your Self. You seek to experience Who You Are through others, rather than allowing others to experience Who They Are through you.

What did You say? Would You say that again?

I said, you seek to experience Who You Are through others, rather than allowing others to experience Who They Are through you.

That may be the most important thing You ever said to me.

It is a fairly intuitive statement.

What does *that* mean? I don't know what that means.

Many of life's most important statements are intuitive. You know that they are true before you know why or how. They come from a deeper understanding that transcends evidence and proof and logic and reason and all those tools with which you try to determine whether something is true or not—and thus, whether it is important. Sometimes you know something is important just from the ring of it. It has the "ring of truth."

All my life I have believed what others have said about me. I have changed my behaviors, altered who I am, in order to change what others were saying about me, and change what they were telling me about myself. I was literally experiencing myself through others, just as You've said.

Most human beings do that. Yet when you reach mastery, you will allow others to experience Who They Are through you. This is how you will know a Master when you see one: the Master is one who sees *you.*

The Master gives you back to your Self, for the Master recognizes you. That is, the Master re-cognizes you—knows you again. And thus do you once again re-cognize your Self. You know your Self, again, as Who You Really Are. Then you pass this on to others. *You* have become a Master, and no longer seek to know your Self through others, but choose to have others know themselves through you.

Thus have I said, a true Master is not the one with the most students, but one who creates the most Masters.

How can I experience the truth of this? How can I stop needing affirmation from without, and find all that I require to be happy within?

Go within. To find what is within, *go* within. If you do not go within, you go without.

You've said that before, too.

Indeed, all of these things have I shared with you before. All of this wisdom has been given you. Do you imagine that I would make you wait to hear the greatest truths? Why would I keep these things secret?

Not only have you heard these things before in your previous conversations with God, you have heard them elsewhere as well. There is no revelation here, except the revelation that all has already been revealed.

Even you have been revealed to your Self. And that revelation, which has been given you, lies deep within your soul.

Once you get a glimpse of that, once you have even a momentary experience of it, you will be very clear that nothing outside of yourself can compare with what is within you; that no feeling you get from any exterior stimulation or source is anything like the total bliss of communion within.

I tell you again, it is within that your bliss will be found. There will you remember once again Who You Are, and there will you experience once more that you have no need of anything exterior to your Self.

There will you see the image of you, in the likeness of Me.

And on that day will your need for *anything* else end, and will you be able, at last, to truly love, and to love truly.

You speak with such force and grace and eloquence. I am so often having my breath taken away by You. But tell me again how I can go within. How can I know myself as he who needs nothing exterior to himself?

Simply be quiet. Be with your Self in the stillness. Do this often. Do this daily. Even hourly in small doses if you can.

Just stop. Stop all of your doingness. Stop all of your thinking. Just "be" for a while. Even for only a moment. It can change everything.

Take an hour every day at dawn and give it to your Self.

Meet your Self there, in the holy moment. Then go about your day. You will be a different person.

You are talking about meditation.

Do not get caught up in labels, or ways of doing things. That is what religion has done. That is what dogma seeks to do. Do not create a label or a set of rules around this.

What you call meditation is nothing more than being with your Self—and thus, ultimately, *being* your Self.

You can do this in many ways. For some of you it may look like what you call "meditation"—that is, sitting quietly. For others it may look like walking alone, in nature. Scrubbing a stone floor with a brush on hands and knees can be a meditation—as many a monk has discovered. Others, outsiders, come to a monastery and see this work and think, oh, what a hard life. Yet the monk is deeply happy, deeply at peace. He is not looking to get out of scrubbing floors, he is looking for another floor to scrub! Just give me another floor! Give me another brush! Give me another hour on my hands and knees, my nose six inches from the cobblestones. I'll give you the cleanest floor you've ever seen! And my soul will be cleansed in the process. Cleansed of any thought that happiness requires something outside of itself.

Service can be a deep form of meditation.

Okay, let's say that I've discovered that I don't need anything from anyone else to be truly happy. Wouldn't this make me anti-social?

On the contrary, it will make you more social than ever, for now you clearly see that you have nothing to lose! *Nothing inhibits your loving each other more than the thought that you have something to lose.*

It is for this same reason that you have found it difficult, and frightening, to love Me. You have been told that if you do not love Me in the right way, at the right time, for the right reasons, I will become angry. For I am a jealous God, you have been told, and I will not accept your love in any way, shape, or form other than that in which I demand it.

Nothing could be farther from the truth, yet the truth has never been farther from your awareness.

I need nothing *from* you, and therefore seek, want, and demand nothing *of* you. My love for you is without condition and without limitation. You will return to Heaven whether you have loved Me in the right way or not. There is no way for you not to return to Heaven, because there is no place else to go. Thus is your eternal life assured, and your eternal reward guaranteed.

You said in *Conversations with God* that even making love, experiencing sexual ecstasy, can be a form of meditation.

That is correct.

But that is not being with the self. That feels like being with another.

Then you do not know what it is like to be truly in love. For when you are truly in love, there is only one of you in the room. What starts out as being with another becomes an experience of being One—of being with the Self. Indeed, that is the whole purpose of sexual expression, and of every form of love.

You have an answer for everything!

I should hope so.

So what about the other two love-enders, expectation and jealousy?

Even if you manage to eliminate need from your relationship with each other, and with Me, you may still have to struggle with expectation. This is a state in which you have an idea that someone else in your life is to perform in a particular way, is going to show up as who you think they are, or who you think they should be.

Like need, expectation is deadly. Expectation reduces freedom, and freedom is the essence of love.

When you love someone, you grant them total freedom to be who they are, for this is the greatest gift you could give them, and love always gives the greatest gift.

It is the gift that I give you, yet you cannot imagine that I am giving it to you, because you cannot imagine a love so great. So you have decided that I must have given you the freedom to do only the things that I want you to do.

Yes, your religions say that I give you the freedom to do anything, to make any choice you wish. Yet I ask you again: if I torture you endlessly and damn you eternally for making a choice I did not want you to make, have I made you free? No. I have made you able. You are *able* to make whatever choice you wish, but you are not *free* to. Not if you care about the outcome. And, of course, all of you do.

So this is how you've got it constructed: if I'm to grant you your reward in heaven, I expect you to do things My way. And this you call God's love. Then, you hold each other in the same place of expectation, and you call *this* love. Yet it is not love, in either case, for love expects nothing save what freedom provides, and freedom knows nothing of expectation.

When you do not require a person to show up as you imagine you need them to be, then you can drop expectation. Expectation goes out the window. Then you love them exactly as they are. Yet this can only happen when you love your Self exactly as you are. And *that* can only happen when you love *Me* exactly as *I* am.

In order to do that, you must know Me as I am, not as you have imagined Me to be.

That is why the first step in having a friendship with God is to know God, the second step is to trust the God that you know, and the third step is to love the God that you know and trust. You do that by treating God as *someone you know and trust.*

Can you love God unconditionally? That is the big question. All this time you may have thought that the question was, Can God love *you* unconditionally, but the big question is, Can you love *God* unconditionally. Because you can only receive My love in the way you give Me yours.

Oh, my, that's an enormous statement. Again, I'm going to ask You to repeat it. I can't let that one just slip past.

You can only receive God's love in the way that you give God yours.

I suppose this is true of human relationships as well.

Of course. You can only receive another's love in the way that you give them yours. They can love you their way as long as they want. You can only receive it your way.

You cannot experience what you do not allow others to experience.

And that brings us to the last element in this answer: jealousy.

Out of your decision to love God jealously, you have created the myth of a God who loves jealously.

Wait a minute. You're saying we are jealous of You?

Where do you think the idea of a jealous God came from?

You have tried as hard as you can to co-opt My love. You have tried to be the sole owner. You have laid claim to Me, and done so viciously. You have declared that I love you, and *only* you. *You* are the chosen people, *you* are the nation under God, *you* are the one true church! And you are very jealous of this standing that you have bestowed upon yourself. If someone claims that God loves all people equally, accepts all faiths, embraces every nation, you call that blasphemy. You say it is a blasphemy for God to love in any way other than the way *you* say God loves.

George Bernard Shaw said that all great truths begin as blasphemies.

He was right.

This jealousy-ridden kind of love is not the way that I love, yet this is the way that you have perceived My love, because this is the way that you have loved Me.

This is also the way you have loved each other, and it is killing you. I mean that literally. You have been known to kill each other, or yourselves, because of your jealousies.

If you love another person, you tell them that they must love you, and only you. If they love another person, you become jealous. And this is not where it begins and ends. For you are not only jealous of other people, you are jealous of jobs, of hobbies, of children, of anything that takes the focus of your loved one away from you. Some of you are jealous of a dog, or a game of golf.

Jealousy takes many forms. It has many faces. Not a one of them is beautiful.

I know. Once, in a moment when I was having jealous feelings about a woman named Dawn with whom I was deeply in love, I was expressing that to her, and she said to me, very quietly, "Neale, this is not a very attractive part of you."

I never forgot that. It was stated so simply, without emotion.

It was just a matter of fact. There was no argument about what I had just said, and no lengthy discussion about what she had just said. She just put that thought out into the room. It was shattering.

Dawn gave you a great gift.

Yes, she did. Still, jealousy has been hard for me to get over. Just when I think I'm rid of it at last, here comes more. It's like it's in *hiding,* and I don't even know that it's there. In fact, I swear that it's *not* there. And then, *boom,* there it is.

I think I experience less of it now, but if I said that I don't ever feel any, I'd be lying.

You're working on it, that's enough. You're recognizing it for what it is, and that's good.

But how can I get rid of it? I know some people who actually have gotten rid of it, completely. How do they do that? I want to do that!

You mean you're jealous of people with no jealousy? That's pretty funny.

Cute. You're cute, You know that?

Of course I do. What do you think keeps Me going?

Okay, so what's the answer?

Get rid of your idea that happiness depends on anything outside of yourself, and you will get rid of jealousy. Get rid of your thought that love is about what you *get* in trade for what you give, and you will get rid of jealousy. Get rid of your claim on any other person's time or energy or resources or love, and you will get rid of jealousy.

Yes, but how do I do *that?*

Live your life for a new reason. Understand that its purpose has nothing to do with what you get out of it, and everything to do with what you put into it. This is also true of relationships.

The purpose of life is to create your Self anew, in the next grandest version of the greatest vision ever you held about Who You Are. It is to announce and become, express and fulfill, experience and know your true Self.

This requires nothing of the other people in your life—or any other person in particular. That is why you can love others without requiring anything of them.

The idea of being jealous of the time that those you love spend playing golf, or working at the office, or in the arms of another is an idea that can only occur to you if you imagine that your own happiness is compromised when the one that you love is happy.

Or that your happiness depends on your loved one always being with you, rather than being with someone else, or doing something else.

Exactly.

But hold on a minute. Do You mean that we shouldn't even be jealous when our loved one is in the arms of another? You mean that infidelity is okay?

There is no such thing as okay and not okay. These are measures that you are making up. You are creating them—and changing them—as you go along.

There are those who say that this is the very problem with society today; that we are being spiritually and socially irresponsible. We are changing our values in the moment, to suit our purposes.

Of course you are. That is the way life is. If you did not do that, life could not proceed. You would never make any progress at all. Do you truly want to hold onto your old values forever?

Some people do.

They want to hang women in the town square, calling them witches, as you did just a few generations ago? They want their church to send soldiers out on crusades, killing people by the thousands for not confessing the one true faith?

But you're using historical examples of human behaviors that arose out of misplaced values, not old values. We've risen above those behaviors.

Have you? Have you looked at your world lately? Yet that is another subject altogether. Let's stick to this one.

Changing values are the sign of a maturing society. You are growing into a larger version of yourself. You are changing your values all the time as you gather new information, as you bring in new experiences, as you consider new ideas and discover new ways of looking at things, and as you redefine Who You Are.

This is a sign of growth, not of irresponsibility.

Let me get this straight. It is a sign of growth to be okay with our loved one hanging out in the arms of another?

It is a sign of growth not to have your peace taken away from you by that. Not to disrupt your life because of that. Not to end your life because of that. Not to kill another because of that. All of these things, humans have done. Even now, some of you are killing others because of that, and most of you are killing your love because of that.

Well, I don't agree with killing, of course, but how can it not kill your love for someone when they are loving another at the same time they say that they are loving you?

Because they love another, does that mean that they do not love you? Must they love you only, in order for their love to be true? Is this how you have it?

Yes, doggone it! That's what many people would say. *Yes, doggone it.*

No wonder you have such trouble accepting a God who loves everyone equally.

Well, we are not gods. Most people need some level of emotional security. And without it, without a mate or partner providing it, love can just die, whether you want it to or not.

No, it is not love that dies. It is the need. You decide that you do not need that person anymore. In fact, you don't *want* to need that person, because it hurts too much. So you make a decision: I don't need you to love me anymore. Go and love whomever you wish. I'm out of here.

That's what happens. You kill the need. You do not kill the love. Indeed, some of you carry the love forever. Friends say that you are still carrying a torch. And you are! It is the light of your love, the flame of your passion, still burning inside of you, shining so brightly that others can see it. But this is not bad. This is as it should be—given who and what you say you are, and what you declare that you choose to be.

You're supposed to never be able to fall in love with anyone else because you're carrying a torch for someone?

Why do you have to let your love for that one person go in order to love another? Can you not love more than one person at a time?

Many people cannot. Not in that way.

You mean sexually?

I mean romantically. I mean, as a life partner. Some people need a life partner. Most people do.

The difficulty is that most people confuse love with need. They think that the two words, and the two experiences, are interchangeable. They are not. Loving someone has nothing to do with needing them.

You can love someone and need them at the same time, but you don't love them *because* you need them. If you love them because you need them, you have not loved them at all, but merely what it is that they have given you.

When you love another for who they are, whether they give you what you need or not, then you truly love them. When there is nothing that you *do* need, then you truly *can* love them.

Remember, love is without condition, without limitation, and without need. This is how I love you. Yet this is a love that you cannot imagine receiving, because it is a love that you cannot imagine expressing. And that is the sadness of all the world.

Now, given that you say that you wish to become Highly Evolved Beings, infidelity, as you call it, is not okay. That is because it will not work. It will not get you where you say you want to go. And that is because infidelity means not being true, and somewhere deep inside your soul you know and understand that Highly Evolved Beings live and breathe and have their being in truth—first, last, and always. Truth is not what they speak, truth is who they are.

To be a Highly Evolved Being, you must always be true. First, you must be true to yourself, then to another, then to all others. And if you are not true to yourself, you cannot be true to anyone else. Thus, if you love someone other than the one who wishes you to love only them, then you must say so, openly, honestly, directly, clearly, and immediately.

And that's supposed to be acceptable?

Nobody is required to accept anything. In highly evolved relationships between Highly Evolved Beings, everyone simply lives their truth—and everyone speaks the truth they are living. If something is happening with someone, that is simply acknowledged. If something is unacceptable to someone, that is simply spoken. The truth is shared with everyone about everything all the time. This is done as a celebration, not an admission.

The truth should be something to celebrate, not to admit.

Yet you cannot celebrate a truth of which you have been told to be ashamed. And you have been told to be ashamed of nothing more than you have been told to be ashamed of who and how and when and why you love.

You have been told to be ashamed of your desires and your passions and your love of everything from dancing to whipped cream to other people.

Most of all, you have been told to be ashamed of your love for your very Self. Yet how can you ever love another if you are not allowed to love the one who is supposed to be doing the loving?

This is the precise dilemma that you face with God.

How can you love Me if you cannot be allowed to love the essence of Who You Are? And how can you see and declare My glory if you cannot see and declare your own?

I tell you this—again: all true Masters have declared their glory, and they have encouraged others to do the same.

You begin on the road to your own glory when you begin on the road to your own truth. This path is taken when you declare that, henceforth, you will tell the truth all the time, about everything, to everyone. And that you will *live* your truth.

In this commitment, infidelity has no place. Yet telling someone that you love another is not infidelity. It is honesty. And honesty is the highest form of love.

Oh, my God. You did it again. There's another one for the refrigerator. Would You repeat that, please?

Honesty is the highest form of love.

I wish I could remember that.

Put it on your refrigerator.

Ha! So You seem to be saying that being in the arms of another is okay, as long as you're honest about it. Am I getting this right?

You are reducing it to its most volatile terms.

Well, we humans like to do that. We like to take great truths and reduce them to simplistic conclusions. Then we can have really good arguments about them.

I see. Is that your intention here? Do you wish to have an argument with Me?

No. I really am trying to get at some wisdom here, in my own stumbling way.

Then it would benefit you to listen to everything I am saying and to place all of My words into that larger context, rather than create a meaning out of only a few of My words.

I stand corrected.

Do not stand corrected. Stand advised. A correction is for someone who has done wrong. Advice is for someone who is seeking direction.

God gives direction, not correction; commendation, not condemnation.

Whew. Oh, boy . . .

I know, I know. Another bumper sticker.

Well, it *is*. It really is!

Make as many bumper stickers as you like. T-shirts, too. Get the word out. Stop at nothing. Do a movie. Go on television. Be shameless!

While you're at it, be shameless about love. Get the shame out of it, and replace it with celebration.

. . . you may want to do the same thing about sex.

Let's not get into that, or we'll never get my question answered. Are You saying that being in the arms of another is okay, as long as you're honest about it?

I am saying that a thing is okay or not okay depending on what you decide about it. I am saying that people in relationship cannot even know if it is okay with them if they do not know that it is occurring.

I am saying that what does not work in highly evolved relationships is lying—about anything. I am saying that lying is lying, whether it is by commission or omission. And I am saying that once the whole truth is told, your decision about whether you can love a person who has loved, or is now loving, another is ultimately based on what you declare to be your most appropriate and comfortable form of relationship—and that this will be based, in most cases, on what you imagine that you need from another person in order to be happy.

I am saying that if you need nothing, then you can love another unconditionally, without any limitations whatsoever. You can grant them total freedom.

Yes, but then you wouldn't be in a life partnership with them.

You wouldn't, unless you would. Mastery is reached when this becomes a decision and a choice based on what is true for you, rather than what someone else has told you ought to be true, or on what your society has established as its current convention around life partnerships, or on what you feel others may think of you.

Masters give themselves the freedom to make any choice they wish—and give those they love the same freedom.

Freedom is the basic concept and construct of life everywhere, because freedom is the basic nature of God. All systems which reduce, restrict, impinge upon, or eliminate freedom in any way are systems which work against life itself.

Freedom is not the *goal* of the human soul, but its very nature. By *nature* the soul is free. Lack of freedom is, therefore, a violation of the very nature of the soul. In truly enlightened societies, freedom is not recognized as a right, but as a fact. It is something that *is,* rather than something that is *given.*

Freedom is not granted, but rather, *taken* for granted.

What is observable in enlightened societies is that all beings are free to love each other, and to express and demonstrate that love to each other, in whatever way is authentic and true and appropriate to the moment.

The people who decide what is appropriate to the moment are the people doing the loving. There are no laws of government, societal taboos, religious restrictions, psychological barriers, tribal customs, or unspoken rules and regulations regarding who, when, where, and how one may love, and who, when, where, and how one may not.

Yet here is the key that makes this work in highly evolved societies. *All* the parties who are in love must decide what love would do now. One party may not decide to do something because he thinks it is loving, if there is no agreement from the other party or parties. All the parties must also be adult and mature and capable of making such decisions for themselves.

This eliminates all the questions you just had in your head about child abuse, rape, and other forms of personal violation.

What if I am a third party, and I don't think that what two other people have decided is loving is very loving toward me?

Then you must tell the other parties how you feel about it, what your truth is. And, depending upon how they respond to your truth, you can decide what changes, if any, you wish to make in the form of your relationship with them.

But what if it's not all that easy? What if I need them?

The less you need from someone, the more you can love them.

How can you need nothing from someone you love?

By loving them not for what they can give you, but simply for who they are.

But then they could walk all over you!

Loving another does not mean that you must stop loving yourself.

Granting another full freedom does not mean granting them the right to abuse you, nor does it mean sentencing yourself to a prison of your own device, in which you live a life you would not choose, in order that another may live a life that they do. Yet granting full freedom does mean placing no limitations of any kind upon another.

Wait a minute. How can you stop another from walking all over you if you don't place any limitations on them?

You do not place limitations on *them,* you place limitations on *yourself.* You limit what *you* choose to experience, not what *another* is allowed to experience.

This limitation is voluntary, and so, in a very real sense, it is not a limitation at all. It is a declaration of Who You Are. It is a creation. A definition.

No one, and nothing, is limited in God's kingdom. And love knows nothing but freedom. Nor does the soul. Nor does God. And these words are all interchangeable. Love.

Freedom. Soul. God. All carry aspects of the other. All *are* the other.

You are free to announce and declare Who You Are in every moment of Now. Indeed, you are doing so, without even knowing it. You are not free, however, to declare who someone else is, or who they must be. This, love would never do. Nor would God, who is the essence of love itself.

If you wish to announce and declare that you are a person who needs and requires the exclusive love of another in order to be happy, in order to feel comfortable and appropriate and secure, you are free to announce that. You will show it with your actions in any event; they will be your announcement.

If you wish to announce and declare that you are a person who needs and requires the largest portion of the time and energy and focus of another in order to be happy, in order to feel comfortable and appropriate and secure, you are free to announce that, too. Yet I will tell you this: if you allow your declaration of Self to translate into jealousy of another, or of another's friends or job or hobby and outside interests, your jealousy will end your love, and may very well end that other's love for you.

The good news is that defining who you are, and who you choose to be, does not have to translate into jealousy of another, nor into control over them. It simply and lovingly states who you are, and how you choose Life to be for you. Your love for another goes on, even as you lovingly and compassionately work through whatever differences may exist between you, and however you change the nature of your relationship as a result of those differences.

You do not have to end a relationship in order to change it. Indeed, you cannot end a relationship, but can only alter it. You always have a relationship with everyone. The question is not whether you have a relationship, but what kind of relationship do you have?

Your answer to this question will affect your life forever—and, indeed, could truly change the world.

Nine

I have learned throughout my conversations with You that my relationships are sacred. They are the most important aspects of life, because it is through relationships that I express and experience who I am, and who I choose to be.

> And not merely your relationships with other people, but your relationships with everything everywhere. Your relationship with Life, and all the elements of Life. Your relationship with money, love, sex, and God—the four cornerstones of the human experience. Your relationship with trees, plants, animals, birds, wind, air, sky, and sea. Your relationship with nature, and your relationship with Me.

My relationship with everything determines who and what I am. Relationship, You have told me, is holy ground. Because in the absence of a relationship with something else, I cannot create, know, and experience anything I have decided about myself. Or, as You have put it, *in the absence of that which I Am Not, that which I Am . . . is not.*

You have learned well, My friend. You are becoming a messenger.

Yet as I try to explain this to others, they sometimes get lost. This concept doesn't always easily translate.

Try using the Parable of Whiteness.

Yes, that helped me immediately.

Imagine that you are in a white room, with white walls, white floor, white ceiling, no corners. Imagine that you are suspended in this space by some invisible force. You are dangling there, in mid-air. You cannot touch anything, you cannot hear anything, and all you see is whiteness. How long do you think that you will "exist" in your own experience?

Not very long. I'd exist there, but I wouldn't know anything about myself. Pretty soon, I'd go out of my mind.

Actually, that's exactly what you would do. You would, literally, leave your mind. Your mind is the part of you that is assigned the task of making sense out of all incoming data, and without any data incoming, your mind has nothing to do.

Now, the moment you go out of your mind, you cease to exist in your own experience. That is, you cease to know anything in particular about yourself.

Are you big? Are you small? You cannot know, because there is nothing outside of yourself with which to compare yourself.

Are you good? Are you evil? You cannot know. Are you even here? You cannot know, because there is nothing over there.

You cannot know anything about yourself in your own experience. You can conceptualize it all you want, but you cannot experience it.

Then something happens to change all this. There appears a tiny dot on the wall. It's as if someone has come along with a fountain pen and squirted a tiny dot of ink. Nobody knows how the dot actually got there, but it doesn't matter, because the dot has saved you.

Now, there is something else. There is You, and there is the Dot On The Wall. Suddenly, you can make some decisions again, you can have some experiences again. The dot is over there. That means that you must be here. The dot is smaller than you. You are bigger than it. You are starting to define yourself again—in relationship to the Dot On The Wall.

Your relationship with the dot becomes sacred, because it has given you back a sense of your Self.

Now a kitten appears in the room. You don't know who is doing this, who is causing all this to happen, but you are grateful, because now some more decisions can be made. The kitten appears softer. But you appear smarter (at least, part of the time!). It is faster. You are stronger.

More things begin appearing in the room, and you begin to expand your definition of Self. Then it dawns on you. Only in the presence of *something else* can you know yourself. This something else is that which you are not. Thus: *In the absence of that which You Are Not, that which You Are . . . is not.*

You have remembered an enormous truth, and you vow never to forget it again. You welcome every other person, place, and thing in your life with open arms. You reject none of it, because you see now that all that appears in your life is a blessing, presenting you with a greater opportunity to define who you are, and to know yourself as that.

But wouldn't my mind figure out what was going on if I was placed alone in that white room? Wouldn't it say, "Hey, I'm in a white room, that's all. Relax and enjoy it"?

It would at first, of course. But soon, in the absence of any more incoming data, it would not know *what* to think. Ultimately, the whiteness, the emptiness, the nothingness, the aloneness would get to it.

Do you know one of the greatest punishments your own world has devised?

Solitary confinement.

Exactly. You cannot stand being alone for extended periods.

In the most inhumane prisons, there is not even light in solitary. The door is closed, and you are in utter darkness. Nothing to read, nothing to do, nothing else at all.

Since thinking is creating, you would stop creating your reality, because your mind must have data in order to create. You call your mind's creations conclusions, and when it could not come to any conclusions, you would leave it—you would go "out of your mind."

And yet, leaving your mind is not always bad. You do it in all your moments of great insight.

Uh, come again?

You don't believe that insight comes from your mind, do you?

Well, I've always thought . . .

That's been the problem, right there! You've *always thought*. Try *not* thinking once in a while! Try simply *being*.

It is when you just "be" with a problem, rather than keep thinking about it, that the greatest insight comes. That's because thinking is a creative process, and being is a state of awareness.

I don't quite understand. Help me understand. I thought not being able to think was the problem. The guy in the white room goes crazy.

I didn't say he goes crazy. You said that. I said he leaves his mind. He stops creating his reality, because he has no data.

Now, if he stopped creating his reality for an extended

period, that would be one thing. But what if he did this for only a moment? For a brief period? Would such a "time out" help him or hurt him?

That's an interesting question.

Thought, word, and deed are the three levels of creation, yes?

Yes.

When you are thinking, you are creating. Every thought is a creation.

Yes.

So when you are thinking about a problem, you are seeking to create a solution.

Exactly. What's wrong with that?

You can either seek to create a solution, or you can simply become aware of the solution that has already been created.

Once more? For those of us who are slow, could You give me that once more?

None of you is slow! But some of you are using a very slow method of creation. You are trying to create by thinking. This can be done, as we have shown. But now I'm telling you something new. *Thinking is the slowest method of creation.*

Remember, your mind must have data to create. Your being needs no data at all. That is because data is the illusion. It is what you are making up, rather than what *is.*

Seek to create from what *is,* rather than from the illusion. Create from a state of being, rather than from a state of mind.

I'm trying to stay with this, to understand it, but I think You're losing me. You're going too fast.

You cannot find the answer—*any* answer—rapidly by thinking about it. You have to get out of your thoughts, leave your thoughts behind, and move into pure beingness. Have you not heard the truly great creators, the truly great problem solvers, say, when you give them a problem, "hmmm . . . let me be with it for a while . . ."?

Of course.

Well, this is what they are talking about. And you can do the same thing. You can be a great problem-solver, too. But not if you imagine you are going to unravel the riddle by thinking about it. No! To be a genius, you have to be *out of your mind!*

A genius is not one who creates an answer, but who discovers that the answer has always been there. A genius does not create the solution, but finds the solution.

This is not really a *dis*covery, but a *re*covery! The genius hasn't discovered anything but has simply recovered what was lost. It "was lost, but now it is found." The genius is someone who has remembered what all of you have forgotten.

One thing that most of you have forgotten is that all things exist in the Eternal Moment of Now. All solutions, all answers, all experiences, all understanding. In truth, there is nothing for you to have to create. All that is necessary is for you to become aware that everything you wish and everything you seek has already been created.

This is something that most of you have forgotten. That is why I have sent others to remind you, saying, "Even before you ask, you have been answered."

I would not tell you these things were they not so. Yet you cannot move to a state of awareness regarding all these things by thinking about them. You cannot "think aware," you can only "be aware."

Awareness is a state of being. Therefore, if you are perplexed or puzzled about something in life, you must not mind. And when you have a problem, pay it no mind. And when you are surrounded by negativity, negative forces, and negative emotions, do not mind a thing.

When you "mind" it, you obey it! Do you not see? You are controlled by it, because you are minding it. Do not be as children, who mind their parents. Get *out of your mind.*

Remember, you are a human *being,* not a human minding. Move, therefore, into beingness.

What does that mean? I don't know what the hell that means!

What are you being right now?

Agitated. I'm agitated because You're losing me with all this mumbo-jumbo.

Ah, so you *do* know what you are being!

No, that's how I'm *feeling*. I'm feeling agitated.

Then that is what you are being. What you are feeling is what you are being. Have I not told you that feeling is the language of the soul?

Well, yes, but I didn't understand it quite in this way.

Good. So now you are being more understanding.

Yes, a little.

Did you hear what I said?

What?

I said, now you are "being" more understanding.

What are You trying to say to me here?

I am saying to you that in every single moment of now you are "being" something. And what you are feeling tells you exactly what you are being. Your feelings never lie. They do not know how to. They tell you exactly what you are being in any moment. And you can change how you are feeling by simply changing how you are being.

I can? How do I do that?

You can choose to "be" a different way!

That doesn't seem possible. The way I feel is the way I feel. I can't control that.

The way you feel is a response to the way you are being. And you *can* control that. That is what I am telling you here. "Beingness" is a state in which you place yourself, it is not a response. "Feeling" is a response, but "being" is not. Your feelings are your response to what you are being, but your being is not a response to anything. It is a choice.

I am choosing to be what I am?

You are, indeed.

How come I am not aware of that? I don't seem to be aware of that.

Most people are not. Because most people have forgotten that they are creating their own realities. But because you have forgotten you are doing it does not mean you are not doing it. It means that you simply do not know what you are doing.

"Father, forgive them, for they know not what they do."

Exactly.

Yet if I don't know what I'm doing, how can I do anything different?

Now you *do* know what you are doing. That has been the purpose of this whole dialogue. I have come here to wake you up. You are awake now. You are aware. Awareness is a state of being. You are "being" aware. From this state of awareness, you can choose any other beingness. You can choose to be wise, or wonderful. You can choose to be compassionate and understanding. You can choose to be patient and forgiving.

Can't I simply choose to be happy?

Yes.

How? How do I do that?

Don't *do* it. Simply *be* it. Do not try to "do" happy. Simply choose to "be" happy, and everything you do will spring from that. It will be given birth by that. What you are being gives birth to what you are doing. Always remember that.

But how can I choose to be happy? Isn't happiness something that happens? I mean, isn't it something that I just am because of something that is happening, or going to happen?

No! It is something that you *choose* to be because of what is happening, or going to happen. You are *choosing* to be happy. Haven't you ever seen two people reacting entirely differently to the same outer set of circumstances?

Of course. But that's because the circumstances meant something different to each one of them.

You determine what something means! *You* give it its meaning. Until you decide what something means, it has no meaning at all. Remember that. Nothing means anything at all.

Out of your state of beingness will meaning spring.

It is you who are choosing, in any moment, to be happy. Or choosing to be sad. Or choosing to be angry, or mollified, or forgiving, or enlightened, or whatever. You are choosing. *You.* Not something outside of yourself. And you are choosing quite arbitrarily.

Now, here is the great secret. You can choose a state of beingness *before* something happens, just as you do after something happens. Thus, you can *create* your experience, not simply have it.

You are, in fact, doing this right now. In every moment. Yet you may be doing it unconsciously. You may be as someone sleep-walking. If so, it is now time to wake up.

Yet you cannot be totally awake while you are thinking. Thinking is another form of being in a dream state. Because what you are thinking about is the illusion. It is okay. You are living in the illusion, you have placed yourself there, so you should give it some thought. But remember, thought creates reality, so if you've created a reality that you don't like, don't give it a second thought!

"Nothing is evil, lest thinking make it so."

Precisely.

So every once in a while, it might be good to stop thinking all together. To get in touch with a higher reality. To pop out of the illusion.

How can I stop thinking? It seems that I'm always thinking. I'm even thinking about *this!*

First, be quiet. By the way, notice that I said *be* quiet, I did not say think quiet.

Oh, that's good. That's very good.

Okay. Now, after being quiet for a while, you will notice that your thinking at least slows down a bit. It starts to simmer down. Now, start thinking about what you're thinking about.

What's that?

You heard Me. Start thinking about where your thoughts are going. Then, *stop your thoughts from going there.* Focus your thoughts. Think about what you're thinking about. This is the first step toward Mastery.

Whoa. This is blowing my mind.

Exactly.

No, that's not what I meant . . .

Yes, it is. You just didn't know it. This really *is* blowing your mind. What is it that you humans say? Let's blow this joint? Well, now you are going to blow your mind! That is, you are going to *leave it.*

Now, when people see you in this state of mindlessness, they may very well ask, "Have you taken leave of your senses?" And you can answer "Yes! Isn't it great?" Because your mind is your sensory input analyzer, and you've stopped analyzing all the incoming data. You've stopped thinking about it. Instead, you're thinking about what you're thinking about. You're beginning to focus your thoughts, and soon, you will focus your thoughts on nothing at all.

How can you focus on nothing?

First, focus on something in particular. You can't focus on nothing until you first focus on something.

Part of the problem here is that the mind is almost always focused on *many* things. It is receiving input data from a hundred difference sources at all times, and it is analyzing this data faster than the speed of light, sending you information about yourself and what is happening to you and around you.

To focus on nothing, you have to stop all this mental noise. You have to control it, limit it, and, ultimately, eliminate it. You want to focus on nothing, but first, you have to focus on something in particular, rather than *everything at once.*

So make it something simple. You can start with the flickering of a candle. Look at the candle, look at the flame, see what you notice about it, stare deeply into it. Be with the flame. Don't think about it. Be with it.

After a bit, your eyes will want to close. They will become heavy, fuzzy.

Is this self-hypnosis?

Try to avoid labels. You see? You're doing it again. You're thinking about this. You're analyzing it and wanting to give it a name. Thinking about something stops you from just being with it. When you do this, don't think about it. Just be with the experience.

Okay.

Now, when it feels like you want to close your eyes, just close them. Don't think about it. Just let them fall shut by themselves. They'll do this quite naturally if you don't fight to keep them open.

You are now limiting your sensory input. This is good.

Now, begin listening to your breathing. Focus on your breath. Especially, listen to your breathing in. Listening to your Self stops you from listening to everything else. This is when great ideas come. When you listen to your in-breath, you are listening to your *inspiration.*

Oh, my God, how do You do that? How do you keep coming up with stuff like that?

Shhh. Be quiet. Stop *thinking* about this!

Now, focus your inner vision. For once you have inspiration, it will bring you great "in-sight." Focus this insight on the space in the middle of your forehead, just above your eyes.

The so-called Third Eye?

Yes. Place your attention there. Look deeply there. Don't look expecting to see something. Look at the nothing, at the no-thing. Be with the darkness. Do not strive to see anything. Relax, and be content with the peace of emptiness. Empty is good. Creation cannot come except into the void. Enjoy, then, the emptiness. Expect nothing more, want nothing more.

What do we do with all the thoughts that keep popping up? Most people are lucky to get three seconds of emptiness. Could

You address the issue of all the constant thoughts that keep popping up—especially for the beginner? Beginners are very frustrated over why they can't silence the mind and get to the nothingness You are talking about. This may be a piece of cake for You, but it sure isn't for most of us.

You're thinking about this again. I invite you to stop thinking about this.

If your mind keeps filling with thoughts, just watch that, make that okay. As the thoughts pop in, just step back and observe that this is happening. Do not think about it, just notice it. Do not think about what you are thinking about. Just step back and notice it. Don't judge it. Don't get frustrated by it. Don't start talking to yourself about it, like, "Well, here we go again! All I get is thoughts! When do I get to the nothingness?"

You can't get to the nothingness by continually complaining that you are not there. When a thought pops in—some extraneous thought about nothing in particular, having nothing to do with the moment—just notice that. Notice that, and bless it, and make it part of the experience. Don't dwell on it. It's part of the passing parade. Let it pass.

Do the same thing with sounds or feelings. You may notice that you never hear as many sounds as when you are trying to experience total stillness. You may notice that you never have as much trouble feeling comfortable as when you are trying to sit totally comfortably. Just notice this. Step back one level and watch yourself noticing this. Include all of this as part of your experience. But don't dwell on it. It's part of the passing parade. Let it pass.

Like the question you asked just now. It's just a question you had. It's a thought that popped in. It's part of the passing parade. Let it pass. Don't try to answer it, don't try to solve it, don't try to figure it out. Just let it be there. Let it be part of the passing parade. Then let it pass. Notice there's nothing you have to do about it.

In this will you find great peace. What a relief. Nothing to want, nothing to do, nothing to be, except exactly what you are being right now.

Let go. Let it be.

But keep looking. Not anxiously, not expectantly. Just . . . keeping a gentle watch. Needing to see nothing . . . ready to see anything.

Now, the first time you do this, or the tenth time, or maybe the hundredth or the thousandth time you do this, you may see what will look like a flickering blue flame, or a dancing light. It may appear in flashes at first, then steady itself in your sight. Stay with it. Move into it. If you feel your Self merging with it, let that happen.

If that happens, nothing more will have to be said to you.

What is this blue flame, this dancing light?

It is you. It is the center of your soul. It is that which surrounds you, moves through you, *is* you. Say hello to your soul. You've just found it, at last. You've just experienced it, at last.

If you merge with it, if you become One with it, you will know a sublime fullness of joy that you will call bliss. You will discover that the essence of your soul is the essence of Me. You will have become one with Me. For just a moment, perhaps. For only a nanosecond. But that will be enough. After that, nothing else will matter, nothing will ever be the same again, and nothing in your physical world will match it. And this is when you will discover that you need nothing and no one outside of yourself.

That seems a little scary, at some level. You mean I won't want to be with anyone else ever again? I won't want to love anyone, because they can't possibly give me what I've found within?

I did not say that you would never *love* anyone or anything outside of yourself. I said you would never *need* anyone or anything outside of yourself. I will say again, love and need are not the same thing.

If you truly have the experience of inner oneness that I have described, the result will be just the opposite of what you fear. Far from not wanting to be with anyone, you will want to be with *everyone*—but now, for the first time, for an entirely different reason.

No longer will you seek to be with others to get something from them. Now you will yearn to give something to them. For you will desire with all your heart to share with them the experience that you have found within—the experience of Oneness.

You will seek this experience of Oneness with everyone,

because you will know that it is the truth of your being, and you will want to know this truth in your own experience.

This is when you will become "dangerous." You will fall in love with everyone.

Yes, and that *is* dangerous, because we human beings *have* created a life in which feeling Oneness with everyone all of the time gets us into trouble.

Yet you now also know the causes so that you can avoid all this.

Well, yes, I do know now that neediness, expectation, and jealousy really *are* the great love-enders. Still, I'm not sure that I can eliminate these from my life, because I'm not sure I know the formula. I mean, it's one thing to say, *Don't do that anymore,* and it's another thing to say, *Here's how.*

That's where your friendship with Me comes in.

A friendship with God allows you to "know the formula"—not only the formula for getting rid of neediness, expectation, and jealousy, but the formula for all of life, the wisdom of the ages.

Your friendship with Me will also allow you to practicalize this wisdom; to make it practical, to make it real, to make it live in your life. It is one thing to know, and another thing to be able to use what you know. It is one thing to have knowledge, and another to have wisdom.

Wisdom is knowledge, applied.

I will show you how to apply all the knowledge I have given you. I am always showing you that. Yet it will be easier for you to hear me if we have a friendship. Then we can really zing! Then we can really fly!

We are talking here about a real friendship with God. Not a pseudo-friendship, not a make-believe friendship, not a part-time friendship, but an important, meaningful, close friendship.

I am taking you through the steps that will help you do that. The first three steps are:

1. Know God
2. Trust God
3. Love God

And now we're looking at Step Four: Embrace God.

Embrace God?

Embrace God. Get close to God.

That's what we've been talking about here. We've been talking about how to get close to God.

I'd like to do that. I'd like to be close to You. I've always wanted to be close to You. I just didn't know how.

And now you do. Now you know one very good way. By being with the silence, being with the Self, for a few golden moments each day. This is where you may most profitably begin.

When you are with the Self—the True Self—you are with Me, for I am One with the Self, and the Self is One with Me.

As I have said to you before, there is more than one way to do this. I have given you one way, I have just described one way, but there is more than one way. There is more than one way to the Self, and more than one way to God, and that is something that every religion in the world would do well to understand—and to teach.

Once you have found your Self, you may wish to begin to move out from the Self, to create a newer world. To do this, touch others as you would have your Self be touched. See others as you would have your Self be seen.

"Do unto others as you would have them do unto you."

Exactly. Embrace others as you would seek to embrace Me, for when you embrace others, you *do* embrace Me.

Embrace all the world, for all the world embraces who and what I am.

Reject nothing of the world, and no one in it. Yet while you are in the world, and the world is in you, remember that you are larger than it. You are the creator of it, for you are creating your own reality as surely as you are experiencing it. You are both the creator and the created, as am I.

I am made "in the image and likeness of God."

Yes. And you can choose to have the experience of being the creator, or that which is created, at any given moment.

I can choose to be "in this world, but not of it."

You are learning, My friend. You are taking the knowledge I have given you, and turning it into wisdom. For wisdom is knowledge applied. You are becoming a messenger. We are beginning to speak with one voice.

Making friends with You really does mean making friends with all people, and with everything—every circumstance and condition.

Yes.

What if there is a person or condition that you would rather not see continue having an effect in your life? What if there is a person or condition that you find hard to love, that you find yourself wanting to resist?

What you resist, persists.
Remember that.

The solution, then?

Love.

Love?

There is no condition, no circumstance, no problem that love cannot solve. This does not mean that you must submit to abuse. We have discussed this before. It does mean that love, for yourself and others, is always the solution.

There is no person that love cannot heal. There is no soul that love cannot save. Indeed, there is no saving to be done at all, for love is what every soul is. And when you give the soul of another what it is, you have given it back to itself.

That's what I have said that You do for *us!* And that has become the mission statement of my foundation. That's what came to me when I was trying to write the mission statement: *To give people back to themselves.*

Do you think this was by accident?

I suppose by now I should know better.

Perhaps you should.

Nothing is by accident, is it?

Nothing.

Not my getting into radio, not my going to live in the South, not my being offered a job at an all-black radio station, and not my meeting with Jay Jackson at *The Evening Capital.* It's all been very *non*-accidental, hasn't it?

Yes.

I think I knew that the first time Jay and I met. There seemed to be something fated between us. I can't explain it; it's just a feeling I had, almost from the moment I stepped into his office. I was nervous, yes, because I desperately needed work. But I had a sense that things were going to turn out all right almost immediately after I sat down.

Jay was a wonderful man. As I grew to know him, I found him to be compassionate, deeply understanding of the human condition, incredibly friendly, and most of all, humanly kind. Everyone loved him.

And Jay saw the positive in everyone. He gave everyone a chance. And then a second chance, and a third. Working for him was a dream. When you did something good, he never missed it. You'd get a note immediately, always in felt-tipped pen: *Nice job on the budget story,* or, *Re: interview with the nun—JUST GREAT!* These notes flew off his desk in a flurry; you could find them all over the newsroom, every day.

I loved Jay, and I couldn't believe it when he died so young.

He was in his mid-forties, I would guess, and had some kind of stomach problem. Or maybe it was something much larger, I don't know. All I know is that in the last months I worked along side him, he was eating nothing but mush. Baby food, mainly. Or oatmeal. That's the only kind of stuff he could eat.

We were at *The Anne Arundel Times* then. *The Evening Capital* had been purchased, and Jay, along with his father and brother, had bought another small paper and turned it into a weekly serving all of Anne Arundel County (Annapolis was the county seat). I was still working at the *Capital* when Jay called and offered me a job as the founding managing editor of the *Times.* It took me two seconds to decide.

I'd received a liberal education at the first paper, but I learned even more at the second. A much smaller publication, with a tiny staff, it required hands-on preparation each week. I learned about layout and paste-up.

I was also the newspaper's photographer (I had to learn fast how to handle a camera, and even how to work my way around a darkroom), and its ace (actually, only) reporter. I also learned a lot about operating under pressure, with all of a newspaper publication's unforgiving time deadlines.

I'm hoping that what you "get" here is that I discovered talents I didn't even know I had. I also discovered that *I could call forth these talents* by simply pressing myself to do so. This was a major revelation for me. This was a major message. A memo from The Top. God was telling me something that I have used countless times since: life begins at the end of your comfort zone.

I have said this before and I will say it again. Don't be afraid in your life to s-t-r-e-t-c-h. Reach higher than your grasp. It may seem scary at first, but you'll come to enjoy it.

As for me, I loved it. I thrived on it. I couldn't get enough of it. And Jay knew that about me. He saw that in me, and he drew it out of me. In those younger years I was often beset by insecurity, but Jay knew what I was made of. He gave me back to myself. All Masters do that, and by so doing they give the greatest blessing.

I blossomed under Jay's tutelage, under his firm but gentle guidance, and his "nothing is impossible" brand of leadership. In fact, I soon adopted it, made it my own. It matched up well with what my father had taught me: *You can do anything you set your mind to.* Or, as my mother would put it, *Where there's a will, there's a way.*

As I said, I really was shocked when Jay died so young. I didn't think that a person that good should have to leave so soon.

His work was done.

I know. I know that now. But I didn't understand that then. I was mystified, hurt. If this is the reward for the really nice ones, what's the point? That's where I was in my head. I wasn't even sure in those days whether there was such a thing as a hereafter. I didn't know if there was life after death. Jay's death shook me. It made me look hard at this question.

Did you find an answer?

Yes. I received my answer the day of Jay's funeral.

How did that happen?

Jay gave me the answer himself. In two words. In the graveyard. In his own voice.

Ten

A graveyard is, perhaps, an unlikely place to find enlightenment, but that's where I found it. A piece of it, anyway.

I'd gone to Jay's funeral service at St. Anne's Church in Annapolis, but arrived late and found just about every seat in the place taken. Half the city must have been there, and I don't know why, but I felt somehow out of place with all the public mourners. I guess I wanted a private moment, just between us. I'd lost a very good friend. We'd become that. He'd been like an older brother to me.

I left the church and decided to have my personal "service" for Jay, my own private good-bye, at his gravesite later that day. Two hours later, when I guessed that everyone would have been to the grave and left, I made my way to St. Anne's Cemetery. My guess was right. There was no one there. I set out to find Jay's grave and say my farewell. Except I couldn't find the gravesite. Anywhere. I looked at row after row of headstones, but no ELMER (JAY) JACKSON, JR. I doubled back and looked again. Nothing.

I was becoming frustrated. Maybe I should have stuck with the funeral party after all. Had I gotten the wrong cemetery? Was I just not looking in the right place? I really wanted to say goodbye to Jay. I really wanted this moment. And now it was starting to drizzle. The wind had come up, and it looked like a storm was brewing. *C'mon, Jay,* I shouted inside my head, *where are you?*

You know how, when you're at a traffic light and you want it to change and it isn't changing, you shout, *C'mon, change, darn it,* inside your head? That's what I was doing here. You don't really expect the light to change, right then, right there, in that instant. And you don't really expect to get an answer in a cemetery. (In fact, you'd rather not.)

Well, I did. And it scared the wits out of me.

Over here.

That's all he said. But it was his voice, Jay's, as crisp and as clear as a bell. It came from directly behind me, and I whipped around so fast I almost left my shoes.

There was no one. Nothing.

I could have *sworn* I'd heard Jay.

Then I heard him again.

Over here.

This time it came from further away, in the direction I was now facing, but up, over a small knoll. A chill ran up my back. It was Jay's voice. It wasn't someone who sounded like Jay. It was *Jay.*

But there was no one there. So then I thought that maybe a groundskeeper had wandered in. Maybe he saw me looking around and guessed that I was searching for a freshly turned grave. Maybe he was someone who *did* sound a lot like Jay.

But there just was no one around. I really wanted there to be someone around. I really did. Because this voice was not something I was imagining. I *heard* it, as loudly and clearly as I heard the beating of my heart a moment later.

I rushed over to the knoll. Maybe there's somebody on the downside, and I just can't see him from here, I reasoned. I found a vantage point at the top of the knoll and looked around.

No one.

Then I heard the voice again—softer now, the words spoken quietly, as if Jay were right behind me.

Over here.

I turned around, slowly this time. I was frightened. I'll admit it. But fright soon turned to amazement. Jay's headstone was square in front of me. I was standing on his grave.

I jumped off that pile of earth as if I'd been standing on an alligator. *Soorreee,* I apologized. I don't know who I thought I was talking to.

Yes, I did. I was talking to Jay. I knew then that he was there. I knew that he had survived his "death," and that he had called me to his grave for a final, private moment.

My eyes filled with tears. I sat on the ground and rested there for a while, catching my breath, looking at Jay's name, freshly carved in the marble. I waited for him to say something else. He didn't.

"Well," I said, after a while, "what's it like being dead?"

I was trying to lighten the moment. Instead, I saw lightening in the distance. The storm was getting closer.

"Listen, Jay," I said in my head, "I want to thank you for all you did for me, and for all that you are, were, for everyone. You've been such an inspiration to so many people. You've touched so many lives in such a kind and caring way. I just wanted to say thank you. I'm going to miss you, Jay."

I began to quietly sob. Then I received my last communication from Jay. It wasn't in the form of words this time. It was a feeling. A feeling that lovingly swept over me, like someone laying a cape over my shoulders and gently squeezing my arms.

I can't describe it further. There are no words. But I just knew then that Jay was going to be all right, that he *was* all right, and that I would be all right, too. And I understood that everything right then was perfect. It was just the way it should be.

I stood up. "Okay, Jay, I get it," I smiled, *"Nothing is impossible."*

As I turned and walked back down the hill, I could have sworn that I heard a chuckle.

You two shared a beautiful moment there. Thank you.

He was there, wasn't he? I did hear him, didn't I? And he did hear me.

Yes.

There *is* a life after death, isn't there?

Life is eternal. Death does not exist.

I'm sorry to have even asked that question. I should, by now, never doubt these things.

Never?

Never. A true Master like The Buddha, a Master like Krishna, like Jesus, never doubts.

What about, "Father, why hast Thou forsaken Me?"

Well, that was . . . I don't know. I don't know what that was.

Doubt, My son. That was doubt. If only for a moment, if only for a second. So, know this, My friend: every Master visits his Garden of Gethsemane. There, she asks the questions every Master asks. Could this be true? Have I made this all up? Is it really God's will that I drink from this cup? Or could it pass from my lips?

I have some of those questions sometimes, and I'm not ashamed to admit it.

It would be easier for you, I know, if you were not talking to Me right now. In many ways, it would be easier. You could release all this, let all this go—all this responsibility that you have taken on to bring a message to the human race, and to help change the world; all this public attention you have drawn to yourself, which has placed your life in such a spotlight.

Yet, I see that it is your will that you go on. It was your will that all that has occurred in your life should occur. All the incidents of your life have led you to this moment.

You were given the perfect mother and the perfect father to prepare you for this assignment you have given yourself; the perfect family situation and the perfect childhood.

You were given raw talents in communication, and the chance to develop those talents. You were put in just the right place at just the right time, and others were put there with you, in just the right way.

That is why you met Jay Jackson, and why he had such a profound impact on your life. It is why you have worked among Blacks in Baltimore, southern whites, the natives of Africa, the people of Ecuador. It is why you have joined in friendship and meaningful conversation with oppressed and fearful people who have nothing, living under totalitarian regimes in foreign lands, and with world-famous movie stars and television personalities and political leaders who have everything, living in your own country.

Nothing has happened to you by accident, nothing has occurred by chance. It has been called forth, all of it, that you may experience and know what you choose to experience and know, that you may experience the grandest version of the greatest vision ever you held about Who You Are.

I take it, then, that out of the same category came my meeting with Joe Alton.

You take it correctly.

You knew that I would one day need to know all about the political arena if I was to carry Your message to the nation—and, indeed, to the world—in every effective way.

It was you who knew that. You've always known that you wanted to bring new hope to the world, and you understood very well at a deep level that politics, as well as religion, were two areas where changes would have to be made if new hope was to be born, much less endure.

I've always been interested in politics, from the time I was a kid. I just happened (ahem) to have been given a father who was steeped in local politics much of his life. He worked for candidates, he made sure that he knew the people holding office, and our house was always filled with judges and aldermen and ward healers and precinct captains, many of whom regularly played cards with my dad.

When I arrived in Annapolis at nineteen, the first thing I did was get to know Joe Griscom, the mayor, and Joe Alton, the county sheriff. Inasmuch as I worked for the local radio station, I was, nominally, a member of the "working press." So I had a little easier time getting to see these men. I also had something to offer—a little airtime never hurt any politician—and I gave both Joe's plenty.

Not long after I met him, Joe Alton ran for the State Senate from our district and won. I liked Joe immensely; most folks did. He won his elections by wide margins, and when some citizens of Anne Arundel County began pushing for a charter form of government, Joe was corralled into heading up the movement. I became involved in the campaign for home rule, and when it was victorious, Joe Alton went on to be elected Anne Arundel's first county executive.

Several years later, when I found myself back in Annapolis at *The Anne Arundel Times,* Joe Alton called one day.

He liked the way I'd been covering county government, and now he was running for another term as county executive and needed a press aid. But his call didn't come to me. It went to Jay.

I guess he didn't want to offend the owners of the local weekly and figured he'd better ask before he offered me a job. Jay walked into my office one afternoon about three or four months before he died—and said, "Your friend Joe wants you to come to work on his campaign."

My heart jumped. I was always being given these incredible opportunities. They were always dropping in my lap. Jay saw my excitement. "I guess you're going, eh?"

I didn't want to disappoint him. "I won't leave if you really need me," I said. "You've been great to me, and I owe you."

"No, you don't," Jay corrected me. "You owe yourself. Always remember that. If you can have something you want without hurting somebody, you owe it to yourself to go after it. Clean up your desk and scram."

"Right now?"

"Why not? I can see where your heart is, and there's no point in keeping you here, counting the days until you can get over there. So go ahead."

Jay stuck his hand out, and I shook it. "I've enjoyed this," he smiled. "Cub reporter to managing editor. It's been quite a ride for you."

"Yeah."

"We've had a good ride, too. Thanks for taking us along."

"No, thanks for taking *me* along." I choked up. "Thanks for giving me a chance. I really needed that job when you gave it to me. I'll never forget that. I don't know how I can ever repay something like that."

"I do," Jay said.

"How?"

"Pass it on."

That was it. How could I leave this guy? How could I abandon the paper? Jay saw the look on my face. "Don't even think about it," he said. "Pack your stuff and get out of here."

Then he was gone. Just like that. Out of my office, and out the door to the street. But as he left, he said over his shoulder, "Don't look back, friend. Never look back."

That was the last time I saw him.

He gave you good advice.

Really? We should never look back, ever? There's nothing to gain from looking back?

He meant, "No second guesses." Move forward with no second-guessing, no guilt trips, no hesitation. Your life is out in front of you, not behind you. What you've done is what you've done. You can't change that. But you can move forward.

Yes, but isn't it okay to have regrets?

As long as you don't confuse regret with guilt. They are not the same. Regret is your announcement that you did not demonstrate your highest idea about who you are. Guilt is your decision that you are not worthy of doing so ever again.

Your society and your religions teach you of a guilt which requires you to be punished without hope of rehabilitation. Yet I tell you this: the purpose of life is to re-create yourself anew in each moment, in the next grandest version of the greatest vision ever you held about Who You Are.

In this, I have joined you as cocreator, seeing where you are going, seeing the path you have set for yourself, and giving you the tools to experience exactly what you needed to experience, to create exactly what you needed to create. All of this has been called forth by you and Me together.

Whose "will" is it, then?

I tell you that it is Divine Will. Remember this, always:

Your Will and Mine
is that will which is Divine.

Oh, man, that's wonderful. Wow. That says it, doesn't it? That puts it all together. You have a way of doing that. You have a way of putting it all in ten words or less. That's another way of saying something You said in *Conversations with God:* "Your will for you is My will for you."

Yes.

But you said something back there that struck me. You said that I have simply been "using God" to make my life happen. Somehow, that doesn't seem right. I mean, it doesn't feel as though that's the kind of relationship I'm supposed to have with You.

Why not?

I don't know, exactly. But somewhere mixed in there are some things I've been taught about being here to serve God. When I was at St. Lawrence Elementary School in Milwaukee and I was really thinking that I was going into the seminary, I remember the nuns talking about God using me to serve God's purpose. There was never any talk about my using God to serve my purpose.

And yet, this is how I would have it be.

It is? You would?

Yes.

You want us to use You? We are not here for You to use us?

Part of the problem in understanding this, in straightening this out, is that this conversation is being constructed on top of a separation paradigm. That is, we are talking as if you and I were somehow separate from each other—which is, of course, how most of the human race thinks of it. It is how most people imagine their relationship with God to be. So it may be useful to talk within that paradigm if it allows for greater understanding, but I just want to note that we are speaking of the illusion here, not reality, not what is real.

I understand. I agree that there may be some benefit in speaking in illusory terms about life inside "the illusion." I am clear that all life on Earth is illusory. I know now, and often deeply experience, the Ultimate Reality of Oneness, with You and with everything and everyone. But it is helpful to sometimes discuss things within the framework of my—and many people's—lesser understandings. Speaking within that framework, are we not here for You to use us?

If you were there for Me to use you, why is the world the way it is? Could it be that this is what I had in mind? *Or could it be that this is what you've had in mind?* I tell you this: it is the latter, and not the former.

The world around you is exactly what you've had in mind.

I'm going to say that again, because there's a possibility you may have missed it. I said, *The world around you is exactly what you've had in mind.*

What you have *carried in your mind* about the world is what you will see around the world. What you carry in your mind about your life is what you will see in your life.

If I have been using you for My purposes (as you have framed them in your limited understanding), I must be a very inefficient God. I can't seem to get anything done! Even using you as My Messenger and assistant, even sending to Earth My only begotten Son (as some of you would have it), I have been unable to turn the tide, to change the course of events, to create the world of My desires. Could it be that My purpose has been to create the world as it is? Of course not . . . unless . . . My purpose has been for *you* to create the world as you *choose.* In *that* case, you *have* served My purpose, and I *have* been "using" you.

Yet you have also been "using" Me, because it is only through the creative power that resides within you—power given to you by Me—that you have been able to create the world of your dreams.

This is the world of my dreams?

If you had not dreamed it, it could not be.

Many days, this seems like the world of my worst nightmares.

Nightmares are dreams as well. They are particular kinds of dreams.

How do I get rid of them?

Change your mind about what you *hold* in mind about the world. It is part of that same process of which I spoke earlier. Think about what you're going to think about. Think on things good and wondrous. Think of moments of splendor, visions of glory, expressions of love.

"Seek ye first the Kingdom of Heaven, and all else will be added unto you."

Exactly.

And use You, use God, in the process?

God *is* the process. The process is what I Am. It is the process you call Life. You cannot *not* use Me. You can only not know that you are. Yet if you use Me consciously, if you use Me with awareness and with intention, all things will change.

This is Step Five in creating a friendship with God.

Use God.

Please tell me how to do that. It still seems so strange to think of it in those terms. I need You to help me understand what it means to use God.

It means to use all the tools and gifts I have given you.

The gift of creative energy, which allows you to form your reality and create your experience with your thoughts, words, and deeds.

The gift of gentle wisdom, which allows you to know the truth in times when it may be good to judge not by appearances.

And the gift of pure love, which allows you to bless others and accept them without condition, granting them the freedom to make their own choices and to live them, and giving your Divine Self the freedom to do the same, each of you re-creating your Self anew in the next grandest version of the greatest vision ever you held about Who You Are.

I tell you, there is a Divine Force in the universe, and it is made up of these: creative energy, gentle wisdom, pure love.

When you use God, you are simply using this Divine Force.

"May the force be with you."

Precisely. Do you think George Lucas came up with that by accident? Do you imagine that idea came out of thin air? I tell you, I inspired George to come up with those words, and the ideas behind them, just as I am inspiring you now to come up with the words and ideas here.

So go now, and do that which you have given your Self to do. Change the world "by force."

And use Me. Use Me all the time, every day. In your darkest hour and your shining one, in your moment of fear and in your moment of courage, in your ups and your downs, your highs and your lows.

I tell you, you will have all of these. And have had them. For everything there is a season, and a time for every purpose under heaven.

A time to be born, and a time to die;

a time to plant, and a time to harvest that which has been planted;

a time to kill, and a time to heal;

a time to break down, and a time to build up;

a time to weep, and a time to laugh;

a time to mourn, and a time to dance;

a time to cast away stones, and a time to gather stones together;

a time to embrace, and a time to refrain from embracing;

a time to seek, and a time to lose;

a time to keep, and a time to cast away;

a time to rend and a time to sow;

a time to keep silence, and a time to speak;

a time to love, and a time to hate;

a time for war, and a time for peace.

What is it time for now? That is the question. What time do you choose for it to be now? You have had all of these times, and now it is time for you to choose which time you wish to experience "this time"!

For all that has ever happened, is happening now, and ever will happen, is happening right now. This is the eternal moment, the time of your new deciding.

The world awaits you, and your decision. It will put into place what you place into being. You will place into being what you *are* being.

This is how it works. This is how it is. And now is the time of your awakening to this truth. Go forth and spread this message to all the world: the time of your deliverance is at hand. For you have prayed to Me, "deliver us from evil," and I am doing so again, with the message found here. I am holding out, again, the hand of friendship.

A friendship with God.

I am here for you, always.

All Ways.

Eleven

Thank You for this wonderful dialogue on how to have a friendship with God. I'm having another marvelous time with You. And these first five steps alone—know God, trust God, love God, embrace God, use God—could change people's lives.

Yes. But, patience. There are two more.

I know. And I need a little help with the next one.

Help God.

Yes. I need a little help understanding why You need help. I thought You were the one who didn't need anything.

I don't need help, but I enjoy having it. It makes things easier.

Easier? I thought there were no levels of difficulty in God's world. Are You going back on Yourself?

No, in Ultimate Reality there are not. When I converse with you here, I most often use terms consistent with your illusion. If I always spoke to you in terms consistent with ultimate reality, we could not have any conversation at all. You could not understand. It is very challenging to you when I do so even occasionally.

The difficulty is that you do not have words for most of what there is to convey, and of that for which you do have words, you do not have a context within which to place them. This is the difficulty with much spiritual and esoteric writing. They are attempts to convey truth about ultimate reality with limited words, taken out of context.

That must be why so much spiritual writing and sacred scripture has been misinterpreted.

You're right.

So within the context of my understanding, what did You mean when you said that Your having my help "makes things easier"?

I meant that it makes things easier for *you.*

Oh. I thought you meant that it makes things easier for You.

In a sense I did, and it does. But, you see, here's where we get into that "context" thing again. I am crossing over into the context of Ultimate Reality when I say things like that. In Ultimate Reality, what helps you, helps Me, because in Ultimate Reality, you and I are One. There is no separation between us. Yet within the separation paradigm in which you live, within the illusion you are experiencing, such a statement has no meaning.

Throughout this dialogue I have had to do that kind of crossing over, moving from one context to another, in order to explain things that cannot be explained simply by staying within the framework of your own Earthly experience.

Thus, it is a challenge for you to *grok in fullness,* as wonderful Robert Heinlein would put it, what I mean when I say "help God."

Most people can't even grok in fullness what "grok in fullness" means!

Well, exactly. That's the problem, right there. You grok it in fullness.

Why don't we just say, then, that it makes things easier for *Us* when I help God? But now, tell me, how does it make things easier?

In order for you to understand that, you have to understand what God is trying to do. You have to understand what I am up to.

I think I do. You are re-creating Yourself anew in every single moment of Now. You are doing this in the next grandest version of the greatest vision You ever held about Who You Are. And You are doing this in, as, and through us. In that sense, we are You. We are members of the body of God. We are God, "Godding."

You have remembered well, My friend. Once again, We begin to speak with one voice. This is good, for you shall be one of many messengers; not only a seeker of the Light, but a bringer of the Light.

And that is how I can best *help* You! I can best help by remembering. Or, as You would put it, *"re-membering."* That is, becoming *a member once again* of the body of God.

You have truly understood. You have grasped this completely, in its every nuance. Now here is how you can help God. Live your life deliberately, harmoniously, and beneficially. These three ways of living you can accomplish by using the gifts I have given you: creative energy, gentle wisdom, and pure love.

Creative energy has been placed by Me in your entire being, and in everything that proceeds from it. Thoughts, words, and deeds are the Three Tools of Creation. When you know this, you can choose to be the *cause* of your experience, rather than being at the *effect* of it.

Life proceeds out of your intentions for it. When you are aware of this, you can live your life deliberately. The things you think, you think deliberately. The things you say, you say deliberately. The things you do, you do deliberately.

When you do something and people say, "You did that

deliberately!" it will not be an accusation, but a compliment.

Everything you do, you do on purpose—and your purpose in every moment of your life is, indeed, to live the grandest version of the greatest vision ever you held about Who You Are. When you use creative energy, you help God be more of what God is, and seeks to experience of Itself.

Gentle wisdom has been placed by Me in your soul. When you use this gift, you live harmoniously in any situation. Your very Being is harmony itself.

Harmony means feeling the vibration of the moment, of the person, place, or circumstance you are now experiencing, and blending with it. Blending does not mean matching. Singing in harmony does not mean singing in unison. It does mean singing together.

When you sing in harmony, you change the way the entire song is sung. It becomes a new song, a different song. This is the song of the soul, and there is none more beautiful.

Bring a gentle wisdom to your moments. Watch it change them. Watch it change you.

You have that gentle wisdom within you. I have placed it there, and it has never left you. Call on it in times of difficulty and stress, in times of decision or enmity, and it will be there. For when you call on it, you call on Me. When you use gentle wisdom, you help God be more of what God is, and seeks to experience of Itself.

Pure love has been placed by Me in every human heart.

It is that which I Am, and which You Are. Your heart is filled with this love to overflowing. It is bursting. Your whole Self is permeated by it. It is *composed of it.* Pure love is Who You Are.

When you express pure love, you give yourself the direct experience of Who You Are. It is the greatest gift. It looks as if you are giving a gift to others, and you are giving it to your Self. That is because there is no one else in the room. It only looks as if there is. Pure love allows you to see the truth.

When you come from a place of pure love, you live a life that is beneficial to everyone. You make sure that everyone benefits from your having been here. "Kindness" becomes an important word to you. Suddenly, you understand its deeper meaning.

Kindness means not only goodness, it means *sameness.* You realize when you live in pure love that you and all others are of "like kind." You are truly *kin,* and now, suddenly, you see that when you express pure love you are expressing *kin-dness.*

This is what it means to be a *kin-dred spirit.* This is what it is to know a Oneness with all things. And when, in any circumstance or situation, you use pure love, you help God be more of what God is, and seeks to experience of Itself.

You help God when you help yourself *to* God. So have a big helping. Help yourself to as much of God as you like. For this is the food of life, by which all things are nourished.

Take, and eat of this, for this is My body.

You are all members of that One body. And it is time, now, to re-member.

I would not tell this to you if it were not so. This is the greatest truth, so help Me/God.

I have never seen words come together like that, so meaningfully. It's all so . . . *symmetrical.*

God is symmetrical. God is perfect symmetry. There is order in the chaos. There is perfection in the design.

I see that. I see the perfection in the design throughout my life—even in my friend Joe Alton going to jail, though I was shocked when it happened. Joe Alton was found to have committed some relatively minor offenses relating to campaign contributions, and he spent a few months in a minimum-security lockup at a federal prison in Allenwood, Pennsylvania.

The lesson for me in it all—something I always knew but had forgotten—was that there are few saints among us. All of us are trying our best, and many of us stumble, and fall.

This remembering has helped me to stay out of my judgments when the weaknesses of others are revealed by their actions—and when *my* weaknesses are revealed by mine. It has not been an easy task, and I have not always succeeded. But since my days in Anne Arundel County politics, I have always tried. They taught me to always try.

There was another reason I'd been thrust into Joe Alton's presence, though, having nothing to do with this. At some level I must have known that I had to train myself for being with the public, for dealing one-on-one with large numbers of people. I couldn't have picked a better trainer.

Joe Alton had a richer understanding of human nature than just about any person I'd met. Working with him, first as a low-level campaign aide, then as a low-level staff member in the county government, I had a chance to see him put that into action, and it dramatically changed my own way of dealing with people.

Joe was besieged by folks wherever he went. At public meetings they would crowd around, pulling and tugging at him, each person wanting one private moment, a chance to ask a small favor, to request his help, or just to bring themselves to his attention.

As they came at him from every direction, I never saw Joe Alton brush off a single person. It didn't matter how late it was, or how long he'd been there, or how much more he had to do after he left. He never failed to look everyone in the eye, or give anyone his full attention.

One night following such a public meeting, I was playing "lead man," making a path through the crowd in the slow trek from the front of the room to the back of the hall and our waiting car. When we climbed into the backseat at last, I turned to Joe incredulously.

"How do you *do it?*" I asked. "How can you give so much of yourself? All those people, hanging all over you, everybody wanting something from you."

"It's very simple to give them what they want, actually," Joe smiled.

"What do they want?" I had to know. "What kinds of things are they asking you?"

"They all want the same thing."

I looked at him quizzically.

"Don't you know what all people want?"

"No," I had to admit.

Joe looked me straight in the eye. "They all want to be heard."

Thirty years later I would be walking out of meeting rooms and lecture halls with people coming at me from every direction, and I would remember Joe.

People want to be heard, and they deserve to be. They've read your book and given you their mind from cover to cover. They've given you a part of themselves, and they want a part of you, and that's fair, and that's what Joe Alton knew. It's what he deeply understood. He wasn't giving anything away. He was *giving back.*

I've learned that again on the lecture circuit from some wonderful people. Author Wayne Dyer always says to his audiences, "I'm going to stay here until the last one of you has had your book signed and I've had a chance to visit with you." So do a lot of other speakers. They hang around. They give back.

What goes around, comes around.

Joe Alton was the first to teach me that wisdom, too. I learned that "what goes around, comes around" thirty years ago in the rough and tumble of a political campaign.

We were in the trailer late one night following a long and difficult debate. Joe's opponent had been ruthless in his denunciations, saying very little about the substantive issues in the campaign, engaging instead in personal attacks. When I got back to the trailer, I headed immediately for the typewriter. My fingers flew across the keyboard as I composed a stinging and concise rebuttal—a rebuke, as I recall, of unmatched eloquence.

Joe lumbered over casually. "What are you writing?"

"Your statement for the press tomorrow in response to those vicious attacks," I replied in a tone that said, "What *else?*"

Joe just chuckled. "You know I'm not going to use any of that, don't you?"

"Why not? We need to come back at him! We can't let him get away with that!"

"Okay," Joe agreed, "then here's my statement. Are you ready?"

Yes, I thought to myself, *now we're cookin'! Joe will say this much better than I ever could.*

"Go," I said, my fingers poised.

Joe dictated a one-sentence statement: "I'm sorry to see my opponent doing this to himself."

"That's it?" I burst out. *"That's it?"*

"That's it," Joe repeated.

"But what about all those things he said?"

"We can drop down to his level," Joe said quietly, "or we can rise above it. Which do you choose?"

"But, but—"

"—Which do you choose?" Joe asked again.

I glanced at the pages I had written. I reread the first couple of paragraphs. Then I tore them up.

"Good choice," Joe said and he patted me on the shoulder. "You grew up tonight."

Now I want to tell you something about that life experience that you may not realize.

What?

When you use the insight that you gained there, you are *using God.* When you use that story in a book like this, you are *using God.* Because you have taken a gift I have given you and sent it to all the world.

Do you see? This is more than an interesting anecdote. This was more than a simple life episode. You brought this to your Self, and now you've shared it with us, for a reason. You seek to change your Self and change the world.

The telling of stories from your life in this book is about much more than satisfying the curiosity of your readers about your past. It is about causing others to remember what they, too, have always known.

Now here is the symmetry, here is the perfection in the design: it was clear to your soul thirty years ago what persons, places, and conditions would provide perfect experiences that would prepare you to play your role in changing the world. It was also known to your soul that should you choose those experiences, what you received from them would have lasting value that *you would use thirty years later.*

Whoa.

Do you really think anything happens by accident?

I tell you again, there is perfection in the design.

Nothing happens in life by accident. Nothing.

Nothing occurs in your life by chance. Nothing.

Nothing takes place without producing the opportunity for real and lasting benefit to you. Nothing at all.

The perfection of every moment may not be apparent to you, yet that will make the moment no less perfect. It will be no less a gift.

Twelve

When I step back far enough to see the design, to see the beauty of the intricate and delicate weavings in the fabric of my life, I am filled with gratitude.

That is the final step, the Seventh Step, in creating a friendship with God:

Thank God.

It is an almost automatic step. It is what naturally occurs, what naturally follows, if you undertake Steps One through Six.

All your life you have not known God as God really is. Now you can.

All your life you have not trusted God as you wished you could. Now you can.

All your life you have not loved God as you've wanted to. Now you can.

All your life you have not embraced God with a closeness that made God a very real part of your experience. Now you can.

All your life you have not used God as you would use your best friend. Yet now, being as close as you are, you know that you can.

All your life you have not helped God in a conscious way, because you did not know that God wanted any help, and even if you did, you did not know how to give it. Now you do.

It is not your fault that you did not know God. How can you know one thing when everyone is telling you another?

It is not your fault that you did not trust God. How can you trust that which you do not know?

It is not your fault that you did not love God. How can you love that which you do not trust?

It is not your fault that you did not embrace God. How can you embrace that which you do not love?

It is not your fault that you did not use God. How can you use that which you do not hold?

It is not your fault that you did not help God. How can you be helpful with that for which you have no use?

And it is not your fault that you did not thank God. How can you be thankful for that which cannot be helped?

Yet today is a new day. Now is a new time. And yours is a new choice. It is a choice to create anew your personal relationship with Me. It is a choice to experience, at last, a friendship with God.

Everybody in the world wants that. Everybody who believes in God, anyway. We've tried our whole lives to have a friendship with You. We've tried to please You, to not offend You, to find the real You, to have You find us—we've tried everything. But we haven't followed these Seven Steps. At least, I certainly haven't. Not the way You've got them laid them out here. So, thank You. But may I ask You a pointed question?

Certainly.

Why is gratitude necessary? Why is it so important that we thank You? Why is it one of the Seven Steps? Are You a God with such ego needs that if we do not show You our gratitude, You will take away all good things?

On the contrary, I am a God of such love that by showing your gratitude, you will *receive* all good things.

That sounds like a backward way of saying the same thing. I have to show my gratitude in order to receive good things.

You do not have to, it is not a requirement. Many people who seem not the least bit grateful enjoy goodness.

Okay, then I am totally confused.

Gratitude is not something I require. It is not an ego salve, a greaser of the skids, an oiler of the wheels. It does not make God more likely to be good to you next time. Life sends you good things whether you are grateful or not. But with gratitude, life sends them to you faster. That is because gratitude is a state of being.

Remember when I said, *"Thinking is the slowest method of creation"?*

Yes. I was very surprised by that.

You shouldn't be. You perform all of your body's most important functions *without thinking about it.* You don't think about blinking an eye, or taking a breath, or beating your heart. You don't think about perspiring, or saying "ouch." These things just happen, because you are a human being. That is, a human, comma, *being.*

Yes, I remember. You said earlier that some life functions and experiences are created automatically, without any effort, at the level of experience called subconscious. Is this where we create most effectively?

No. You create most effectively, most efficiently, and most rapidly when you create not from the *sub*conscious, but from the *supra*conscious.

The *supra*conscious is the name given to that level of experience reached when the superconscious, conscious, and subconscious, are all rolled into One—and then transcended. This is a place above thought. It is your true state of being, and this true state is Who You Really Are. It is unperturbed, unmoved, unaffected by your thoughts. Thought is not first cause. True Being is.

We are exploring now, very deeply, the most complex

esoteric understandings. The differences here, the *nuances,* become very delicate.

That's okay, I think I'm ready for it. Go.

All right. But remember, here is where we get into some languaging problems. What I'm going to have to do here is cross over into a larger context, and speak from a standpoint of ultimate reality, and then cross back over into the illusion, which is the reality in which you are now living, and hope you can make the translation.

I understand. Let's give it a whirl.

Are you sure? This is going to be rough going here. This is going to be tough sledding; the toughest part of our dialogue so far. You may want to skip over this, just take My word for all this, and go right on.

I want to understand it. At least, I want to try.

Okay. Here we go.

Try on this statement:

Beingness is, thought does.

What does that say to you?

It says that beingness is not an action, it is not an undertaking, it is not something that occurs. Rather, it is an "is-ness." It is what is. It is a "so-ness"—it is what is so.

Good. And what about thought?

It says that thought is a process, a "doingness," something that happens.

That's very good. So what are the implications of that?

Anything that "happens" takes time. It may happen very fast, like thought, but it still takes what we call time. Something that "is," however, simply is. It is right now. It's not "going to be"; it is right here, right now.

In short, "is-ing" is faster than "doing," and "being" is therefore faster than "thinking."

You know what? I should have hired you as My interpreter.

I thought You did.

Ah, good one. Okay, now try this statement:

Being is first cause.

What does that say to you?

It says that being causes everything. What you are "being," you experience.

Excellent. Yet does being cause thought?

Yes. If the proposition is correct, then yes, being would cause thought.

So, what you are being affects how you think.

Yes, you could say that.

Yet I have said that "thought is creative." Is this true?

It is, if You say that it is.

Good. I'm glad you have come to trust Me. Now, if "thought is creative," can thought create a state of being?

You mean, *which comes first, the chicken or the egg?*

Exactly.

I don't know. I suppose if I am "being" sad, I can change my mind about that. I can decide to think happy thoughts, to dwell on positive things, and suddenly, I can "be" happy. You have told me that I can do this. You have said that my thought creates my reality.

So I have.

Is it true?

Yes, it is. Yet, let Me ask you this. Do your thoughts create your True Being?

I don't know. I've never heard You use that phrase before. I don't know what my True Being is.

Your True Being is All of It. It is Everything. It is the All-in-All. The Alpha and the Omega, the beginning and the end, the Oneness.

In other words, God.

That's one other word, yes.

So You're asking me if my thought creates God?

Yes.

I don't know.

Then let Me pick it up from here and unravel it for you.

Please.

We're limited here by language and context, as I have explained now several times.

I understand that.

Okay. Your thought about God does not create God. It merely creates your *experience* of God.

God *is*.

God is the All-in-All. The Everything. All that ever was, is now, and ever will be.

So far, so good?

So far, so good.

> When you think, you do not *create* The All. You reach *into* The All to create whatever experience *of* The All that you choose.
>
> All of It is *already there.* You are not *placing it there* by thinking about it. Yet by thinking about it, you are placing *in your experience* that part of the All about which you are thinking.
>
> Did you follow that?

I think I did. Go slowly. Go very slowly. I'm trying to keep up.

> Your True Being, which is Who You Really Are, precedes everything. When you think about who you wish to now *be,* you are reaching into your True Being, into your Total Self, and focusing on a part of your Total Self that you now wish to experience.
>
> Your total Self is All of It. It is the happiness *and* the sadness.

Yes, yes! You have said this before! You have said of me, "You are the up and the down of it, the left and the right of it, the here and the there of it, the before and the after of it. You are the fast and the slow, the big and the small, the male and the female, and what you call the good and the bad. You are all of it, and there is none of it that you are not."

I have heard You say that to me before!

You are right. I have. Many times have I said this to you. And now you understand it better than you ever have before.

And so, does "thinking" affect "being"? No. Not in the largest sense. You are What You Are, no matter what you think about it.

Yet can thinking create an immediately different *experience* of your being? Yes. What you think about, what you focus on, will be made manifest in your individual present reality. Thus, if you are being sad, and you think positive, joyful thoughts, you will very easily "think your way" to being happy.

You are simply moving from one part of your Self to another!

Yet there is a "shortcut"—and this is what we have been trying to get at here. This is what we've been talking about.

You can move to any state of being you wish—that is, you can call forth any part of your True Being—at any moment, instantly, by simply knowing it to be so, and declaring it to be so.

You once said to me, "What you know is what is so."

Yes, I did. And this is exactly what I meant by that. What you know of your True Being is what will be so of your state of being right now. When you declare what you know, you make it so.

Declarations are made most powerfully with "I Am" statements. One of the most famous of these was a statement made by Jesus, "I am the way and the life." The most sweeping such statement ever made was one made by Me: I Am That I Am.

You can make "I Am" declarations, too. In fact, you do so every day. "I am sick and tired," "I am up to my ears," and so forth. These are statements of being. When you make these statements of being consciously, rather than unconsciously, you live from Intention; you live deliberately. Remember, I have suggested that you live . . .

Deliberately
Harmoniously
Beneficially

Your whole life is a message, did you know that? Every act is an act of self-definition. Every thought is a film on the movie screen of your mind. Every word is voice mail for God. Everything you think, say, and do sends a message about you.

Think of your "I Am" declarations, therefore, as a sort of State of the Union message. This is your State of the Being message. You are making a statement about how it is with you. You are saying "what is so."

Hey, wait a minute! I just thought of something! We're all One anyway, so it really *is* a State of the *Union* message!

That's good. That's very good.

Now when you make a declaration, that is the short route to your state of being. Declarations are a *calling forth* of Who You Really Are—or, more accurately, of that portion of Who You Really Are that you wish to experience right now.

This is beingness being creative, rather than thought being creative. *Beingness is the fastest method of creation.* That is because what *is,* is *right now.*

A true declaration of being is made without thinking about it. If you think about it, you will, at best, delay it, and, at worst, deny it.

Delay will occur simply because thinking takes time, and being takes no time at all.

Denial could occur because thinking about what you choose to be often convinces you that you aren't that—and can't ever become that.

If that's true, then the worst thing I can do is to think!

In a sense, that is correct. All spiritual Masters are out of their minds. That is, they do not consciously think about what they are being. They simply *are* it. The moment you think about it, you can't be it. You can only delay being it, or deny being it.

To use a very down-home illustration, you can only *be* in love when you *are* in love. You cannot be in love if you are thinking about it. If someone who loves you asks, "Are you in love with me?" and you say, "I'm thinking about it," that will probably not go over very well.

Excellent! You are understanding very well.

Now, if time is not critical, if it's not a matter of inches and seconds (and few things are), if it isn't important how long it takes before you are experiencing what you choose (such as "being in love"), then you can take all the time you want to "think about it."

And thinking is a very powerful tool. Don't get Me wrong. It is one of the Three Tools of Creation.

Thought, word, and deed.

Precisely. Yet today I have given you another method by which you can experience Life. This is not a tool of creation, this is a new *understanding* of creation: that it is not a process by which things occur, but by which you become aware of what already *has* occurred—an awareness of *what is,* always was, and always will be, world without end.

Do you understand?

I am beginning to, yes. I am beginning to see the whole cosmology, the whole construction.

Good. I know this has not been simple. Or rather, it *has* been simple, but it has not been *easy.*

Just remember this: Being is instant. Compared to that, your thought is very slow. As fast as thought is, it is very slow compared to being.

Let's use your very human example of being in love.

Remember a time when you fell in love. There was a moment, a magical split second, when you first felt that love. It may have hit you, as you are fond of saying, "like a ton of bricks." Suddenly, it came over you. You looked at that person across the room, across the dining table, across the front seat of the car, and all at once you *knew* that you loved them.

It was sudden. It was instant. It was not something you had to think about. It just "happened." You may have thought about it later. You may even have thought about it beforehand—I wonder what it would be like to be in love with that person—but in that moment when you first felt it, first knew it in your heart, it just swept over you. It happened much too fast for you to have "thought" it there. You simply found yourself there, *being in love.*

You can be in love before you've even thought about it!

Boy, don't I know that.

It's the same with gratitude. When you feel gratitude, no one has to tell you, "It's time to feel gratitude." You simply, quite spontaneously, feel grateful. You find yourself *being grateful* before you even think about it. Gratefulness is a state of being. There is no word like "lovefulness" in your language, but there should be.

You're a poet, you know that?

So I've been told.

Okay, so I'm clear that being is faster than thinking, but I still don't see why "being grateful" for something brings it to you faster than . . . wait a minute—even as I'm saying this, I think I'm getting the answer . . .

You've said before that gratitude is a state of being which announces my clarity that I already have what it is I think I need. In other words, if I am *thanking* God for something, rather than *asking* God for something, I must know that it is already in place.

Exactly.

That is why the Seventh Step is, "Thank God."

Exactly.

Because when you thank God, you are "being" aware that all good things in life have already come to you; that everything you need—the right and perfect people, places, and events—to express and experience and evolve as you have chosen has already been put in place for you.

Even before you ask, I will have answered. Yes, that's it.

Then maybe thanking God should be the first thing you do, not the last!

That could be very powerful. And you have just uncovered a great secret. The wonder of the Seven Steps to God is that they may be turned around. They can be *reversed.*

If you are thanking God, you are helping God to help you.

If you are helping God to help you, you are using God.

If you are using God, you are embracing God in your life.

If you are embracing God, you are loving God.

If you are loving God, you are trusting God.

And if you are trusting God, you are knowing God for sure.

Amazing. Absolutely amazing.

You now know how to create a friendship with God. A true friendship. A real friendship. *A practical, working* friendship.

Great! Can I begin using it right away? And don't say, "You can, but you may not."

What?

Oh, I had a third-grade teacher who was always correcting our grammar. When we would raise our hand and say, "Sister, can I go to the bathroom?" she would always say, "You can, but you may not."

Ah yes, I remember her.

Can you ever forget?

I can, but I may not.

Ba-da-*boom.* Cymbal crash, please.

Thank you—thank you—thank you very muuuuch.

But seriously, folks . . . I'd like to begin using this friendship. You said that You would help me understand how to practicalize, how to make functional, the wisdom in *Conversations with God;* how to use it in our daily lives.

Well, that's what a friendship with God is for. It's for helping you to remember these things. It's for making your day-to-day life easier, your moment-to-moment experience more of an expression of Who You Really Are.

This is your greatest desire, and I have established a perfect system whereby all of your desires may be realized. They are being realized now—in this very moment. The only difference between you and Me is that I know this.

In the moment of your total knowing (which moment could come upon you at any time), you, too, will feel as I do always: totally joyful, loving, accepting, blessing, and grateful.

These are the Five Attitudes of God, and I promised you that before our dialogue was over, I would show you how the application of these attitudes in your life now can, and will, bring you to Godliness.

You did make that promise, long ago, in book 1 of *Conversations with God,* and I think it's about time You kept it!

And *you* promised to tell *us* about your life, and especially your experiences since the release of those *Conversations with God* books, and you've only given us a smattering. So maybe we should *both* keep our promises!

Coolness.

Thirteen

I left the county government for a job in the school system, after ten years went to work on the West Coast with Dr. Elisabeth Kübler-Ross, eighteen months later started my own advertising company in San Diego, signed on with Terry Cole-Whittaker Ministries there, moved to the State of Washington a couple years later, migrated to Portland, then to Southern Oregon, where I wound up living under the open sky without a nickel to my name, finally found a job back in radio, three years later got fired, had a miserable time, then became a nationally syndicated talk show host, wrote the *Conversations with God* books, have had an amazing time ever since, and here I am.

Okay, I kept my promise, now You keep Yours.

I think people want a little more than that.

No, they don't. They want to hear from You. They want You to keep Your promise.

Fine.

I made the world, created Adam and Eve, put them in the Garden of Eden, told them to be fruitful and multiply, had some trouble with a serpent there, watched as they blamed each other and misunderstood everything, later gave an old man a couple of stone tablets to try to clear things up, did a little sea-splitting and miracle working, sent some messengers to tell My story, noticed that nobody was listening, decided to keep trying, and here I am.

Okay, I kept My promise.

Cute. Very cute.

What's good for the goose is good for the gander.

Nobody has said that in thirty years.

I'm old, I'm old. What do you want from Me?

I want You should stop being such a comedian. Nobody's going to believe a word in here if You keep being such a comedian.

Listen to this. I've got the pot calling the kettle black here.

Okay, have we gotten it out of our systems now? Can we get back to the book?

If you insist.

I'd like to know about the Five Attitudes of God—one of which was *not*, I notice, "hilarious."

Maybe it should have been.

Will You *stop?*

No, I'm serious. People have this idea that God is never humorous, cannot laugh, and that everybody has to act very sacred around the Divine. I wish you would all lighten up a bit. All of you. Laugh at yourself. Someone once said, "You grow up the day that you have a good laugh at yourself."

Don't take yourself so seriously. Give yourself a little slack. And while you're at it, give each other a little, too.

You want to know about the Five Attitudes of God? Take a look at the first one.

"Totally joyful."

That is the *First* Attitude. Did you notice that? I listed that *first.*

So what are You saying?

I'm saying that it comes before anything else. It is what makes everything possible. Without joy, there is nothing.

I'm saying that unless you get a little humor in your life, none of it is going to make any sense. I'm saying that laughter is the best medicine. I'm saying that joy is good for the soul.

I'll go further than that. Joy *is* the soul. The soul is that which you would call joy. Pure joy. Endless joy. Unadulterated, unlimited, unrestricted joy. That is the *nature* of the soul.

A smile is a window to your soul. Laughter is the door.

Oh, wow.

Wow, indeed.

Why is the soul so happy? *People* aren't that happy. I mean, the people whose souls these *are* don't seem all that happy, so what's going on here?

That's a wonderful question. If the soul is so joyous, why aren't you? That's a perfectly wonderful question.

The answer lies in your mind. You must "be of a mind" to be joyful if you are to release the joy that is in your heart.

I thought the joy was in your soul.

Your heart is the corridor between your soul and your mind. The joy in your soul must move through your heart, otherwise it will "not even enter your mind."

Feelings are the language of the soul. They will back up in your heart if you have a closed mind. That is why, when you are feeling very, very sad, you say that your heart is breaking. And that is why, when you are feeling very, very happy, you say that your heart is bursting.

Open your mind, allow your feelings to be expressed, to be *pushed out,* and your heart will neither break nor burst, but be a free-flowing channel of the life energy in your soul.

But if the soul is joy, how can it ever be sad?

Joy is life, expressing. The free flow of life energy is what you call joy. The essence of life is Oneness—unity with All That Is. This is what life is: unity, *expressing.* The feeling of unity is the feeling that you call love. Therefore, in your language, it is said that the essence of life is love. Joy, then, is love, expressing freely.

Whenever the free and unlimited expression of life and love—that is, the experience of unity and oneness with all things and with every sentient being—is prohibited or limited by any circumstance or condition, the soul, which is joy itself, is not fully expressed. Joy not fully expressed is the feeling that you call sadness.

I'm confused. How can a thing be one thing if it is another? How can a thing be cold if its essence is that which is hot? How can the soul be sad if its essence is joy?

You misunderstand the nature of the universe. You are still seeing things as separate. Hot and cold are not separate from each other. *Nothing is.* There is nothing in the Universe that is separate from anything else. Hot and cold are, therefore, the same thing *in varying degrees.* So, too, are sadness and joy.

What a terrific insight! I never thought of it that way. Sadness and joy are just two *names.* They are *words* we have used to describe *different levels of the same energy.*

Different expressions of the Universal Force, yes. And that is why these two feelings can be experienced in the same moment. Can you imagine such a thing?

Yes! I *have* felt sadness and joy at the same time.

Of course you have. It is not unusual at all.

The television show *M*A*S*H* was a perfect example of this kind of juxtaposition. And, more recently, an extraordinary motion picture called *Life is Beautiful.*

Yes. These are incredible examples of how laughter heals, of how sadness and joy can intermingle.

This is the life energy itself, this flow that you call sadness/joy.

This energy can be expressed in a way that you call joy at any time. That is because *the energy of life can be controlled.* Like turning a thermostat from cold to hot, you can speed up the vibration of life energy, from sadness to joy. And I tell you this: if you carry joy in your heart, you can heal any moment.

But how do you carry joy in your heart? How do you get it there if it's not there?

It is there.

Some people do not experience that.

They do not know joy's secret.

What is the secret?

You cannot feel joy until you let it out.

But how do you let it out if you are not feeling it?

Help another to feel it.

Release the joy that is inside of another, and you release the joy that is inside of you.

Some people don't know how to do that. That is such a huge statement, they don't know what that looks like.

It can be done with something as simple as a smile. Or a compliment. Or a loving glance. And it can be accomplished with something as elegant as making love. With these devices can you release joy in another, and with many more.

With a song, or a dance, or the stroke of a brush, or the molding of clay, or the rhyming of words. With the holding of hands, or the meeting of minds, or the partnering of souls. With the mutual creation of anything good and lovely and useful. With all these devices can you release another's joy, and with many more.

With the sharing of a feeling, the telling of a truth, the ending of anger, the healing of judgment. With the willingness to listen, and the willingness to speak. With the decision to forgive, and the choice to release. With the commitment to give, and the grace to receive.

I tell you there are a thousand ways to release the joy in the heart of another. Nay, a thousand times a thousand. And in the moment you decide to do so, you will know how.

You're right. I know You're right. It can be done even on someone's deathbed.

I sent you a great teacher to show you that.

Yes. Dr. Elisabeth Kübler-Ross. I couldn't believe it. I couldn't believe that I actually got to meet her, much less work on her staff. What an extraordinary woman.

I'd left the Anne Arundel County government *(before* Joe Alton's troubles began. *Whew!)* to take a job in the school system there. Its long-time press aide retired, and I applied for the position. Once again, I was in the right place at the right time. I received more incredible life training, working on everything from the Crisis Intervention Team to the curriculum development committee. Whether preparing a 250-page report on school desegregation (once more touching the Black Experience) for a Congressional subcommittee, or traveling from school to school holding first-of-their-kind family meetings with teachers, parents, students, administrators, and support staff, I was in the thick of things.

I spent the decade of the seventies there—the longest I'd ever worked anywhere—and enjoyed the first two-thirds of it immensely. But eventually, the bloom fell off the rose, and my tasks began getting repetitious and uninspiring. I was also starting to glimpse what looked more and more like a dead end ahead—I could see myself doing the same job for thirty more years. Without a college degree, I didn't stand much chance for advancement (I was lucky, in fact, to have the high-level job I did have), and my energies began to flag.

Then, I was kidnapped in 1979 by Dr. Elisabeth Kübler-Ross. And a kidnapping it was, make no mistake about it.

I'd begun helping Elisabeth that year as a volunteer, partnering with a friend, Bill Griswold, in coordinating some East Coast fund-raising lectures for Shanti Nilaya, the non-profit organization that supported her work. Bill had introduced me to Dr. Ross a few months earlier, when he'd asked me to help with some P.R. for an appearance he'd managed to talk her into making in Annapolis.

I'd heard of Elisabeth Kübler-Ross, of course. A woman of monumental achievement, her groundbreaking 1969 book, *On Death and Dying,* had altered the world's view of the dying process, lifting the taboo from the study of thanatology, spawning the founding of the American hospice movement, and changing the lives of millions forever.

(She's written many other books since, including *Death: The Final Stage of Growth,* and, her most recent, *The Wheel of Life: A Memoir of Living and Dying.*)

I was taken with Elisabeth immediately—as was nearly everyone who met her. She has an extraordinarily magnetic and deeply compelling personality, and no one whom I have seen touched by her is ever really quite the same. I knew after sixty minutes with her that I wanted to assist in her work, and volunteering to do so was not something that anyone had even to ask me to do.

Nearly a year after that first meeting, Bill and I were in Boston setting up another lecture. Following her talk, a few of us found ourselves in a quiet corner of a restaurant, enjoying a few rare moments of private conversation with Elisabeth. I'd had two or three such conversations with her before, so she'd already heard what I told her again that night: I would do anything to join in her work

Elisabeth was at the time presenting Life, Death, and Transition Workshops around the country, interacting with terminally ill people and their families, and others who were doing what she called "grief work." I'd never seen anything like it. (She later wrote a book, *To Live Until We Say Goodbye,* describing with great emotional force what went on at these retreats.) This woman was touching people's lives in ways that were meaningful and profound, and I could see that her work made sense of her own life.

My work did not. I was just doing what I thought I had to do in order to survive (or make sure that others survived). One of the things I learned from Elisabeth is that none of us has to do that. Elisabeth would teach such gargantuan lessons in the simplest way: single-sentence observations with which she permitted no argument. At the restaurant in Boston that night, I was gifted with one of these.

"I just don't know," I was whining, "there's nothing exciting about my job anymore, and it feels as if my life is wasting away, but I guess I'll be working there until I'm sixty-five, and get my pension."

Elisabeth looked at me as if I were crazy. "You don't have to do that," she said very quietly. "Why do you do that?"

"If it were just me, I wouldn't, believe me. I'd be out of there tomorrow. But I have a family to support."

"And tell me, what would they do, this family of yours, if you died tomorrow?" Elisabeth asked.

"That's beside the point," I bickered. "I am not dead. I'm still living."

"You call that living?" she replied, and turned away to talk with someone else, as if it was perfectly obvious that there was nothing more to say.

The next morning over coffee at her hotel with her Boston helpers, she turned to me abruptly. "You drive me to the airport," she said.

"Oh, okay," I agreed. Bill and I had driven up from Annapolis, and my car was right outside.

On the drive, Elisabeth told me she was headed to Poughkeepsie, New York, for another five-day intensive workshop. "Come with me inside," she said. "Don't just drop me off. I need help with my bags."

"Sure," I said, and we wheeled into the parking lot.

At the ticket counter Elisabeth presented her own ticket, then laid down a credit card. "I need another seat on this flight," she told the agent.

"Let me see if we have space," the woman replied "Ah, yes, just one seat left."

"Of course," Elisabeth beamed as if she knew some inside secret.

"And who will the other traveling party be, please?" the agent inquired.

Elisabeth pointed at me. "This one," she muttered.

"I beg your pardon?" I choked.

"You're coming to Poughkeepsie, no?" Elisabeth asked, as if we'd discussed the whole thing.

"No! I have to be at work tomorrow. I only took three days off."

"That work will get done without you," she said matter-of-factly.

"But I've got my car here in Boston," I protested. "I can't just leave it out there in the parking lot."

"Bill can come and get it and drive it up."

"But . . . I have no clothes to wear. I didn't plan on being away so long."

"There are stores in Poughkeepsie."

"Elisabeth, I can't do this! I can't just get on a plane and go flying off somewhere." My heart was pounding, because that was exactly what I wanted to do.

"The woman needs your driver's license," she said, blinking heavily.

"But, Elisabeth . . ."

"You're going to make me miss the plane."

I gave the woman my driver's license. She handed me a ticket.

As Elisabeth hiked off to the gate, my voice trailed after her. "I have to call the office and tell them I'm not going to be there. . . ."

Elisabeth buried herself in some reading on the plane, barely saying ten words to me. But when we got to the workshop site in

Poughkeepsie, she presented me to the assembled participants as "my new P.R. man."

I called home to tell my wife I'd been abducted and would be home on Friday. And for the next two days I watched Elisabeth work. I saw people's lives change right in front of me. I saw old wounds being healed, old issues being resolved, old angers being released, old beliefs being overcome.

At one point a woman sitting very near me in the process room "went up." (Workshop staff talk for someone who breaks into prolonged tears, or in some other way loses control of the moment.) Elisabeth, with a slight gesture of her head, signaled me to take care of it.

I gently guided the weeping woman from the room and walked her to a small space which had been set aside down the hall. I'd never done this kind of thing before, but Elisabeth had given very specific instructions to everyone who staffed (she generally brought three or four people with her). One thing she was very clear on. "Don't try to *fix it,"* she said, "just listen. If you need help, call for me, but being there to listen is almost always enough."

She was right. I was able to "be there" for that workshop participant in a quality way. I was able to hold the space of safety for her, to give her a place to just let it all out, to let go of what she'd been carrying around that had been triggered in the larger room. She cried and wailed and spat out her anger and talked quietly, and then went through the whole cycle again. I never felt so useful in my life.

That afternoon I called the school board office back in Maryland.

"Personnel, please," I said to the operator, and when I'd been connected to the right department, I took a deep breath.

"Can a person," I asked, "resign over the phone?"

My time as a member of Elisabeth's staff was one of the greatest gifts of my life. I saw, up close, a woman working in saintly ways, hour after hour, week after week, month after month. I stood by her in lecture halls, in workshop rooms, and at the bedside of people who were dying. I saw her with old folks and with little children. I watched her with the fearful and the brave, the joyful and the sad, the open and the closed, the furious and the meek.

I watched a Master.

I watched her healing the deepest wounds that can be inflicted upon the human psyche.

I watched, I listened, and I tried very hard to learn.

And, yes, I did come to understand that what You've said is true.

> There are a thousand ways to release the joy in the heart of another, and in the moment you decide to do so, you will know how.

And it can be done even on someone's deathbed.

Thank You for the teaching, and for the master teacher.

> You are welcome, My friend. And do you know, now, how to live joyfully?

Elisabeth advised us all to love unconditionally, to forgive quickly, never to regret the pains of the past. *"Should you shield the canyons from the windstorms,"* she would say, *"you would never see the beauty of their carvings."*

She also urged us to live fully now, to stop and taste the strawberries, and to do whatever it took to finish what she called "your unfinished business," so that life could be lived fearlessly and death could be embraced without regret. *"When you are not afraid to die, you are not afraid to live."* And, of course, her biggest message was: *"Death does not exist."*

That is much to receive from one person.

Elisabeth has much to give.

Go, then, and live these truths, and those I have brought to you through other sources, that you may spread the joy in your soul, feel it in your heart, and know it in your mind.

God is life, at its highest vibration, which is joy itself.

God is *totally joyful,* and you will move to your own expression of godliness when you express this First Attitude of God.

Fourteen

I never met anyone more joyful than Terry Cole-Whittaker. With a smile that could knock your eyes out, a wondrous, eruptive, liberated laughter that was utterly infectious, and an unparalleled ability to touch people deeply with her understandings of the human condition, this sensational woman took Southern California by storm in the early 1980s with a brand of optimistic spirituality that brought hundreds of thousands back into happy relationship with themselves and with God.

I first heard about Terry when I lived in Escondido and worked for Dr. Kübler-Ross at Shanti Nilaya. I've never been more occupationally fulfilled, and close contact with a person of such compassion and spiritual wisdom brought me back to a place I had not been in years: a place of yearning to have a personal relationship with God; to know God in my life as a direct experience.

I hadn't gone to church since my twenties when, for the second time in my life, I'd almost become a member of the clergy. Missing out on the priesthood in my teens, I cycled back to my desire to minister when I continued my theological investigations in the years after I left Milwaukee at nineteen.

In searching for a God of whom I did not have to be afraid, I abandoned Roman Catholicism for good after turning twenty. I began scouring books on theology and made visits to a number of churches and synagogues in Anne Arundel County, finally settling on the First Presbyterian Church in Annapolis as the place I would attend.

Almost immediately, I joined the choir, and within a year I'd become a Lay Reader in the church. As I stood at the lectern on Sundays and read the week's scriptural passages, I became aware once more of my childhood longing to spend my life in close relationship with God, teaching all the world of His love.

Presbyterians did not seem to be nearly as fear-based in their faith as Catholics (there were far fewer rules, rituals, and, therefore, pitfalls), so I had a much higher comfort level with their theology. I became so comfortable, in fact, that I began to put some real passion into my Sunday-morning Bible readings—so much so that the congregation began to look forward to my turn in the rotation. This became apparent not only to me, but to the leadership of the church as well, and it was not long before I was brought in for a chat with the pastor, one of the nicest people I've ever known.

"Tell me," the Rev. Winslow Shaw asked after pleasantries had been exchanged, "have you ever thought of entering the ministry?"

"I sure have," I replied. "I thought for certain that I was going to enter the seminary and become a priest when I was thirteen, but that didn't happen."

"Why not?"

"My dad stopped it. He said that I wasn't old enough to decide."

"Do you think you are old enough now?"

For some reason at that point I almost broke down and cried.

"I was always old enough," I whispered, and worked to gather my composure.

"Why are you not still in the Catholic Church, then?" Rev. Shaw asked gently.

"I . . . had some problems with its theology."

"I see."

We sat quietly for a moment.

"How do you feel about Presbyterian theology?" the minister asked at last.

"Comfortable."

"It would seem so. We've had a few people around here comment on your Scripture readings. You seem to get quite a bit of meaning out of them."

"Well, there's quite a bit of meaning *in* them."

Rev. Shaw smiled. "I agree," he said, then looked at me intently.

"May I ask you a personal question?"

"Of course."

"Why haven't you pursued your obvious love of theology? You're able, now, to make your own decisions. What's kept you out of the clergy? Some clergy, somewhere. Surely you could find a spiritual home."

"It isn't as simple as finding a home. There's also the challenge of finding the money. I'm in the middle of a career, with a wife and two small children. It would take a miracle at this stage to find a way to just drop everything and take this up."

Rev. Shaw smiled again.

"Our church has a program through which, if we identify a member of our congregation we think is particularly promising, we sponsor that person in studies at seminary. Usually Princeton."

My heart jumped.

"You mean you give them the money to attend?"

"Well, it's a loan, of course. There's a commitment to come back here and serve for a few years as an associate to the pastor. You could work with a youth ministry, or a street ministry, or whatever your personal interest is, in addition to offering spiritual counseling, providing leadership in the Sunday School programs, and, of course, spelling the pastor in the pulpit now and then. I think that's something you could handle."

It was my turn to be silent. My mind was spinning.

"How does that sound to you?"

"It sounds fantastic. Are you offering it to me?"

"I think the Presbytery seems ready to do that, yes. They're certainly ready to explore it. They'd want to talk with you personally, of course."

"Of course."

"Why don't you go home and think about it? Talk to your wife about it. And pray on it."

I did just that.

My wife was totally supportive. "I think it would be wonderful," she said, beaming. Our second child had been born twenty-one months after the first. The two girls were barely toddlers. "What would we live on?" I asked. "I mean, this is just tuition they're talking about."

"I could get back into physical therapy," my wife offered. "I'm sure I'd find something. Everything would work out."

"You mean you'd support us while I went back to school?"

She touched my arm. "I know this is something you've always wanted," she said softly.

I don't deserve the people who have come into my life. I certainly didn't deserve my first wife, one of the kindest human beings I have ever met.

But I didn't do it. I couldn't. Everything was in place, everything was perfect—except the theology. In the end, it was the theology that stopped me.

I'd done as Rev. Shaw suggested. I'd prayed about it. And the more I prayed, the more I realized that I could not preach—no matter how quietly—a sermon about natural-born sinners and the need for salvation.

From the earliest days of my youth I'd had trouble seeing people as "bad." Oh, I knew that people did bad things. I could see it all around me as I grew up. But even as a teenager, and then a young man, I held to a stubbornly positive understanding of human nature at its basis. It seemed to me that all people were *good,* and that some of them did bad things for reasons having to do with their upbringing, their lack of understanding or opportunities, their desperation and their anger, or, in some cases, just plain laziness . . . but not because of any inherent evilness.

The story of Adam and Eve made no sense to me, not even as an allegory, and I knew that I couldn't teach it. Nor could I ever teach a theology of exclusion, no matter how benign, because something deep inside my soul caused me to know, from the time I was small, that all people were my brother and sisters, and that no one and no thing was ugly or unacceptable in the sight of God—least of all, I grew certain as I grew older, for having committed the "sin" of adopting the "wrong" theology.

If this was not true, then everything that I knew intuitively at the deepest part of my being was false. I could not accept that. But I didn't know what to accept. The opportunity to enter the Christian ministry, very real and very present for the second time in my life, threw me into spiritual crisis. I so earnestly wanted to do God's work in the world, and yet I couldn't accept that God's work was to teach a gospel of division, and a theology of punishment for the divided.

I begged God for clarity—not simply on whether I should enter the ministry, but on the largest questions surrounding the relationship of human beings to Deity. I received insights on neither. Then I abandoned both.

Now, as I approached forty, Elisabeth Kübler-Ross was bringing me back to God. Over and over she spoke of a God of unconditional love, who would never judge, but would only accept us just as we were.

If only people could understand this, I thought, and apply the same truth in their lives, the problems and the cruelties and the tragedies of the world would evaporate. "God does not say, 'I love you IF . . .' " Elisabeth insisted, and thus took the fear out of dying for millions of people the world over.

Now this was a God I could believe in. This was the God of my heart, of my childhood's deepest inner knowing. I wanted more of this God, so I decided to go back to church. Maybe I'd been looking in the wrong place, in the wrong way. I went to a Lutheran Church, then to the Methodists. I tried the Baptists and the Congregationalists. But I was right back in fear-based theology. I ran out. I explored Judaism. Buddism. Every other "ism" I could find. Nothing seemed to fit. Then I heard about Terry Cole-Whittaker, and her church in San Diego.

A housewife in the vapid California suburbs of the sixties, Terry, too, had yearned for an outward experience of the spiritual connection she felt deep in her heart. Her own search led her to stumble on something called The United Church of Religious Science. She fell in love with it, and throwing everything to the wind, she began formal religious studies. Eventually, she became ordained and received a letter of call from a struggling congregation of less than fifty people in La Jolla, California. Then she had to choose between her dream and her marriage. Her husband did not fully support her sudden transformation, and he certainly was not okay with leaving his own good job and moving the family to a new community.

So Terry left the marriage. And within three years she turned the La Jolla Church of Religious Science into one of the largest in the denomination. Over a thousand people were coming to hear her at two services each Sunday morning, and the throng was growing. Word of this spiritual phenomenon spread quickly throughout Southern California, even to Escondido, a very conservative, traditional wine-growing and farming community to the north of San Diego.

I went down to check it out.

Terry's congregation had grown so large that she'd had to move her services into a rented movie theater. *A Celebration of Life with Terry Cole-Whittaker,* the marquee read, and as I approached, I thought, "Oh, brother, what's this?" Ushers handed out carnations to everyone as they filed in, and greeted each person as if they'd known them for a lifetime.

"Hello, how *are* you? It's so *great* to have you here!"

I didn't know what to make of it. I'd been greeted nicely at churches before, of course, but never quite so effusively. There was an energy in the space that felt enlivening.

Inside, the moving, rousing theme from *Chariots of Fire* was playing. An air of expectancy filled the theatre. People were chattering and laughing. Finally, the house lights went down and a man and woman appeared on the stage, the man taking a seat at one side and the woman at the other.

"Now is the time to become quiet, to go within," the man said into a microphone. A choir in the back of the room softly sang an invocation about "peace," and the service began.

I'd never experienced anything quite like this. It certainly wasn't what I'd anticipated, and I was feeling a bit out of place, but I decided to hang in there. After a few opening announcements, Terry Cole-Whittaker stepped to the center of the stage behind a see-through, Plexiglas podium, and chirped, "Good morning!" Her smile was radiant, her cheerfulness contagious.

"If you came here this morning expecting to find something that looks like a church, or feels like a church, or sounds like a church, you came to the wrong place." She was certainly right about that. The audience laughed its agreement. "But if you came here this morning hoping to find God, notice that God arrived the moment you walked through the door."

That was it. I was hooked. Even if I didn't know exactly what she was driving at yet, anyone who had imagination and courage enough to open a Sunday service with a line like that had my attention. It was the beginning of a nearly three-year relationship.

As with the first time I met Elisabeth, I was captivated by Terry Cole-Whittaker and her work within ten minutes. As I did with Elisabeth, I made that clear very quickly by volunteering my enthusiastic assistance. And as with Elisabeth, I was on staff with Terry's organization very soon, accepting a position in the ministry's outreach department (writing newsletters, creating the weekly church bulletin, etc.).

It "just happened" that I was out of work within a few weeks of crossing paths with Terry. Elisabeth fired me. Well, fired seems like a harsh term. She let me go. It wasn't in anger; it was just time for me to move on, and Elisabeth knew it. She said simply, "It is time for you to go. I give you three days."

I was flabbergasted. "But why? What have I done?"

"It is not what you have done. It is what you will *not* do if you stay here. You will not realize your full potential. You cannot possibly do so, standing in my shadow. Get out. Now. Before it is too late."

"But I don't want to leave," I pleaded.

"You have played in my backyard long enough," Elisabeth said matter-of-factly. "I give you a little kick. Like the bird from its nest. It is time for you to fly."

And that was that.

I moved to San Diego and got back into the commercial public relations and marketing game, starting my own firm called *The Group.*

There was no group actually, there was only me. But I wanted it to sound like something of substance. And I acquired quite a few clients within the next few months, including a man running for Congress as an independent candidate whose name did not even appear on the ballot. Ron Packard was the former mayor of Carlsbad, California, and became the first man to win a seat in Congress on a write-in vote in this century—and I helped him do that.

But, with the stunning Packard victory the notable exception, my days in marketing and advertising once again proved vacuous. After working with Elisabeth, helping someone sell weekend hotel stays, restaurant food, or home remodeling was singularly and predictably unsatisfying. I was going crazy again. I had to find some way to return meaning to my life. I poured all of my energy into volunteering at Terry's church. I spent days, evenings, weekends in church work, letting my business (forgive me, I can't resist this) go to hell. My energy, enthusiasm, and creativity quickly brought an offer of full-time employment as Director of Outreach. That's church-ese for public relations and marketing.

Terry left her denomination shortly after I'd gone to work for her, however, feeling, she told us, that formal religious affiliations were often limiting, confining, restrictive. She formed Terry Cole-Whittaker Ministries, and her Sunday services were eventually televised in cities across the country, expanding her "congregation" to hundreds of thousands.

As in my time with Elisabeth, my connection with Terry provided me with invaluable training. I learned much, not only about dealing with people, including those facing emotional and spiritual challenges, but also about non-profit organizations and how they best functioned to meet human needs and send spiritual messages. I didn't know then how invaluable this experience would prove to be—although I should have guessed that my life was once again preparing me for my own future. I see now that I have been led to just the right people at just the right time, in order to continue my education.

Like Elisabeth, Terry spoke of a God of unconditional love. She also spoke of the power of God, which she said resided within all of us. This included the power to create our own reality and to determine our own experience.

As I've said in the introductions to all the *Conversations with God* books, some of the ideas in that trilogy are ideas I have been exposed to before. Many, including some of the most startling, are not. They are insights that I've never heard anywhere, never read anyplace, never before entertained, or even imagined. Yet, as *CWG* has made clear, my whole life has indeed been a teaching, *and that is true for all of us.* We have to pay attention! We have to keep our eyes and ears wide open! God is sending us messages all the time, having a conversation with us every moment of every day! God's messages are coming to us in a variety of ways, from a variety of sources, in endless profusion.

In my life, Larry LaRue was one of those sources. Jay Jackson was one of those sources. Joe Alton was one of those sources. Elisabeth Kübler-Ross was one of those sources. And Terry Cole-Whittaker was one of those sources.

My mother was one of those sources, too, as was my father. Each taught me life lessons, and brought me life wisdoms that have served me to this very day. Even after I "threw out" all the stuff that I got from them—and from other sources—which did not serve me, which did not resonate with me, and which did not feel like my inner truth, there was still plenty of treasure left.

In fairness to Terry, who I am sure would want this stated for accuracy sake, I need to point out that she long ago closed her ministry. She has since embarked on a different spiritual path, distant from traditional Judeo-Christian constructions, but distant, too, from the largest part of her own former message. I honor that decision by Terry, who has resolved to make her life a never-ending and courageous search for a spiritual reality with which her soul deeply resonates. I wish that all people would seek divine truth with such fervor.

That is what Terry taught me above all else. She taught me to seek Eternal Truth with never-ending determination, no matter how it upsets the apple cart, no matter which of my former beliefs it overturns, no matter how much it might put off others. To this mission, I hope I have remained faithful.

You have. Believe Me, you have.

I have some more questions on this business of joyfulness, however.

Go ahead.

Well, You said that the way to feel joyful is to cause another to feel joyful.

That's right.

So how do I feel joyful when there's no one else around?

There's always a way to contribute to Life, even when you are alone. Sometimes, especially when you are alone. For instance, you do your best writing when you are alone.

Okay, but supposing you're not a writer? Supposing you're not an artist, or a poet, or a composer, or someone who creates in solitude? Supposing you're just a regular person, with a regular job, a homemaker, perhaps, or a dentist, and now all of a sudden, you're alone. Maybe you're a retired priest, living in the retired priests' home, and your time of contributing to the lives of others seems over. Or actually, a retired *anything.* Retirement is often a time of depression for people, who sometimes feel their self worth slipping, their usefulness reduced, and themselves abandoned.

And it isn't just people in retirement. There are others. People who are ill, who are shut in, who for many reasons do not—and cannot—have much of a sense of life beyond themselves. Then there are the ordinary, everyday folks who do just fine when they are active and with other people, because they do as you say—they bring joy to others. But even they have times when they are by themselves, alone with their thoughts, with no one else around and no obvious way to bring joy to others.

I guess what I'm asking is, how do you find joy inside yourself? Isn't this idea of finding joy by bringing joy to others a little dangerous? Isn't it a bit of a trap? Couldn't it lead to the creation of little martyrs—people who feel that the only way they can deserve happiness is to make others happy?

Those are good questions. Those are very good observations, and good questions.

Thank you. So what are the answers?

First, let's clarify something. There is no time that you are ever alone. I am always with you, and you are always with Me. That's number one. And it's an important place to begin, because it changes everything. If you think you are really alone, it could be devastating. Just the thought of total aloneness itself, without anything else going on, could be devastating. That's because the very nature of the soul is unity and Oneness with All That Is, and if it appears that there is nothing and no one else, then an individual could feel just that—*individual,* and not One with anything else at all. And that would be devastating, because it violates your deepest sense of Who You Are.

So it is important to understand that, in fact, you are never alone, and that "aloneness" is impossible.

People who have been prisoners of war in solitary confinement, or shut-ins who've suffered debilitating strokes and are trapped in their own minds, might disagree with you. I know I'm using extreme examples, but I'm saying that there are cases when "aloneness" would very *much* be possible.

You can create the *illusion* of aloneness, yet the experience of something does not make it a reality.

I am always with you, whether you know it or not.

Yet if we don't know it, then You may as well *not* be with us, because the effect, for us, is the same.

I agree. Therefore, to change the effect, know that *I am with you always, even unto the end of time.*

How can I know this if I don't "know it"? (Do You understand the question?)

Yes. And the answer is that it is possible for you to know, and yet not "know that you know."

Could You explain that further, please?

In life, there appear to be those who do not know, and who do not *know* that they do not know. They are as children. Nurture them.

Then there appear to be those who do not know, and who *know* that they do not know. They are willing. Teach them.

Then there appear to be those who do not know, but who *think that they know*. They are dangerous. Avoid them.

Then there appear to be those who know, but who do not *know* that they know. They are asleep. Wake them.

Then there appear to be those who know, but who pretend that they do *not* know. They are actors. Enjoy them.

Then there appear to be those who know, and who *know that they know*. Do not follow them. For if they know that they know, they would not have you follow them. Yet listen very carefully to what they have to say, for they will remind you of what *you* know. Indeed, that is why they have been sent to you. That is why you have called them to you.

If a person knows, why would he pretend that he does not know? Who would do that?

Nearly everybody. At one time or another, nearly everybody.

But why?

Because you all love the drama so much. You have created an entire world of your illusion, a kingdom in which you can reign, and you have become the drama king and the drama queen.

Why would I want the drama, rather than an end to the drama?

Because it is in the deliciousness of the drama that you get to play out, at the highest level and with the greatest intensity, all the various versions of Who You Are, and may then select who you choose to be.

Because it is juicy!

You're kidding. Isn't there an easier way?

Of course there is. And you will ultimately choose that, the moment you realize that all the drama isn't necessary. Yet sometimes you will continue to use drama, to remind yourself, and to instruct others.

All Wisdom Teachers do this.

What are they reminding and instructing about?

The illusion. They are reminding themselves and instructing others that all of life is an illusion, that it has a purpose, and that once you know its purpose, you can live within the illusion or outside of it, at will. You can choose to experience the illusion, and make it real, or you can choose to experience Ultimate Reality, in any given moment.

How can I experience Ultimate Reality in any particular moment?

Be still, and know that I am God.

I mean that literally.

Be still.

That is how you will know that I am God, and that I am always with you. That is how you will know that *you* are One with Me. That is how you will meet the Creator inside of you.

If you have come to know Me, to trust Me, to love Me, and to embrace Me—if you have taken the steps to having a friendship with God—then you will never doubt that I am with you always, and all ways.

So, as I have said before, embrace Me. Spend a few moments each day embracing your experience of Me. Do this now, when you do not have to, when life circumstances do not seem to require you to. Now, when it seems that you do not even have time to. Now, when you are not feeling alone. So that when you *are* "alone," you will know that you are not.

Cultivate the habit of joining Me in divine connection once each day. I have already given you directions on one way that you may do this. There are other ways. Many ways. God is not limited, and neither are the ways to reach God.

Once you have truly embraced God, once you have made that divine connection, you will never want to lose it, for it will bring you the greatest joy you ever had.

This joy is What I Am, and What You Are. It is Life Itself, expressing at the highest vibration. It is *supraconsciousness.* It is at this level of vibration that creation occurs.

You might even say it's the *Creation Vibration!*

Yes, it is! That is it, exactly!

But I thought that joy was something that you could only feel when you were giving it away. How can you feel this joy if you are simply being alone with yourself, connecting only with the God within?

Only? Did you say "only"?

I tell you, you are connecting with *All That Is!*

You are not being "alone with yourself," and you never can be! It is not possible! And when you actually feel your eternal connection with the God within, you *are* giving away joy. You are giving it to Me! For My joy is to be One with you, and My *greatest* joy is for you to know it.

So I bring joy to You when I let You bring joy to me?

Has there ever been a more perfect description of love?

No.

And is love not what God is—what We Are?

Yes.

Good. Very good. You are putting it all together now. You are getting it. You are preparing again, as you have been doing during so much of your life. You are a messenger. You, and many others like you, who are coming to these same understandings with you—some through this dialogue, some in ways uniquely their own, all toward the same end: to no longer be a seeker, but a *bringer,* of the Light.

Soon, you will all speak with One Voice.

The role of messenger is given to everyone, in truth. You all send a message to the world about life and how it is, and about God. What is the message you have been sending? What is the message you now choose to send?

Is it time for a New Gospel?

Yes. Yes, it is. But I sometimes feel so alone in this. Even as I accept the truth that I am never really alone, I wonder, how does that change things when I *feel* alone? If I am feeling all alone, and I am not feeling very much joy, what do I do?

What you can do if you are *imagining* that you are alone is to come to Me.

Come to Me in the depths of your soul. Talk to Me from your heart. Companion with Me in your mind. I will be with you, and you will know it.

If you have been making daily contact with Me, this will be easier. Yet even if you have not, I will not fail you, but be with you the moment you call to Me. For this is My promise: Even before you call My name, I will be there.

That is because I am always there, and your very decision to call My name merely elevates your awareness of Me.

Once you are aware of Me, your sadness will leave you. For sadness and God cannot exist in the same place, because God is Life Energy, turned up as high as it will go, and sadness is Life Energy turned down.

Therefore, when I come to you, *do not turn Me down!*

Oh, wow, that's amazing. There You go again, putting things in amazing ways so that we can "get" them. But I don't think people do that, do they? I don't think people actually turn You down.

Every time you have a hunch about something and ignore it, you turn Me down. Every time you receive an offer to put an end to bad feelings, or cease a conflict, and ignore it, you turn Me down. Every time you do not return the smile of a stranger, walk under the awesome wonder of a night sky and don't look up, pass a flower bed without stopping to behold its beauty, you turn Me down.

Every time you hear My voice, or feel the presence of a departed loved one, and say it's just your imagination, you turn Me down. Every time you feel love for another in your soul, or feel a song in your heart, or see a grand vision in your mind, and do nothing about it, you turn Me down.

Every time you find yourself reading just the right book,

or hearing just the right sermon, or watching just the right movie, or running into just the right friend, at just the right time in your life, and write it off to coincidence or serendipity or "luck," you turn Me down.

And I tell you this: before the cock crows three times, some of you will deny Me.

Not me! I will never deny You again, nor will I ever turn You down when You invite me to experience communion with You.

That invitation is continual and everlasting, and more and more humans are feeling this Life Energy at full force, and not turning it down. You are letting the force be with you! And that is good. That is very good. For as you move into the next millennium, you will plant the seeds of the greatest growth the world has ever seen.

You have grown in your science and in your technologies, yet now you will grow in your *consciousness.* And this will be the greatest growth of all, making all the rest of your advances look insignificant by comparison.

The twenty-first century will be the time of awakening, of meeting The Creator Within. Many beings will experience Oneness with God and with all of life. This will be the beginning of the golden age of the New Human, of which it has been written; the time of the universal human, which has been eloquently described by those with deep insight among you.

There are many such people in the world now—teachers and messengers, Masters and visionaries—who are placing this vision before humankind and offering tools with which to create it. These messengers and visionaries are the heralds of a New Age.

You may choose to be one of them. You, to whom this message is now being sent. You, who are reading this right now. Many are called, but few choose themselves.

What is your choice? Shall We speak now with One Voice?

To *say* the same thing, we must all *know* the same thing. Yet You have just said that there are those who do *not* know. I'm confused.

I did not say that there are those who do not know. I said there *appear to be* those who do not know. Yet, judge not by appearances.

All of you know everything. No one is sent into this life without the knowing. That is because you *are* the knowing. The knowing is What You Are. Yet you have forgotten who and what You Are in order that you might create it again. This is the process of re-creation of which we have spoken now many times.

Book 1 of the *Conversations with God* trilogy explains this all in wonderful detail, as you are aware. And so it *appears* that you "do not know." In wholly accurate terms, it would be said that you "do not remember."

There are those who do not remember, and they do not remember that they've not remembered.

There are those who do not remember, but they remember that they're not remembering.

There are those who do not remember, but think they have remembered.

There are those who remember, but do not remember that they've remembered.

There are those who remember, but pretend that they have not remembered.

And there are those who remember, and remember that they've remembered.

Those who have fully *Re-membered* have become a Member Once Again of the Body of God.

Fifteen

I wish to fully re-member. I wish to be re-united with God. Isn't that what every human soul longs for?

Yes. Some do not know it, some do not "remember that they remember," but they have a longing in their hearts nonetheless. Some do not even believe in the existence of God, yet the longing deep within them will not disappear. They think it is a longing for something else, but, in the end, they will discover that it is a longing to return home, to become a Member Once Again of the Body of God.

They will discover this, the unbelievers, when they discover that nothing else for which they reach, nothing else which they acquire, can satisfy their deepest inner longing. Not even the love of another.

All Earthly loves are temporary and short-lived. Even the love of a lifetime, a partnership which lasts for half a century or more, is short-lived compared to the life of the soul, which is without end. And this the soul will realize, if not before, then at the moment of what you call death. For the soul will know in that moment that there is no death; that life is everlasting, and that You have always been, are now, and always will be, world without end.

When the soul realizes this, it will also realize the temporary nature of what it thought to be a permanent love. And then, on its next journey into physical life, it will understand more deeply, it will remember more easily, and it will know that all that one loves in physical life is short-lived, transient.

Somehow, that seems so desolate. It seems to take the joy out of love for me. How can I love someone or something fully if I know that it is so temporary, so . . . so meaningless on the overall scale of things.

I did not say anything about it being meaningless. Nothing about love is meaningless. Love *is* the meaning of life itself. Life is love, expressed. That *is* life. Therefore, every act of love is life expressing, at the highest level. The fact that something, some experience, is temporary, or relatively short, does not render it meaningless. Indeed, it may give it more meaning.

Let me explain a bit more about love, and then you will understand more fully.

Experiences of love are temporary, but love itself is eternal. These experiences are only here-and-now expressions of a love that is everywhere, always.

That does not seem to make it more joyful for me.

Let us see if we can bring the idea of joy back into it. Do you have someone in particular that you love right now?

Yes, many people.

And one, in particular, with whom you partner?

Yes. Nancy. As you know.

Yes, I do know that, but I am leading you through this one step at a time, so just dialogue with Me.

Okay.

Now this Nancy with whom you feel a particular love, do you have sexual experiences with her?

Do I ever.

And these experiences, are they continual, constant, and never-ending?

Don't I wish.

No, I don't think you really do. Not if you think about it. But for now, I am accepting that these experiences are temporary, is that correct?

Yes. Periodical and temporary.

And short-lived?

It depends how long it's been.

What's that?

A little joke. Just a little joke. Yes, relatively speaking, the experiences are short-lived.

Does that give them any less meaning?

No.

Does it make them any less enjoyable?

No.

So you are saying that your love for Nancy is forever, but your expressions of love for her in this particular way are periodical, temporary, and short-lived, is that correct?

I see where You are going.

Good. Then the question is, where are *you* going?

Are you going to a place where you cannot enjoy or have meaning in your expressions of love as an eternal being simply because the experiences themselves are temporary? Or are you going to a place of greater understanding that allows you to love "full out" what you love when you love it, even knowing that the experience of love in that particular form is temporary?

If you go to the latter place, then you are heading for mastery, for Masters know that *it is the full-out loving of life, and of all that life presents in every moment, that is the expression of Godliness.*

This is the Second Attitude of God. God is totally loving.

Yes, I know about this Second Attitude, and how it can change my life. This is one I don't need explained to me. I understand what fully loving means.

Do you?

I think I do, yes.

You understand what it means to be totally loving?

Yes. It means to love everyone without condition and without limitation.

What does that mean? How does that work?

Well, I am trying to figure that one out. That is a day-to-day exploration for me. It's a moment-to-moment discovering.

You would do better to make it a moment-to-moment creating. Life is not a process of discovery; it is a process of creation.

How do I create, then, moment-to-moment, the experience of unconditional and unlimited love?

If you do not have the answer to that question, then you cannot say that you understand what it means to be totally loving. You understand what the words are saying, but you do not know what they mean. As a practical matter, they have no meaning.

That is the problem today with the word "love."

And the phrase "I love you."

And the phrase "I love you," yes. People say it, but many people do not understand what it means—what it *really* means—to love another. They understand what it means to *need* another, to *want* something from another, and even to be willing to give something in return for what they need and want, but they do not understand what it means to really love, to truly love.

Many people have had a real challenge, a real problem, with this word "love," and this phrase "I love you."

Including me, of course. My life has been a disaster when it comes to love. I didn't understand what it meant to be fully loving, and I guess I don't understand now. I can say the words, but I don't seem to be able to live them. Can anybody be truly loving, without any condition, without any limitation? Can human beings do that?

Some can, and have.

These beings are called Masters.

Well, I am not a Master, by this or any other measure.

You *are* a Master! All of you are! You are simply not experiencing that. Yet you are well on your way to experiencing mastery, My son.

I wish I could believe that.

So do I.

Until my most recent years, I didn't understand anything at all about love. I thought I knew it all. But I knew nothing, and my life was a demonstration of that. And you've just proven to me here that I don't really understand it yet. I mean, I *talk* a good game, but I'm not what you'd call a championship player.

I haven't gone into my important relationships and my marriages in my narrative here, because I want to honor the privacy of those people whose lives I've touched in hurtful ways. I've kept my "story" limited to my own personal wanderings. But I can say in a general sense that just about everything one can do to hurt a person (except injure someone physically), I've done in my love relationships. Just about every mistake one can make, I've made. Just about every selfish, insensitive, non-caring thing one can do, I've done.

I married for the first time when I was twenty-one. Of course, I thought I was a grown man, understanding all there was to understand about love. I understood nothing. About selfishness I knew a great deal, but about love I knew nothing.

The woman who was unlucky enough to marry me thought she was getting a self-assured, sensitive, caring guy. And what she got was a self-centered, egotistical, domineering man who, like his father, assumed that he was "the boss," and who inflated himself by making others look small.

It was just after we were married that we moved to the South for our short stay, then headed back to Annapolis again. I became deeply involved in the town's cultural life, with the Colonial Players, and helping put on the first productions at the Annapolis Summer Garden Theatre. I was one of the founders of Maryland Hall for the Creative Arts, as well as part of the small group that conceived and coordinated the first Annapolis Fine Arts Festival there.

Between my full-time job and my other "obligations," however, I was away from my wife and children three or four nights a week, and most weekends, throughout the year. In my world, "love" meant "providing," and being willing to do what it takes to accomplish that. This willingness I had, and no one ever had to convince me of my responsibilities. Yet I thought they began and ended with my pocketbook—because that's where they seemed to begin and end for my father.

Only later, as I grew older, was I able to admit and acknowledge that my father was far more involved in my life than I wanted to give him credit for—making pajamas (he was incredibly handy with a sewing machine), baking apple pies (the world's best), taking me camping (he became a pack leader when we joined the Cub Scouts), hauling me on fishing trips to Canada and expeditions to Washington, D.C., and elsewhere, teaching me photography and typing, the list is endless.

What I did lack from my father was any verbal or physical

show of love. He simply never said "I love you," and actual bodily contact was unheard of, except on Christmas and birthdays, when Mom would instruct us, after we received our always-wonderful gifts, to "go hug your father." We did it as fast as we could. It was a Cursory Closeness.

To me, Dad was the source of authority in the house. Mom was the source of love.

Dad's edicts and decisions, his wieldings of power, were often arbitrary and heavy-handed, and Mom was the voice of compassion and patience and leniency. We went to her with our pleas that she help us get around Dad's rules and restrictions, or get him to change his mind. She often did. Together, they played a very good game of Good Cop/Bad Cop.

I imagine that this was a fairly typical model of parenting in the 1940s and 1950s, and I simply adopted the model in the sixties, with some modifications. I made it a point to constantly tell my children that I loved them, and to hug and kiss them a lot, whenever I was around them. I simply was not around them very much.

In the model I was given, it was the woman's job to "be with the kids," while the man went out into the world and "did things." One of the things I eventually wound up "doing" was having flings with other women, and finally, a full-fledged affair. That led to the end of my first marriage, and turned into my second.

I was never proud of the way I behaved, and my deep sense of guilt only ripened through the years. I've apologized to my first wife many times, and, because she is and has always been a gracious person, we have maintained cordiality for many years. But I know that I hurt her deeply, and I wish there were some way a person could go back and redo, or undo, or at least *do a different way,* what was done.

My second marriage failed, and led to a third—which also ultimately failed. I didn't seem to know how to hold onto a relationship, and the reason was that I didn't seem to know how to *give.* I held (although not consciously, I don't think) the extraordinarily selfish and immature view that relationships existed to bring me pleasure and convenience, and that the challenge was to keep them going while giving up as little of myself as possible.

In truth, that is what romantic relationships felt like to me: interactions requiring me to give up bits and pieces of myself until I had all but disappeared. I didn't want that, and yet I didn't seem to know how I could be happy without a "significant other" in my life. So it was always a question of how much of myself I was willing to "sell out" in order to have the security of a permanent source of love, companionship, and affection (read, sex) in my life. As I said, I'm not very proud of any of this. I'm trying to be transparent here. My friend Rev. Mary Manin Morrissey, founder of the Living Enrichment Center in Wilsonville, Oregon, calls me a Recovering Male.

By the end of my third marriage I thought I was ready to quit, but I was actually to go through this *two more times* before I was able to make a long-term relationship work. In the process I fathered seven more children—four with a woman with whom I had a long-term relationship without becoming married.

To say that I have acted irresponsibly would be generous in the extreme, yet in each instance I believed that (a) this was finally the relationship that was going to last, and (b) I was doing everything I could to make it work. Given my complete misunderstanding then of what love really is, I realize now how empty those words were.

And I wish that I could say that these behaviors were limited to those partnerships, but that would not be telling the half of it. Along the way and in between, I involved myself with many other women, conducting myself with equal immaturity and selfishness.

Now, I fully realize that there are no victims and no villains in these matters, and that all life experiences are co-creations, but I acknowledge the huge role that I played in these scenarios. I see the pattern that it took me thirty years to break, and those are ugly realities I am unwilling to try to cover up with New Age aphorisms.

So it is not suprising, then, that in my late forties I found myself alone. And, as I have said before, my career and health were in no better shape than my love life. It was with hopelessness that I watched my fiftieth birthday approaching. This was the state of things when I awoke in utter despair in the middle of a February night in 1992 and wrote an angry letter to God.

I can't tell you how much it's meant to me that God answered.

> It meant a lot to Me, too.

But I often wonder, why did this happen to me? I'm not worthy.

> Everyone is worthy of having a conversation with God! That was the whole point! Yet I could not make that point by "preaching to the choir."

Okay, but why me? There are many people who have led less than perfect lives. Why choose me? That's the question so many people ask. "Why you, Neale, and not me?"

And what do you say?

I say that God talks to everyone, all of the time. The question is not, To whom does God talk?, but, Who listens?

Excellent. That is an excellent answer.

It should be. You gave it to me. But now I have to ask You to answer my earlier question. How do I create, moment-to-moment, the experience of unconditional and unlimited love? How can I adopt the godly attitude of being fully loving?

To be fully loving is to be completely natural. Loving is the natural thing to do. It is not normal, but it is natural.

Explain that difference to me again.

"Normal" is a word used to denote what is usual, commonplace, consistent. The word "natural" is used to denote the basic nature of a thing. Your basic nature as a human being is to be loving, to love everyone and everything, though it is not *normal* for you to do so.

Why not?

Because you have been taught to act *against your basic nature*—to not be natural—in the way you move through the world.

And why is *that?* Why have we been taught that?

Because you have believed that your Natural Self is bad, is evil, is something which must be tamed, restrained, subdued. And so you have required your race to exhibit and adhere to "normal" behaviors that are not natural. To be "natural" was to be sinful, indulgent, perhaps even dangerously evil. Even to allow yourself to be seen in a "natural" state was said to be sinful.

That is true to this day. Certain magazines are still considered by some to be "dirty." Nude sunbathing is labeled by many as "deviant." Naked bodies, in general, are to be avoided, and people who walk around naked even in their own homes or around their own backyards or pools are often called "perverted."

And it goes far beyond exposing our "private parts." In some cultures we won't even allow a woman to show her *face*, or her wrists, or her ankles.

This, of course, is understandable. If you've ever seen a really attractive pair of woman's ankles, you can understand why some people believe that they must be hidden from public view. They can be very provocative, and even lead a person to think of S - E - X.

Okay, so I'm kidding. But it's almost that repressive in some homes, and in some cultures.

And that is not the only natural aspect of your being that many of you have discouraged. You have discouraged *telling the truth,* even though it is very natural for you to do so. You have discouraged basic trust in the universe, although it is very natural for you to have it. You have discouraged singing and dancing and rejoicing and celebration, though every bone in your body is aching to explode with the pure wonder of Who You Are!

You have done these things because you are afraid that if you "give in" to natural tendencies, you will be hurt, and if you give in to natural pleasures, you will hurt yourself and others. You carry this fear because you hold a Sponsoring Thought about the human race which says that your species is basically evil. You imagine that you were "born in sin," and that it is your nature to be bad.

This is the most important decision you have ever made about yourselves, and since you are creating your own reality, it is a decision you have implemented. Not wanting to make yourselves wrong, you have gone to extraordinary lengths to make yourselves right. Your life has *shown* you that you are right about this, and so you have adopted this as your cultural story. This is just the way it *is,* you say, and by continually saying it, you have made it so.

Yet unless you change your story, change your idea of who you are and *how* you are as a race, as a species, you can never be fully loving, because you cannot even fully love yourself.

That is the first step in being fully loving. You must fully love your Self. And this you cannot do so long as you believe that you were born in sin, and are basically evil.

This question—what is the basic nature of man?—is the most important question now before the human race. If you believe that humans are by nature non-trustworthy and evil, you will create a society that supports that view, then enact laws, approve rules, adopt regulations, and impose restraints that are justified by it. If you believe that humans are by nature trustworthy and good, you will create an entirely different kind of society, in which laws, rules, regulations, and restraints are rarely required. The first society will be freedom *limiting,* the second, freedom *giving.*

God is fully loving because God is fully free. To be fully free is to be fully joyful, because full freedom creates the space for every joyful experience. Freedom is the basic nature of God. It is also the basic nature of the human soul. The degree to which you are not fully free is the degree to which you are not fully joyful—and that is the degree to which you are not fully loving.

You have discussed this before, and so I get that it must be pretty important. You are saying that to be totally loving means to be fully free.

Yes, and to allow others to be fully free.

You mean everyone should be able to do anything they want?

That is what I mean. To the degree that it is humanly possible to allow that, yes. That is what I mean.

That is how God loves.

God allows.

I allow everyone to do anything they want.

Without consequence? Without punishment?

The two are not the same thing.

As I have now told you repeatedly, there is no such thing as punishment in My Kingdom. On the other hand, there is such a thing as consequence.

A consequence is a natural outcome, a punishment is a normal one. It is normal in your society to punish. It is abnormal in your society to simply allow a consequence to assert itself, to reveal itself.

Punishments are your announcement that you are too impatient to await a natural outcome.

Are You saying that no one should be punished for anything?

That is something you have to decide. Indeed, you are deciding it every day.

As you continue to make your ongoing choices about this, you may feel it beneficial to consider what method you find most effective in causing your society, or anyone within it, to change behaviors. This is, after all, your presumed reason for imposing punishments. To punish for purposes of retribution—for, basically, "getting even"—will not create the kind of society you say you wish to create.

Highly evolved societies have observed that little is learned from punishments. They have concluded that consequences are the better teacher.

All sentient beings know the difference between punishments and consequences.

Punishments are artificially created outcomes. Consequences are naturally occurring outcomes.

Punishments are imposed from the outside by someone with a value system different from the one being punished. Consequences are experienced on the inside, by the Self.

Punishments are someone else's decision that one has done wrong. Consequences are one's own experience that something does not work. That is, it did not produce an intended result.

In other words, we do not learn quickly from punishments, because we see them as something that someone else is doing to us. We learn more readily from consequences, because we see them as something that *we are doing to ourselves.*

Precisely. You have it exactly.

But can't a punishment be a consequence? Isn't that the point?

Punishments are artificially created outcomes, not naturally occurring results. The attempt to convert a punishment into a consequence by simply calling it that does not make it that. Only the most immature being can be fooled by such a verbal contrivance, and, even that being, not for very long.

This has not stopped many of those among you who have parented offspring to use the contrivance. And the biggest punishment that you have devised is the withholding of your love. You have shown your offspring that if they behave in a certain way, you will withhold your love. It is by the granting and the withholding of your love that you have sought to regulate and modify, to control and to create, your children's behaviors.

This is something that God would never do.

Yet you have told your children that I do it, too—no doubt to justify your own actions. But I tell you this: true love never withdraws itself. And that is what loving fully means. It means your love is full enough to hold the biggest wrong behavior. It means more than that. It means that no behavior is even *called* "wrong."

Erich Segal had it right. Love means not having to say you're sorry.

That is exactly correct. Yet it is a very high principle, not practiced by many human beings.

Most human beings cannot even imagine it being practiced by God.

And they are right. I do not practice it.

I beg Your pardon?

I *am* it. One does not have to practice what one is, one simply *is* it.

I am the love that knows no condition, nor limitation of any kind.

I am totally loving, and to be totally loving means to be willing to give every mature sentient being total freedom to be, do, and have that which they wish.

Even if you know it will be bad for them?

It is not for you to decide that for them.

Not even for our children?

If they are mature sentient beings, no. If they are grown children, no. And if they are not yet mature, the fastest way to lead them to their own maturity is to allow them the freedom to make as many choices as possible as early as practical.

This is what love does. Love lets go. That which you call need, and which you often confuse with love, does the opposite. Need holds on. This is the way you can tell the difference between love and need. Love lets go, need holds on.

So to be totally loving, I let go?

Among other things, yes. Let go of expectation, let go of requirements and rules and regulations that you would impose on your loved ones. For they are not loved if they are restricted. Not totally.

Nor are you. You do not love yourself totally when you restrict yourself, when you grant yourself less than total freedom, in any matter.

Yet remember that choices are not restrictions. So do not call the choices you have made restrictions. And lovingly provide for your offspring, and all your loved ones, all the information that you feel you may have, to help them make good choices—"good" being defined here as those choices most likely to produce a particular desired result, as well as what you know to be their largest desired result: a happy life.

Share what you know about that. Offer what you have come to understand. Yet do not seek to impose your ideas, your rules, your choices upon another. And do not withhold your love should another make choices you would not make. Indeed, if you believe their choices to have been poor ones, that is precisely the time to *show* your love.

That is compassion, and there is no higher expression.

What else does it mean to be totally loving?

It means to be fully present, in every single moment. To be fully aware. To be fully open, honest, transparent. It means to be fully willing, to express the love that is in your heart full out. To be fully loving means to be fully naked, without hidden agenda or hidden motive, without hidden *anything.*

And You say that it is possible for human beings, for regular people like me, to achieve such love? This is something of which we are all capable?

It is more than that of which you are capable. It is that which you *are.* This is the nature of Who You Are. The most difficult thing that you do is to deny that. And you are doing this difficult thing every day. It is why your life feels so difficult. Yet when you do the easy thing, when you decide to come from, to be, Who You Really Are—which is pure love, unlimited and unconditioned—then your life becomes easy again. All the turmoil disappears, all the struggle goes away.

This peace may be achieved in any given moment. The way to it may be found by asking a simple question:

What would love do now?

The magic question again?

Yes. This is a marvelous question, because you will always know the answer. It is like magic. It is cleansing, like a soap. It takes the worry out of being close. It washes away all doubt, all fear. It bathes the mind with the wisdom of the soul.

What a good way of putting that.

It is true. When you ask this question, you will know *instantly* what to do. In any circumstance, under any condition, you will know. You will be given the answer. You *are* the answer, and asking the question brings forth that part of you.

What if you fool yourself? You cannot fool yourself?

Do not second-guess this answer when it instantly comes to you. When you second-guess is when you fool yourself—and can make a fool *of* yourself. Go into the heart of love, and come from that place in all your choices and decisions, and you will find peace.

Sixteen

What does it mean to be totally accepting, blessing, and grateful? These last three of the Five Attitudes of God are not quite as clear to me—especially three and four.

To be totally accepting means not to quarrel with what is showing up right now. It means not to reject it, or throw it back, or walk away from it, but to embrace it, hold it, love it as if it were your own. Because *it is* your own. It is your own creation, with which you are well pleased—unless you are not.

If you are not, you will resist owning what you have created, and *what you resist persists.* Therefore rejoice, and be glad, and should the present circumstance or condition be one which you now choose to change, simply choose to experience it in another way. The outward appearance, the outward manifestation, may not be altered at all, but your inner experience of it can and will be changed forever, simply out of your decision about it.

Remember, this is what you are after. You are not concerned with outer appearances, only with your inner experience. Let the outer world be what it is. Create your inner world as you would have it be. This is what is meant by being in your world, but not of it. This is mastery in living.

Let me get this straight. You should accept anything, even those things you disagree with?

Accepting something does not mean refusing to change it. In fact, the opposite is true. You cannot change that which you do not accept—in yourself especially, and outside of yourself as well.

Accept everything, therefore, as the divine manifestation of the divinity within you. Then you declare yourself to be its creator, and only then can you "uncreate" it. Only then can you recognize—that is, know again—the power within you to create something new.

To accept something is not to agree with it. It is simply to embrace it, whether you agree with it or not.

You would have us embrace the devil himself, wouldn't You?

How else will you heal him?

We have had this exchange before.

Yes, and we will have it again. Over and over will I share with you these truths. Over and over will you hear them, until you *hear* them. If you catch Me repeating Myself, it is because you are repeating *yourself.* You are repeating every behavior, every action, every thought, which has brought you over and over again to sadness, to misery, to defeat. Yet the victory can be won, the victory over this devil of yours.

Of course, there is no devil—as we have also discussed many times before. We are speaking metaphorically here.

How can you heal that which you will not even hold? You must first hold something firmly in your grasp, firmly in your reality, before you can let it go.

I'm not sure I understand. Help me to understand that.

You cannot drop something you do not hold. Therefore, *Behold!* I bring you glad tidings of great joy.

God is totally accepting.

Humans are very excepting.

Humans love each other *except* when those others do this or do that. They love their world *except* when it does not please them. They love Me *except* when they don't.

God is not excepting, God is accepting. Of everyone and everything.

There are no exceptions.

Being totally accepting sounds a lot like being totally loving.

It is all the same thing. We are using different words to describe the same experience. Love and acceptance *are* interchangeable concepts.

In order to change something, you must first accept that it is there. In order to love something, you must do the same thing.

You cannot love the part of yourself that you claim is not there, that you disown. You have disowned many parts of yourself that you do not wish to claim. In disclaiming those parts of yourself, you have made it impossible to totally love yourself—and thus, to totally love another.

Deborah Ford wrote a wonderful book on this subject called *The Dark Side of the Light Chasers.* It is about people who are seeking the Light, but don't know how to deal with their own "darkness," don't see the gift there. I recommend this book to everybody. It can change lives. It explains in very clear and understandable terms why acceptance is such a blessing.

It *is* a blessing! Without it, you would be damning yourself, and others. Yet through love and acceptance, you bless all those whose lives you touch. When you become totally loving and totally accepting, you become totally blessing—and this renders you and everyone else totally joyful.

Everything flows together, everything connects to everything else, and you are beginning to see and to understand that all of the Five Attitudes of God are really one and the same. They are what God *is.*

The aspect of God that is totally blessing is that aspect which condemns nothing. In God's world there is no such thing as condemnation, only commendation. You are all to be commended for the work you are doing, for the job you are doing, getting to know and to experience Who You Really Are.

Whenever anything bad would happen around my mother, she would always say, "God bless it!" Everyone else would say, "God dammit!", but Mom would say, "God bless it!"

One day I asked her why. She looked at me as if she couldn't quite comprehend how I could ask the question. Then, with the love and patience of one explaining something to a small child, she answered, "I don't want God to *damn* it. I want God to *bless* it. That's the only thing that will make it any better."

Your mother was a very "aware" person. She understood many things.

Go now, and bless all things in your life. Remember, I have sent you nothing but angels, and I have brought you nothing but miracles.

How does one go about blessing things? I don't understand what that's about, what those words mean.

You give something your blessing when you give it your best energies, your highest thoughts.

I should give my best energies, my highest thoughts, to things I hate? Like war? Violence? Greed? People who are unkind? Policies that are inhumane? I don't understand. I can't give these things my "blessing."

But it is precisely your best energies and your highest thoughts which those things need if they are to be changed.

Do you not understand? You change nothing by condemning it. Indeed, you literally condemn it to be repeated.

I am not to condemn wanton killing, rampant prejudice, widespread violence, unchecked greed?

You are to condemn nothing.

Nothing?

Nothing. Have I not sent My teachers to tell you, "Judge not, and neither condemn"?

Yet if we condemn nothing, we seem to be approving of everything.

Failure to condemn does not mean failure to seek change. Because you have not condemned something does not mean that you approve of it. It simply means that you refuse to judge it. You may still, on the other hand, choose something else.

A choice to change does not always have to come out of anger. In fact, *your chances of affecting very real change rise in direct proportion to the decrease in your anger.*

Humans often use anger as their justification to seek change, and judgments as their justification for anger. You have created a lot of drama around this, perceiving injury in order to justify your judgments.

Many of you end your relationships this way. You have

not learned the art of simply saying, "I am complete. The present form of this relationship no longer serves me." You insist on first perceiving injury, then moving into judgment, then coming from anger in order to somehow justify the change you seek to make. It is as if, without anger, you cannot have what you want; you cannot change what you don't like. So you build up all sorts of drama around it.

Now I tell you this: bless, bless, *bless* your enemies, and pray for those who persecute you. Send them your best energies, and your highest thoughts.

You will not be able to do this unless you see every person and every life circumstance as a gift; as an angel, and a miracle. When you do, you will move into the fullness of gratitude. You will be totally grateful—the Fifth Attitude of God—and the circle will be complete.

This is an important element, this feeling of gratitude, isn't it?

Yes. Gratitude is the attitude that changes everything. To be grateful for something is to stop resisting it, to see it and acknowledge it as a gift, even when the gift is not immediately apparent.

In addition, as you have already been taught, gratitude for an experience, condition, or outcome *in advance* is a powerful tool in the creation of your reality, and a sure sign of Mastery.

It is so powerful that I think the Fifth Attitude should almost have been listed first.

In fact, the magnificence of the Five Attitudes of God is that, like the Seven Steps to Friendship with God, *their order may be reversed.* God is totally grateful, blessing, accepting, loving, and joyful!

This is another good place for me to mention my favorite prayer; the most powerful prayer I ever heard. *Thank you, God, for helping me to understand that this problem has already been solved for me.*

Yes, that *is* a powerful prayer. The next time you are confronted with a condition or circumstance you judge to be problematical, express your immediate gratitude not only for the solution, but for the problem itself. By so doing, you instantly change your perspective on it, and your attitude about it.

Next, bless it, just as your mother did. Give it your best energies and your highest thought. In this, you make it your friend, and not your enemy; that which supports you, rather than that which opposes you.

Then, accept it, and resist not evil. For what you resist, persists. Only what you accept can you change.

Now, envelop it with love. Whatever you are experiencing, you can literally love any undesired experience away. In a sense, you can "love it to death."

Finally, be joyful, for the exact and perfect outcome is at hand. Nothing can take your joy away from you, for joy is Who You Are, and who you will always be. So, in the face of every problem, *do a joyful thing.*

Like Anna sang in the musical story of *The King and I:*

"I whistle a happy tune, and every single time, the happiness in the tune, convinces me that I'm not afraid!"

There you have it. You have it perfectly.

I have a friend who uses these attitudes every day, in every moment. He heals other people by helping them to see how easily and quickly they can change their attitudes, and showing them what a difference such a change will make in their lives. His name is Jerry Jampolsky—Gerald G. Jampolsky, M.D., to be formal—and he wrote a ground-breaking book called *Love Is Letting Go of Fear.*

Jerry founded the Center for Attitudinal Healing, in Sausalito, California, and there are now over 130 such centers in cities throughout the world. I have never known a kinder, more gentle man. He holds a positive attitude about everything. *Everything.* In his home, I have never "heard a discouraging word." In this, he is remarkable, and his attitude about life is inspiring.

Nancy and I were spending several days with Jerry and his wonderful and accomplished wife, Diane Cirincione, when, as life would have it, I found myself experiencing a personality clash with one of his other house guests. I'm sorry to say that I was not "on top of it" during this time. Tired and drained from many months on the road, I was not dealing with the situation very peacefully.

Jerry saw that I was agitated, and he asked if there was anything he could do to help. As anyone who knows him will tell you, this is a common question from Jerry whenever he sees anyone around him experiencing any kind of discomfort.

I told him that I was having some negative feelings about an earlier interaction with the other house guest, and Jerry immediately suggested that it might be beneficial to sit down with himself, Diane, and the other person to take a look at it and "see what it would take to heal it."

Then he asked me a probing question. "Do you want to heal it, or do you want to hang onto the negative feelings?"

I told him I didn't think I was making a conscious decision to hold onto the negativity, but that I was having some trouble getting past it. "Well, everything is going to depend here on your attitude about it," Jerry replied in a very kind, quiet voice. "There's probably something very positive going to come from all this. Let's look to see what it is."

We had the talk he suggested, and, with his facilitation and Diane's, the other house guest and I took the first steps on the road back to love. I was really grateful to have Jerry around, during a time when I just plain lost touch with my Center, and Who I Really Am. Without taking sides, without making judgments, without any drastic interventions other than a continuing suggestion to look at things in a different way and give myself permission to see another's point of view, Diane and Jerry not only played a huge role in healing the moment, but gave me tools with which to apply *attitudinal healing* principles to everyday life.

Not all of us can be lucky enough to be around Jerry Jampolsky when we're having a rough moment, but we can be around Jerry's wisdom. That's why I am excited about his new book, *Forgiveness: The Greatest Healer of All.*

What makes Jerry Jampolsky stand out is his remarkable attitude. It heals everything in sight; it even healed *Jerry's* sight.

It happened that during the time we spent together, Jerry was experiencing some medical complications involving his eyesight, which was deteriorating. In fact, on one of the days we were there, he was scheduled to have some outpatient surgery, and there was a real possibility that the procedure could cause his eyesight to be diminished, rather than improved. In fact, there was a chance that he might lose his sight in one eye altogether.

None of this seemed to bother Jerry. He wasn't giving it a second thought. He simply wasn't going to dwell on it. He avoided any discussion of it during the days before the surgery, and I remember that he left for the hospital with the biggest smile. "Everything is going to be just fine," he announced, "no matter how it turns out."

I learned something that day from a Master.

> To accept something is not to agree with it. It is simply to embrace it, whether you agree with it or not.

Yes. I could see that Jerry was accepting and blessing the experience he was having.

> You give something your blessing when you give it your best energies, your highest thoughts.

That's why I think immediately of Jerry when I hear about the Five Attitudes of God. He's a person who practices those attitudes consistently.

People are always asking me how my life has changed since my books have come out. Meeting and becoming friends with people like Jerry Jampolsky is one change that has blessed me deeply. Connecting and developing personal relationships with many people who I have personally admired through the years has been one of the most instructive and humbling outcomes of having produced the *Conversations with God* trilogy. I have seen in these extraordinary people what I have yet to master, and they have inspired me.

There have been other changes, of course, and the most important of these is in my relationship with God.

I now have a personal relationship with God, and that has resulted in an experience of continued well-being, of quiet empowerment, of personal growth and expansion, of deeply enriching inspiration, and of sure and certain love. As a result of this, every other important aspect of my life has changed as well.

Everything about the way I hold the experience of relationship is different, and my personal relationships are reflecting that. My personal interactions with others have become joyful and satisfying. As for life partnership, I am at this writing in the fifth year of my marriage to Nancy, and ours has been almost a fairytale romance. It was wonderful at the beginning, and it has become even more wonderful with every passing day. That does not mean it is guaranteed to last forever in its present form. I am not going to predict that, because I am not going to put that kind of pressure on either Nancy or myself. But I believe that even if the form of our relationship should ever change, it will always remain wonderfully honest, caring, compassionate, and loving.

Not only have my relationships improved, and thus, my emotional health, but so has my physical health. I am now in better condition than I was ten years ago, and feeling enlivened and energized. Again, I am not going to predict that it will always stay that way, because I am not going to put that pressure on myself, but I can tell you that even if my health does change, my inner peacefulness and my deep joy will not, for I have seen the perfection of my life, and I no longer question outcomes, nor struggle against them.

My understanding of abundance has also shifted, and I now experience a world without lack or limitation. While I know that this is not the experience of the majority of my fellow humans, I work consciously every day to help others change their experience, and I share of my abundance freely, supporting causes and projects and people with whom I am in agreement, as another means of expressing and experiencing and re-creating Who I Am.

And yes, I have been inspired by the many wonderful teachers and visionaries I have come to know on a personal level. I've learned from them what makes human beings stand out, what lifts them above the crowd. This is not about star worship or name dropping, because I am clear that what lifts these remarkable individuals can lift us as well. The same magic resides in all of us, and the more we learn about people who have made life's magic work, the more we can make it work in our own lives. In this way we are all each other's teachers. We are guides, calling each other not really to learn, but to remember, to know again, Who We Really Are.

Marianne Williamson is such a guide. Let me tell you what I've learned from Marianne.

Courage.

She has taught me grandly of bravery, and of commitment to a higher walk. I have never known a person with more personal strength or spiritual stamina. Or of greater vision. But Marianne does not merely talk of her vision for the world, she walks that vision, every day, working tirelessly to put it into place. That is what I have learned from her: to work tirelessly to put into place the vision you have been given, and to do so courageously. *Act now.*

I was in bed with Marianne Williamson once. She's going to kill me for telling you this, but it's true. And I learned many wonderful things in those moments we shared.

Okay, maybe not *in* bed, but *on* the bed. And my wife, Nancy, was in and out of the room, chatting away with us as she went about packing. The fact is, we were hanging out at Marianne's home, enjoying some precious and rare personal time together. And early on the morning of my departure, Marianne and I wound up sitting on her bed together, sharing orange juice and sneaking a pastry, talking about life. I asked her how she managed to keep going, how she had continued her breakneck pace for so many years, touching so many lives in such an extraordinary way. She looked at me softly, but with a strength behind her eyes that I remember to this day. "It's about commitment," she said. "It's about *living* the highest choices you make, the choices many people only talk about."

Then, she challenged me. "Are you ready to do that?" she asked. "If you are, wonderful. If you're not, get out of the public eye, and stay out. Because if you give hope to people, you become a model, and you've got to be willing to provide a certain amount of leadership, you've got to be willing to live up to the model. Or at least to try, with all your being. People can forgive you if you fail, but they will find it hard to forgive you if you fail to try.

"Sharing your own evolutionary process with others puts you on the fast track. If you tell somebody else that something is possible for them, you have to be willing to demonstrate that it is possible for you. You have to commit your life to this."

Surely this must be what is meant by living life "deliberately."

Yet even when we set our intentions deliberately, sometimes things seem to happen coincidentally. But I have learned that there is no such thing as coincidence, and that synchronous events are simply God's way of putting things into place for us, once our intentions are clear. It turns out that the more deliberately you live, the more coincidences you notice in your life.

Once *Conversations with God, book 1,* was published, for instance, it became my intention to see it placed into the hands of as many people as possible, because I believed it contained important information for all humankind. Two weeks after its release, Dr. Bernie Siegel was in Annapolis, lecturing about the connection between medicine and spirituality. In the middle of his presentation he said, "All of us are talking to God all the time, and I don't know about you, but I'm writing my dialogue down. In fact, my next book is called *Conversations with God,* and it's about a man who asks God every question he ever had, and God gives him the answers. He doesn't understand all of them, and he even argues a little with God, and so they have this conversation. It's really my own experience."

Everyone in the audience chuckled—except one young woman.

My daughter.

Samantha just "happened" to be in the audience that day, and at the first break rushed down to the podium. "Dr. Siegel," she began, breathlessly, "were you serious about writing that book you talked about?"

"Sure was," Bernie smiled. "I'm halfway through it!"

"Well, that's very interesting," Samantha managed, "because

my father has just had a book published that's exactly the one you've described, *right down to the title.*"

Bernie's eyes widened. "Really? That's fascinating. Although I'm not surprised. Once an idea is 'out there,' anyone can tap into it. I think all of us should write our own personal bible anyway. I'd love to talk with him about his."

The next day, I spoke with Dr. Siegel at his home in Connecticut. We shared our experiences, and it turned out that he was, indeed, writing the same book I'd just had published. At that point, I didn't see the perfection of what was happening, but fell into fear. I began to imagine the worst-case scenario: two months after Bernie's book comes out, people find mine on some back shelf somewhere and *accuse me of copying his.*

I was too embarrassed to share any of these thoughts during our conversation. After all, my own book warned against fear-based thinking, saying repeatedly to throw out negative ideas and replace them with positive ones. Bernie kindly said that he'd love to read my book, and I promised to send him a copy. I hung up, and tried to apply some positive thinking. For several weeks I alternated between worrying and wondering. Wondering is the opposite of worrying. It is to something wonderful as "worrying" is to something worrisome. These days I wonder a lot—that is, produce, with my mental energy, a lot of *wonder.* In those early days I was still caught up in worrying at least half the time.

Half-time wondering must have been enough, because do you know what Bernie Siegel did? Not only did he retitle and rework his own book—*he turned around and endorsed mine.* His was the first celebrity endorsement which *Conversations with God* received, and it helped book buyers, who might have been skittish about a previously unpublished author, see the value of what I had produced.

Now, folks, that's class. That's the action of a big person, who knows he has nothing to lose by lifting up a fellow human being. Even when that fellow human being is walking all over the same territory, covering the same ground, here is a man capable of saying not only, hey, there's room enough for all of us, but, even, *I'll give this person some of my space.*

I've since come to know Bernie on a personal level. We've even made presentations together. He is a sheer delight, with a sparkle in his eyes that lights up every room. That is the sparkle of selflessness, or what I have come to call, in my personal shorthand, the Bernie Factor.

Your eyes will sparkle, too, when you go through life as Bernie does, lifting up everyone whose life you touch. Surely this must be what is meant by living life "beneficially."

Elisabeth Kübler-Ross used to say, "All true benefits are mutual," and that was a great teaching, for when we benefit others, we benefit ourselves. I know a man who understands this perfectly.

Gary Zukav lives an hour from me. We've spent some time together—Gary and his spiritual partner, Linda Francis, and Nancy and me—at my home in Southern Oregon. He told me over dinner once about how, ten years before, he'd written *The Seat of the Soul.* Of course, I was familiar with the book, and had read it shortly after it came out. He also wrote *The Dancing Wu Li Masters.* Both were big sellers, and Gary was suddenly a celebrity. Except that he was not. In his heart, he felt that he wanted to be treated just like everyone else. But authoring bestsellers does not always allow that, so Gary had to make a conscious effort to move himself out of the spotlight. He "disappeared" for a few years, declining lecture invitations and interview requests, retreating instead to a quiet place to mull over what he had done. Had his books made a real contribution? Were they worthy of all the attention? Had he added something of value? What was his place in all of this?

As Gary was sharing his process, I realized that I had not taken the time to ask myself those same questions. I'd just plunged ahead. I knew I'd have to learn from those who have granted themselves a longer look at deeper issues, and I set my intention to do so—though I didn't know how or when I would be given the opportunity.

Jump ahead ten months. I am hopping on a plane to Chicago. As I turn the corner into the cabin, there is Gary Zukav. We "just happened" to catch the same flight, and be seated in the same section, though we were going to the city for entirely different reasons—and we discovered while chatting across the aisle that we were *booked into the same hotel.* Okay, I said to myself, what's going on here? Is this another one of those "coincidences"?

When we got to the hotel, we thought it might be nice to have dinner together. I was in the process of producing the book you are now reading, and it was not going well. Everything had come to a complete halt. As we scanned our menus, I was sharing this with Gary. I told him that I was worried, because I was including stories from my life in the book, and I didn't know if my readers would be interested.

"What they are interested in is *truth,*" Gary said simply. "If you tell anecdotes just to tell anecdotes, they have limited value. But if you describe experiences in your life in order to share *what you learned from them,* they become invaluable."

Of course, he added quietly, you have to be willing to show yourself completely in order to do that. You can't hide behind a *persona.* You have to be willing to be authentic, transparent, and to say things the way they are. If you're not responding to a life situation from a place of mastery, say so. If you're falling short of your own teachings, admit it. People can learn from that.

"So," Gary said, "tell your anecdotes, but always include where you are, and what you have learned. Then we can stay with your story, because it becomes *our* story. Don't you see? We're all walking the same path." He smiled warmly.

Gary Zukav had returned to the public eye by then, of course, accepting invitations to appear on *Oprah,* and even going out now for book signings and lectures. And his book about the soul is a bestseller all over again. I asked him how he was dealing with his fame. He understood, of course, that I was really asking for some advice on how I might deal with mine. And so he thought for a moment. His eyes glazed over just briefly, and I watched him go somewhere else. He spoke, quietly again.

"First, I have to find my center, my inner truth, my authenticity. I search for this every day. I seek it actively. I went looking for it before I answered your question. Then, I try to move from there in everything I do, whether it's my writing, or a media interview, or a book-signing somewhere. If I'm on *Oprah,* for instance, I try to forget that I'm talking to 70 million people. I've got to keep talking to the people right in front of me, to the audience right there in the studio. And if I never abandon my center, I stay in tune with myself, and that allows me to stay in tune with others, and with everything around me."

Surely this must be what is meant by living life "harmoniously."

My authentic truth is that life *has* been exciting since the *Conversations with God* trilogy was published—and one of the exciting parts of it has been learning that most people of fame and importance are *not* inaccessible and unapproachable and self-inflated, as I sometimes imagined them to be. In fact, it's just the opposite. The people of high profile whom I've met have been wonderfully "real," genuine, sensitive, and caring—and I'm coming to see that these are qualities which are common to people who stand out.

One day the phone rang at my home, and it was Ed Asner. He, along with Ellen Burstyn, read the words of God on the audio tapes of *CWG*. We got to talking about the eight-column, top-of-the-page excoriation of me that morning in *The Wall Street Journal.* "Hey," Ed growled, "don't let 'em get to you, kid." I could sense his energy shift as he sought to give me some words of encouragement at what he knew must have been a low point for me. I said that I was thinking of writing a letter to the *Journal* in response to its hit piece.

"Naw," he said, "don't do that. That's not who you are. I know a little bit about the press tearing you apart," he said, chuckling; then he became serious. "They don't know who you are, but you do. Stay close to that, because that's what's most important. They'll come around. They all come around. As long as you *stay who you are.* Don't let anyone or anything pull you out of your truth." Ed Asner, like Gary, is a gentle, loving person, who understands all about authenticity. And lives it.

So does Shirley MacLaine.

I met Shirley through Chantal Westerman, then the entertainment correspondent for *Good Morning, America.* We were going to be filming an interview for *GMA,* and on the day of the shoot Chantal and Nancy and I were lunching in Santa Monica. "I know someone who you should know, and who should know you, and I'm sure she'd be interested in meeting you," Chantal offered over salad. "Can I call her?"

"Who are we talking about?" I asked.

"Shirley MacLaine," Chantal replied casually.

Shirley MacLaine? I shouted inside my head. *I get to meet Shirley MacLaine?* Outwardly, I tried to remain cool. "Well, if you'd like to arrange it," I said in my best off-handed manner, "go ahead."

Do you suppose that if we show people that we're really excited about something, we imagine that we're somehow going to be more vulnerable? I don't know. I don't know what that is. I just know that I'm giving it up. I'm throwing away all the protective wrappers I've had around me so that people would never know what I'm thinking, how I'm feeling, or what's going on with me. What's the point of living if I'm spending half my life hiding out? I've tried to learn from people like Gary and Ed and Shirley.

We had dinner with Shirley that night in the private dining room at the Beverly Hills Hotel. Shirley MacLaine is a very real person—one of the "real-est" I've ever met—and she gets right down to compelling you to be real with her, too. By that I mean, she doesn't have time for a lot of meaningless pleasantries. She's not much into small talk.

"So," she said as I slid into the booth next to her, "did you really talk to God?"

"I think so," I replied modestly.

"You think so?" She was incredulous. "You *think so?*"

"Well," I stammered, "that was my experience."

"Then don't you think you should say that? Isn't that what *happened?*"

"That is what happened. It's just that some people have a hard time accepting that if I just pop right out with it."

"Oh, you care what people think?" Shirley probed, her face now very close, her eyes searching mine. "Why?"

Shirley is always asking questions. What do you think about this? What do you know about that? What makes you think that you know what you think you know? How is it for you when so-and-so happens? I've enjoyed several visits with Shirley since, and I'm pretty clear why she is such an incredible actress. She seems to make every person she meets a case study, taking a very real interest in them, and she *gives* to each person a very real part of herself. She holds nothing back. Her joy, her laughter, her tears, her truth—it's all there, given as a gift from a genuine person being genuinely herself. She does not tailor her behavior, her personality, her comments, or conversation to anybody for any reason.

And here's what Shirley has shared with me, not from anything in particular that she has said during our times together, but just from her beingness: never take someone else's answer for your own, never give up who you are, and never stop exploring who you could be if you moved to the next level.

That takes courage.

Which brings me to two of the most courageous people I know: Ellen DeGeneres and Anne Heche.

It was in December of 1998 that Nancy and I received an invitation to spend a few days with these two remarkable women. They asked if we could arrive in time for a day-long gathering they were planning with a few friends for January first. "We're starting a new life in this new year, and we couldn't think of anyone we'd rather spend New Year's Day with than you," their message said. "The books have inspired us so much."

Nancy and I flew in from Estes Park, Colorado, where we'd just finished, that morning, our annual Year-End Re-creating Yourself Retreat.

I don't think there's any place on Earth where I have felt more comfortable, more rapidly, than I did in Ellen and Anne's home. It's difficult *not* to feel instantly comfortable, because in their space all pretense is gone, all things disingenuous disappear, and what's left is unconditional acceptance of who you are, as you are, no excuses required, no explanations needed, no guilt or shame or fear or feeling of being "not enough." The experience is not the result of anything in particular that Ellen and Anne are doing, but what they are *being.*

First, they are being loving. Openly, honestly, continuously. This shows up as warmth and an easy affection, shared with each other, and with everyone else in the room. Then, they are being transparent—which is, of course, another way of being loving. There isn't a hidden agenda, there isn't an unspoken truth, there isn't a single deception in the space. They are what they are, and you are what you are, and it is all okay, and the *fact* that it is all okay makes every moment delicious.

Anne and Ellen's home, and Anne and Ellen's heart, say, simply, "Welcome, you're safe here."

That is such a special gift to give to another. I only hope that I can always provide such safety in my own space, with everyone I touch. I have had it modeled for me now by many Masters.

I just wish I could have met these wonderful people a few years earlier.

Everything is perfect. You met them at just the right time.

Yes, but a few years earlier and I could have learned what their lives have taught me before I did so much damage to others.

You have done no damage to others, any more than others have done damage to you. Have you not had people who you've imagined to be villains in your life?

Well, maybe one or two.

And have you been irrevocably damaged by them?

No, I guess not.

You *guess* not?

You're sounding like Shirley.

Beats sounding like George Burns.

Cute.

The point is, you have *not* been damaged by others in your life who did what you wish they had not done, or who didn't do what you wish they had.

I tell you this—again: I have sent you nothing but angels. These people all brought you gifts, wonderful gifts, designed to help you remember Who You Really Are. And *you* have done the same for others. And when you all get through with this grand adventure, you will see that clearly, and you will thank each other.

I tell you, the day will come when you will review your life and be thankful for every *minute* of it. Every hurt, every sorrow, every joy, every celebration, every moment of your life will be a treasure to you, for you will see the utter perfection of the design. You will stand back from the weaving and see the tapestry, and you will weep at the beauty of it.

So love each other. *Every* other. *All* others. Even those you have called your persecutors. Even those you have cursed as enemies.

Love each other, and love yourself. For God's sake, love *yourself.* I mean that literally. Love your Self, *for God's sake.*

That has sometimes been very hard to do. Especially when I think about how I have been in the past. I wasn't a very nice person during most of my life. I spent thirty years, my twenties, thirties, and forties, being an utter—

—Don't say it. Don't indict yourself that way. You were not the worst person who ever walked the face of the Earth. You were not the devil incarnate. You were, and are, a *human being,* making mistakes, trying to find your way back home. You were confused. You did what you did because you were confused. You were lost. You were lost, and *now you are found.*

Do not lose yourself again, this time in the labyrinth of your own self-pity, in the maze of your own guilt. Rather, call yourself forth, in the next grandest version of the greatest vision ever you held about Who You Are.

Tell your story, yes, but do not *be* your story. Your story is like everyone's life story. It is just who you *thought* you were. It is not Who You Really Are. If you use it to remember Who You Really Are, you will have used it wisely. You will have used it exactly as it was intended to be used.

So tell your story, and let us see what else you have remembered as a result of it, and what there is for all people to remember.

Well, maybe I wasn't an utter—*whatever* . . . but I certainly wasn't very good at making people feel safe. Even in the early eighties, when I thought I'd learned a little about personal growth, I wasn't applying what I was learning.

I'd married again, left Terry Cole-Whittaker Ministries, and moved away from the hubbub of San Diego, to the tiny town of Klickitat, Washington. But life didn't work out very well there either, largely because I was simply not very safe to be around. I was selfish, and manipulated every moment and person that I could, in order to get what I wanted.

Not much changed when I moved to Portland, Oregon, hoping to get a fresh start. Instead of improving, my life went from complicated to more complicated, the crushing blow being a huge fire in the apartment house where I was living with my wife, destroying just about everything we owned. But I hadn't hit rock bottom yet. I blew my marriage apart, then formed other relationships, and blew them apart. I was struggling like a drowning man trying to stay afloat, nearly taking everyone around down with me.

By this time I knew that things couldn't get worse. Except they did. An eighty-year-old man in a Studebaker hit the car I was driving head-on, leaving me with a broken neck. I wound up in a Philadelphia Collar for over a year, undergoing intensive physical therapy daily for months, every other day for more months, finally dropping off to two visits a week, and then, at last, it was over—but so was everything else in my life. I'd lost my earning power, lost my latest relationship, and I walked outside one day to find that my car had been stolen.

It was a classic case of "when it rains, it pours," and I will remember that moment for the rest of my life. Still reeling from everything else that was going wrong, I walked up and down the street in the vain hope that I'd simply forgotten where I'd parked. Then, with utter resignation and deep bitterness, I dropped to the sidewalk on my knees and wailed away my anger. A passing woman gave me a wide-eyed look and scurried to the other side of the street.

Two days later I took the last few dollars I had and bought a bus ticket to Southern Oregon, where three of my children were living with their mother. I asked if she could give me some help, maybe let me stay in an empty room she had in the house for a few weeks until I could get on my feet. Understandably, she turned me down—and turned me out. I told her that I had no place else to go, and she said, "You can have the tent and the camping gear."

That's how I wound up on the center lawn at Jackson Hot Springs, just outside Ashland, Oregon, where the space rental was $25 a week that I didn't have. I begged the campground manager for a few days to get some money together, and he rolled his eyes. The park was already filled with transients, and the last thing he needed was one more, but he listened to my story. He heard about the fire, the accident, the broken neck, the stolen car, and the incredible unending run of bad luck, and I guess his heart went out to me. "Okay," he said, "a few days. See what you can work out. Put your tent down over there."

I was forty-five years old, and I felt my life had come to an end. I had gone from being a well-paid professional in the broadcasting industry, managing editor of a newspaper, public information officer for one of the nation's largest school systems, and a personal assistant to Dr. Elisabeth Kübler-Ross, to picking up beer cans and soda bottles on the streets and in the park to claim the five-cent deposit. (Twenty cans make a dollar, one hundred make a fiver, and five fivers a week keeps me in the campground.)

I learned a few things about life on the streets during the better part of a year that I spent at the hot springs. I wasn't exactly on the street, but I was the next closest thing to it. And I found out that there's a code out there in the open air, on the streets and under the bridges and in the parks, that, if the rest of the planet followed it, would change the world: Help Each Other.

If you're out there for more than a few weeks, you get to know the others who are out there with you, and they get to know you. Nothing personal, mind you, nobody asks about how you came to be there. But if they see you in trouble, they won't pass you by, as so many under-roof people will. They'll stop, ask, "You okay?" and if you need something they can help you with, you've got it.

I've had guys on the street give me their last pair of dry socks, or half the day's can pickings, when it looked like I wasn't going to make my "quota." And if somebody made a big score (a fiver or a ten spot from a passerby), he'd come back to the campsite with food for everybody.

I remember trying to set up that first night. It was already dusk when I got to the grounds. I knew I had to work fast, and I didn't exactly have tons of tent-pitching experience. The wind was whipping up, and it looked like rain.

"Tie 'er down to that tree," came a gruff voice out of nowhere. "Then send a line back over to the telephone pole. Put a marker on the line, so you don't kill yerself in the middle of the night goin' to the john."

The rain began falling lightly. Suddenly, we were putting the tent up together. My unnamed friend said nothing that wasn't necessary, limiting his comments to "need a stake over here," and "better get the fly up, or you'll be sleeping in a lake."

When we were finished (he did most of the work, actually), he tossed my hammer to the ground. "That oughtta hold ya," he muttered and walked away.

"Hey, thanks," I called after him. "What's your name?"

"Don't matter," he said and didn't look back.

I never saw him again.

My life became very simple in the park. My biggest challenge (and my biggest desire) was staying warm and dry. I wasn't yearning for a big promotion, worrying about "getting the girl," fretting over the phone bill, or asking myself what I was going to do with the rest of my life. It was raining a lot, and the chill winds of March were blowing, and I was simply trying to keep warm and dry.

Once in a while I wondered how I was going to get out of there, but mostly I wondered how I was going to get to stay there. Twenty-five dollars a week was a lot of money to come up with out of thin air. I intended to look for work, of course. But this was right here, right now. This was about tonight and tomorrow and the day after that. I was mending a broken neck, had no car, no money, very little food, and no place to live. Then again, it was spring, moving into summer. That was on the plus side.

Every day I rummaged through the trash cans in hopes of finding a newspaper, half an apple that somebody didn't finish, a lunch bag with a sandwich that Junior wouldn't eat. The newspaper was for extra padding under the tent. It kept the warmth in, the seepage out, and was softer and more level than the lumpy ground. Most important, though, it was a source of information about jobs. Every time I got my hands on a paper, I scoured the classifieds, looking for work. With my neck injury, I couldn't do anything very physical, and most of the jobs immediately available for men were physical. Day laborer. Helper on this crew, or that. But two months into the search, I hit pay dirt.

RADIO ANNOUNCER/WEEKEND FILL-IN,
must have previous experience.
Call etc. etc.

My heart jumped. How many guys could there be in Medford, Oregon, with experience in broadcasting who weren't already working? I raced to the telephone booth, flipped the thank-God-they-were-there yellow pages to broadcast stations, dropped in one of my precious quarters, and called the number. The program director, who I knew would be doing the hiring, was not in. Can he get back to you? a lady's voice was asking.

"Sure," I said casually, mentioning—in my best radio voice—that I was calling in reference to the help-wanted ad. "I'll be here until four o'clock." I gave her the pay phone number and hung up, then sat on the ground next to the booth for three hours, waiting for the call back that never came.

The next morning I found a paperback romance novel in the trash, snatched it up, and headed back to the phone booth. I wanted to be prepared to wait out the day, if need be. Sitting down at nine o'clock and cracking open my book, I told myself that if no call came before noon, I'd invest another quarter and call the station after lunch. The phone rang at 9:35.

"Sorry I couldn't get back to you yesterday," the PD said. "I got tied up. So, I'm told you saw the ad for a weekend jock. You got experience?"

Again, I went deep into my lower register. "Well, I've done some work on-the-air here and there," I said nonchalantly, then added, "over the last twenty years." While this exchange was taking place, I prayed that a big RV didn't rumble into the park as I was standing there talking. I didn't want to have to explain why a huge vehicle was driving through my living room.

"Why don't you come in?" the program director offered. "You got an air check?"

An air check is a tape recording, edited to exclude the music, of a disc-jockey's on-air work. I'd definitely peaked his interest.

"No, I left all my stuff in Portland," I fibbed. "But I can do a 'live read' on any copy you give me, and I think you'll get an idea of what I can do."

"All right," he agreed. "Drop in around three. I go on at four, so don't be too late."

"Got it."

I actually jumped in the air and let out a whoop as I stepped out of the phone booth. A couple of the boys were walking by. "That good, eh?" one of them drawled.

"I think I've found a job!" I crowed.

They were genuinely happy for me. "Doin' what?" one of them wanted to know.

"Weekend disc-jockey! I go in for an interview at three."

"Lookin' like that?"

I hadn't thought about my appearance. There'd been no haircut for weeks, but I could probably get away with that. Half the disc-jockeys in America had pony tails. But I would have to do something about my clothes. There was a laundry room on the grounds, but I didn't have the money to buy soap, get something washed and dried and ready to wear, plus pay the bus fare up to Medford and back.

It hadn't hit me until then just how poor I was. I couldn't make a basic maneuver, like running into town for a quick job interview, without some sort of miracle occurring. I got an experience right then and there of the obstacles people on the street face just trying to get back on their feet and lead a regular life again.

The two men looked at me as if they knew exactly what I was thinking.

"You got no money, right?" one of them half-snorted.

"A couple of bucks, maybe," I guessed, probably overestimating.

"Okay, c'mon, kid."

I followed them to a circle of tents where a number of other men were camped. "He's got a chance to work his way out of here," they explained to their friends, and mumbled something else I didn't hear. Then, turning to me, the older of the two men growled, "You got something decent to wear?"

"Yeah, in my duffel bag, but nothing clean, nothing ready."

"Bring it back over here."

By the time I returned, a woman I'd seen around the springs had joined the men. She lived in one of the small trailers that dotted the park. "You get those things washed and dried and I'll iron 'em for you, honey," she announced.

One of the men stepped forward and handed me a small brown paper bag, jingling with coins. "The fellas dipped in and pulled this together," he explained. "Go do yer laundry."

Five hours later I showed up at the radio station bright-eyed and bushy-tailed, and looking like I'd stepped out of my uptown apartment.

I got the job!

"We're talking $6.25 an hour, for two eight-hour days," the program director said. "I'm sorry I can't offer you more. You're overqualified, and I'd understand if you decided you can't take it."

A hundred dollars a week! I was going to make *a hundred dollars a week.* That's *four hundred a month*—at that time in my life, a *fortune.* "No, no, it's just what I was looking for right now," I offered off-handedly. "I've enjoyed my career in radio, and now I've gone on to something else. I just wanted to find a way to keep my hand in it. This'll be fun for me."

And I wasn't lying, because fun it was. The fun of surviving. I lived in my tent for a couple more months, and I saved up enough to buy myself a '63 Nash Rambler for $300. I felt like a millionaire. I was the only one in our group at the campsite with wheels, and the only one with a regular income, and I shared both freely with all the others, never forgetting what they had done for me.

Nervous about the dropping temperature, I moved in November into one of the tiny, one-room cabins at the park that rented for $75 a week. I felt guilty leaving my friends outside—none of them had that kind of money—so I'd invite one or two of them to share the space with me on the really cold or rainy nights. I tried to rotate the guys around, so everyone had a chance to get out of the weather.

Just when it looked like I'd be working part-time forever, I received a surprise offer from another radio station in town to come over and do their afternoon drive-time show. They'd caught my weekend gig and liked what they heard—but Medford is not exactly a big radio market, and I was offered $900 a month to start. Still, I was working full-time again, and able to leave the campground. I'd lived there over nine months. It was a time I will never forget.

I bless the day I trudged to that park, lugging my camping gear with me, for it was not the end of my life at all, but the beginning. I learned in that park about loyalty and honesty and authenticity and trust, and about simplicity and sharing and surviving. I learned about never resigning myself to defeat, yet accepting and being grateful for what is true right here, right now.

So it isn't just from movie stars and famous authors I have learned. It's from homeless people who befriended me, and from people I see every day, people I encounter as I go through life. The mailman, the grocery clerk, the lady at the dry-cleaner's.

> All have something to teach you, something to bring you as a gift. And here is a great secret. Every one of them came to receive a gift from you as well.
>
> What is the gift you have given them? And if you have,

in your confusion, done what you imagine to have hurt them, do not assume that this is not, too, a gift. It may have been a great treasure, as was your time in the park.

Have you not learned from your greatest hurts, sometimes even more than from your greatest pleasures? Who, then, is the villain, and who is the victim in your life?

You will have reached real mastery when you can come to clarity about this before, rather than after, the outcome of an experience is known to you.

Your time of destitution and desolation taught you that your life is never over. Never, ever, *ever* think that your life is over, but know always that each day, each hour, each *moment* is another beginning, another opportunity, another chance to re-create yourself anew.

Even if you do this at the last possible moment, at the moment of your death, *you will have justified your entire experience, and glorified it before God.*

Even if you are a hardened criminal, a murderer living on death row or walking to your execution, this will nonetheless be true.

You must know this. You must trust it. I would not tell it to you were it not so.

Seventeen

That is the most hopeful thing I have ever read. It means that all of us—even the "worst" of us—have a home in Your heart, if we will but claim it. And this must be what it means to have a friendship with God.

When I began this book I said I hoped to focus on two things: how to turn a conversation with God into a real, working friendship, and how to *use* that friendship to apply the wisdom of *Conversations with God* in day-to-day life.

> And now you are learning what I said to you before—that your relationship with God is no different from your relationship with each other.
>
> As in your relationships with other humans, you begin with a conversation. If the conversation goes well, you develop a friendship. If the friendship goes well, you experience true Oneness. This is what all souls desire with each other. It is what all souls seek with Me.

The idea behind this book was to show you how to develop that friendship, once you've had the conversation. You've had the conversation in three books that preceded this. Now it is time to have a friendship.

I am sorry to say that many people, however, will not take the first step in their relationship with Me. They find it impossible to believe that I would have a real conversation with them, and so they limit their experience of Me to one-way interactions—what most would call prayer. They talk *to* Me, but not *with* Me.

Some of those who talk to Me have a high level of faith that I am hearing their words. Yet even they do not expect to hear *Mine.* So they look for signs. They say, "God, give me a sign." Yet when I give them a sign in the most common way that they can think of—by using the very language which they speak—they deny Me. And I tell you this: some of you will yet deny Me. Not only will you deny that this is a sign, you will deny that receiving such a sign is even possible.

Yet I tell you this: *nothing is impossible in God's world.* I have not stopped talking directly with you, and I never will.

You may not always hear clearly, or interpret with complete accuracy, what I have to say, but as long as you try, as long as you keep the dialogue open, you give our friendship a chance. And as long as you give God a chance, you will never be alone, never face any important question by yourself, never be without an instant resource in a time of need, and, yes, always have a home in My heart. This *is* what it means to have a friendship with God.

And that friendship is open to everyone?

Everyone.

Regardless of their beliefs, regardless of their religion?

Regardless of their beliefs, regardless of their religion.

Or lack of religion?

Or lack of religion.

Anybody can have a friendship with God, at any time, is that right?

You all *do* have a friendship with God. Some of you just don't know it. As I have already said.

I know that we are repeating ourselves, but I want to make sure, I want to make absolutely certain that I get this right. You just talked about how we don't always interpret everything completely accurately, and this is one thing I want to get as accurately as I can. I want there to be no mistake about this. You are saying that there is no "right way" to God?

That is what I am saying. Exactly, precisely, unequivocally. There are a thousand paths to God, and every one gets you there.

So we can, at last, bring an end to "better" about God. We can stop saying that "ours is the better God."

Yes, you can. But will you? That is the question. It will require you to give up your ideas of *superiority,* and that is the most seductive idea human beings ever had. It has seduced the entire human race. It has justified the wholesale slaughter of members of your own species, and every other species of sentient being on your planet.

This one single thought, this one idea that you have, that you are somehow *better* than someone else, has caused all the heartache, all the suffering, all the cruelty, all the inhumanity that you have inflicted upon each other.

You've made this point before.

And like many other points I have made with you in this dialogue, I will make it over and over again. This point, in particular, I want to emphasize now, in such stark terms, in such clear and specific language, that you can never forget it. For throughout the ages humans have asked Me, what is the way to a more perfect world? How can we live together in harmony? What is the secret to lasting peace? And throughout the ages I have given you the answer. Throughout the ages I have brought you this wisdom, a thousand times in a thousand ways. Yet you have not listened.

Now I declare it over and over here, in this dialogue, in language so plain that you can never again ignore it, but will understand it completely, and internalize it so deeply, that you will hereafter and forevermore reject any suggestion that one group of you is somehow better than another group of you.

Again I say: *put an End to Better.*

For this is The New Gospel: There *is* no master race. There *is* no greatest nation. There *is* no one true religion. There *is* no inherently perfect philosophy. There *is* no always right political party, morally supreme economic system, or one and only way to Heaven.

Erase these ideas from your memory. Eliminate them from your experience. Eradicate them from your culture. For these are thoughts of division and separation, and you have *killed* each other over these thoughts. Only the truth I give you here will save you: WE ARE ALL ONE.

Carry this message far and wide, across oceans and over continents, around the corner and around the world.

I will. Wherever I go, and wherever I am, I will say it loud and clear.

And with this declaration of The New Gospel, dispel forever the second-most dangerous idea on which human beings have based their behaviors: the thought that there is something you have to do to survive.

There is nothing you have to do. Your survival is guaranteed. It is a *fact,* not a hope. It is a reality, not a promise.

You have always been, are now, and always will be.

Life is eternal, love is immortal, and death is only a horizon.

I heard that line in the lyrics of a wonderful song recorded by Carly Simon.

Have I not told you that I will communicate with you in many ways—an article in a three-month-old magazine at the hair-styling salon, a chance utterance by a friend, the lyrics to the next song you hear?

It is through these kinds of continuing "conversations with God" that I send you My eternal message: your survival is guaranteed.

The question is not whether you will survive, but what shall be your experience while you are surviving?

You are answering that question now, in what you call this lifetime, and what you call the next. For what you experience in the next lifetime can only be a reflection of what you have created in this lifetime, because, in truth, there is *only One Everlasting Life,* with *each moment creating the next.*

And so we create our *own* heaven, and *our own hell!*

Yes—now, and even forevermore. Yet once you are clear that your survival is not in question, you can stop worrying about which one of you is better. You don't have to punish yourself forever, scramble to get to the top, or destroy others to ensure that you are one of the fittest. And so, at last, you can "get the hell out of there." *Literally.*

Come, then. Join with Me now in a deep and abiding friendship. I have given you the steps here. And I have shared with you the Attitudes of God, which will change your life.

Come then. Get the "hell" out. Bring the blessing and the joy and the heaven in. For thine *is* the Kingdom and the power and the glory, forever.

I would not tell this to you if it were not so.

I accept! I accept Your invitation to enter into true *friendship with God!* I will follow the Seven Steps. I will adopt the Five Attitudes. And I will never again believe that You have stopped talking to me, or that I can't speak directly to You.

Good.

And, since we are now close friends, I have a favor to ask of You.

Anything. Ask, and you shall receive.

Will You explain here how to implement some of the grandest truths in *Conversations with God?* I want everyone to understand how to render that wisdom functional in daily life.

What part of the wisdom do you wish to discuss? Let's focus in on some particular portion of the message, and I will tell you how to use it functionally in your moment-to-moment interactions.

Good! Now we are getting down to it! Okay, at the end of the *Conversations with God* trilogy, You said that the entire 800-plus-page dialogue could be summarized in Three Points: (1) We are all One, (2) There's enough, and (3) There's nothing we have to do. You've kind of circled back to Points One and Three here, just now, when You talked about the end of better—

Yes.

But could You tell me how this would work in everyday life? Also, what about Point Two? How do I apply that in everyday living? How do I apply *all* of these points?

Thank you for asking. We are now, indeed, "getting down to it."

The first message is very easy to apply. Simply move through your life as if everyone, and indeed, everything, is an extension of you. Treat all other people as if they were part of you. Treat all other things the same way.

Wait, wait. There. Right there. That is a good example of what I mean. How do I apply a statement like that to my everyday life? Does that mean that I cannot swat a mosquito?

There are no cans or cannots here. There are no shoulds or shouldn'ts. You may do as you wish. Every decision is a statement of Who You Are.

Well, "who I am" is a person who does not want a mosquito bite!

Fine. Then do what it takes to experience yourself as that. It is simple, you see?

But if I am one with everything, am I not killing a part of myself when I swat the mosquito?

> Nothing dies, but only changes form. Yet let us use your definitions for the moment, for the purposes of this discussion. Yes, by your definition, you are killing a part of yourself when you swat the mosquito. You are doing the same thing when you cut down a tree. Or pick a flower. Or slaughter a cow and eat it.

Then I can't touch *anything!* I have to leave everything exactly the way it is! If termites are destroying my house, I have to just move out and give them the house, because, after all, I don't want to *murder them.* How far do you take this?

> That is a good question. How far *do you* take this? Does the fact that you don't kill people mean that you don't kill termites? Conversely, does the fact that you kill termites mean that it is okay to kill people?

No, of course not.

> Well, then, there you have it. You have answered your own question.

Yes, because I have used *a different value system.* It's not the one you are suggesting here. I'm not saying that "we are all One." I'm saying that people and termites are *not* One, nor are people and trees. And so, having made that distinction, I am treating them differently! Under *Your* value system, I could not do that.

Of course you could. Remember, I have said you are all One, but I have not said you are all *the same.* Is your hair the same as your heart?

I beg your pardon?

Because you cut your hair off, does that mean you will cut your heart out?

I see what You're saying.

Do you? Do you, really? Because many human beings act as if they don't. They treat everyone and everything as if it were the same. They treat human life as if it were worth nothing more than the life of a mosquito. A termite. If they see that it is okay to cut their hair off, they cut their heart out. They bite their nose to spite their face.

Not many people act like that.

I tell you this: *every one of you has acted like that,* in one way or another. Every one of you has acted indiscriminately, treating one thing as if it were the same as another—even treating one *person* as if he or she were another.

You walk down the street and see a white person and think that she is the same as you imagine all white people to be. You walk down the street and see a black person and think he is the same as you imagine all black people to be. In this you make two mistakes.

You have stereotyped Whites and Blacks, Jews and Gentiles, men and women, Russians and Americans, Serbs and Albanians, bosses and workers, even blondes and brunettes . . . and you will not *stop* stereotyping, because to stop stereotyping means that you will have to stop *justifying* your treatment of each other.

Okay, so where are we with all this? How *do* I treat everyone and everything as if it were a part of Me? What if I decide that someone, or some group, is a cancer on my body? Do I not cut it out? Is that not what we call ethnic cleansing, the wiping out, or the displacement, of a whole people?

Indeed, you have made such decisions.

Yes, about the Albanians in Kosovo. About the Jews in Germany.

I was thinking more about the native peoples of America.

Oh.

Oh, indeed. Wiping out a people is wiping out a people, whether at Auschwitz or at Wounded Knee.

As You have observed before.

As I have observed before.

Yet if we are all part of the same body, what if I decide that something or someone *is* a "cancer?" How do I deal with that? That's what I am asking here.

You might attempt to heal the cancer.

How do I do that?

You could try love.

But some things and some people don't respond to love. Sometimes healing a cancer means killing it, getting it out of the body. It is the *body* we are trying to heal, not the cancer.

What if the body doesn't need healing?

What?

Always you are justifying cruelty to others, even the killing of others, as a means of surviving, yourself. Yet this takes us back to another question, another issue. I spoke before about the second-most dangerous idea human beings hold. Now, let's close the circle here. What do you imagine will happen to you if you do not get rid of this cancer you are talking about?

I will die.

And so to avoid dying, you cut the cancer out. It is a matter of survival.

Exactly.

And that is the same reason that people kill other people, wipe out whole *groups* of other people, displace entire populations and ethnic minorities. They think that they must do so, that it is a matter of their very survival.

Yes.

Yet I tell you this: *there is nothing that you have to do to survive.* Your survival is guaranteed. You always have been, are now, and always will be, world without end.

Your survival is a fact, not a hope. A reality, not a promise. Therefore, everything you have been doing in order to "survive" has been unnecessary. You have been creating a living hell for yourself in order to avoid the hell that you imagine that you will avoid by creating the hell that you are creating.

You are talking about one form of surviving—eternal life—and I am talking about another form: Who We Are right now, right here. What if we like who we are right here, right now, and we don't want to see anything or anybody change that?

You do not know Who You Really Are, right here, right now. If you did, you would never do the things you do. You would never have to.

But you aren't addressing the issue. What if we happen to like who we are right here, right now, and *don't want to see anything or anybody change that?*

Then you would not be Who You Really Are. You would only be who you *think* you are, here and now. And you would be attempting the impossible, which is to *always remain* who you think you are. This you cannot do.

I don't get it. You've lost me.

Who You Are is life. You are life itself! And what is life? It is a process. And what is that process? It is *evolution* . . . or what you would call *change.*

Everything in life changes! Everything!

Life *is* change. That is what Life *is.* When you put an end to change, you put an end to life. Yet that you cannot do. And so you create a living hell, trying to do something you cannot do, efforting and straining to remain unchanged, when Who You Are is change itself. You are that which changes.

But some things change for the better, and some things change for the worse! All I am doing is trying to stop the changes for the worse.

There is no such thing as "better" or "worse." You just made that all up. You *decide* what to call better and what to call worse.

Okay, but what if I call it better to stay alive in my present physical form than to die? I call that a change for the worse! Surely You are not saying that if I do have cancer in my body I should do nothing, because life is eternal, and if my life in this body ends because of my inaction, so what? Surely You're not saying that—are You?

I am saying that every act is an act of Self-definition. That is all you are doing here. You are defining and creating, expressing and experiencing, who you think you are. In short, you are *evolving.* How you evolve is *your* choice. *That* you evolve is not.

If you are a being who chooses to cut out a cancer within you in order to preserve your larger life form, then you will demonstrate that.

If you are a being who sees others of your species as a cancer because they are different from you, or disagree with you, you will demonstrate that. Indeed, many of you already have demonstrated that.

I am going to now invite you to see life in an entirely new way. I am going to invite you to view life as nothing more than a continuing process of change.

Think of it this way: everything is changing, all of the time. That includes you. You are both the changer and the changed. That is because, even as you are changing, you are causing the change in your Self and in the world around you.

When you arise in the morning, I invite you to think of one thing. What is going to change today? Not, *will* there be a change today? That is a given! But what is that change going to be? And what part will you play in creating that change, in being the conscious cause of it?

Every second of every minute of every hour of every day you are making decisions. These choices are about what will change, and how. They are about nothing else.

Even a choice as simple as combing your hair. Let's use that, because it's an easy one. You imagine that you are combing your hair the same way every day, and so you are changing nothing at all. Yet the very act of *combing* it is an act of change. You go to the mirror and look at your hair just after you wake up, and you say, "Ugh." It's a mess. You can't go out like that. You've got to change it. You've got to change the way you look. So you wash your face, comb your hair, get ready for the day.

All the while, you are making decisions. Now some of these are decisions to change things *back,* the way they *were.* And so you create the illusion of *keeping things the way they are.* Yet you are simply *re-creating yourself anew,* in the grandest version of the greatest vision ever you held about Who You Are!

All of life is a process of re-creation! This is God's greatest joy. This is God's *recreation!*

Now the implications this has on your life are phenomenal. When you think about it, this is an extraordinary revelation. *You are doing nothing but changing.* You are doing nothing but evolving. How you are changing is up to you. What you are evolving *into* is up to you. Yet the fact that you *are* is not something that is open to question. It is a *given.* That is just what is going on. That is what Life *is.* It is what God is. It is what you are.

Life, God, You = That Which Changes.

But You still haven't resolved the dilemma. If I am One with everything, what about swatting the mosquito?

What kind of change do you choose to create in that part of your Self that you call the mosquito? That is the question you are asking, and that is the implication of the We Are All One wisdom.

You are "changing" the part of The All that you call the mosquito. You cannot "kill" the mosquito, do you see? Life is eternal, you cannot end it. You do have the power to change your form. As in your popular science fiction entertainments, you might call yourself a shape shifter. Yet know this: all of consciousness acts together. In the highest sense, it is impossible for one of you to have dominion or control over another. Every aspect of divinity has co-creative control over its destiny. Therefore, you cannot kill a mosquito against its will. At some level, the mosquito has chosen that. All of the change in the universe occurs with the consent of the universe itself, in its various forms. The universe cannot disagree with itself. That is impossible.

This is dangerous talk. This is a dangerous teaching. People could use this to say, "Well, then I can do anything to anyone I want, since they've given me their permission! After all, they're 'co-creating' it with me!" It would be behavioral anarchy.

You already *have* that. Life *is* what you call "behavioral anarchy," do you not see? You are all doing what you want, when you want, how you want, and *I am not stopping you.* Are you not seeing that? The human race has done what it has called hideous things, and it has done them over and over again, and God is not stopping it from doing so. Have you not ever wondered why?

Of course I have. We all have. We have cried out in our hearts, "God, why are you allowing this?" Of course we have asked.

Well, do you not want the answer?

Of course I want the answer.

Good, because I have just given it to you.

If that's true, I'm going to have to think about this. If that's true, it feels as though there is now nothing in place to stop us from doing incredible damage to each other, all under the guise of simply believing that everything in the Universe agrees with what we are doing. I am just deeply troubled by that. I don't know how to deal with it. The doctrine of right and wrong, of crime and punishment, good and evil, everlasting reward and everlasting damnation—all those things which control us, all those things which give hope to the oppressed, all of them are wiped out by this message. If we don't have a new message to replace it, I'm afraid for the human race, and the new depths of depravity to which it could go.

But you *do* have a new message. It is, at last, The Truth. And this message is the *only* message that can save the world. The old message has not done that. Do you not see this? Is this not clear to you? The old message, which you say has given humanity hope, has brought you *none of the results you've hoped for.*

That old message of right and wrong, crime and punishment, good and evil, everlasting rewarding and everlasting damnation, has done nothing to end the suffering on your planet, to end the killing on your planet, to end the torture that you are inflicting upon yourselves. And that is because it is a message of separation.

There is only one message that can change the course of human history forever, end the torture, and bring you back to God. That message is The New Gospel: WE ARE ALL ONE.

From this New Gospel emerges a new message of total responsibility, telling you that you are *totally responsible* for what you are choosing, that you are choosing it all together, and that the only way to change your choices is to change them all together.

You will not end the torture of yourselves so long as you imagine yourselves to be merely torturing another. You will only end the torture when you are clear that you are, in fact, torturing yourself.

This you can only see when you understand, completely, that it is impossible to do anything against the will of another. Only in that moment of clarity can you glimpse what you would have thought to be an impossible truth. *You are doing all of this to yourselves.*

And *this* truth you cannot see unless you understand, embrace, and live The New Gospel.

WE ARE ALL ONE.

Therefore, of *course* you cannot do anything to another

that has not at some level been co-created with you. *That would be possible only if we are not All One.* Yet, WE ARE ALL ONE. There is only one of Us. We are creating this reality together.

Do you understand the implications of this? Do you see its awesome impact?

Go now, therefore, and teach ye all nations. Teach that what you do for another, you do for your Self, and what you fail to do for another, you fail to do for your Self. Do unto others as you would have it done unto you, because it *is* being done unto you!

That is the Golden Rule. And now you understand it, completely.

Eighteen

Why are these wonderful truths not taught to us in this way from the beginning? As beautiful as the Golden Rule was before, now it makes even more sense. It is perfectly symmetrical. The circle of logic is complete. We see the *reason* for it. We see why it is in *our own best interest* to apply this wisdom. It is no longer an act of altruism, but of practicality. It is simply *what works*—for *Us.* Why is the Golden Rule not taught this way from the very beginning, to little children?

The question is not, Why hasn't this been done in the past? The question is, What do you intend to do in the future? Go, therefore, and teach ye all nations, spreading far and wide *The New Gospel:*

WE ARE ALL ONE.

OURS IS NOT A BETTER WAY, OURS IS MERELY ANOTHER WAY.

Speak it not only from your pulpits, but from the halls of

your governments as well; not only in your churches, but in your schools; not only through your collective conscience, but through your collective economies.

Make your spirituality *real,* right here, right now, *on the ground.*

It sounds like You're talking about politicizing our spirituality. Yet there are those who say that spirituality and politics should not mix.

You cannot *avoid* politicizing your spirituality. Your political viewpoint is your spirituality, *demonstrated.*

Yet perhaps it is not a matter of politicizing your spirituality, but of spiritualizing your politics.

But I thought that there was to be a separation of Church and State. Don't we get into trouble when we try to marry religion and politics?

Indeed, you do, and I am not talking about that.

You may decide that Church and State are best left separate. Based on your results, you may decide that religion and politics do not mix. *Spirituality,* on the other hand, may be another matter.

The reason you may decide that Church and State should be separate is that Church means a particular point of view, a particular religious belief. You may have observed that when such beliefs inform your politics, you create great controversy and political strife. This is because all people do not hold the same religious beliefs. And, in fact, not all people even participate in religion or church, in any form.

Spirituality, on the other hand, is universal. All people participate in it. All people agree with it.

They do? You could have fooled me.

They do, even if they do not know it, even if they do not call it that. This is because "spirituality" is nothing more than life itself, as it is.

Spirituality says that *all things are part of life,* and that is a statement with which no one can disagree. You can argue all you want about whether there is a God, and whether all things are part of God, but you cannot argue about whether there is Life, or whether all things are part of Life.

The only discussion left then is whether life and God are the same things. And I tell you, they are.

Even an agnostic—even an atheist—would agree that there is some force in the Universe that is holding it all together. There is also something that *started* it all. And if there is something that started it all, there has to have been something existing before the universe as you now know it existed.

The universe didn't just burst into being out of thin air. And even if it did, "thin air" is *something.* And even if you say that the universe burst into being out of nothing at all, still you must deal with the question of first cause. What *caused* something to arise out of nothing at all?

This first cause is life itself, expressing in physical form.

It is life, *in formation.* No one can disagree with this, because this is obviously "what's so." You can, however, argue forever (and you have!) over how to describe this process, what to call it, what to infer from it, what to conclude.

Yet I have told you, this is God. This is what you mean, what you have always meant, by the word God. God is first cause. Unmoved Mover. That Which Was before That Which Is, was. That Which Will Be after That Which Now *Is,* is no longer. The Alpha and the Omega. The Beginning and the End.

Again I tell you, the words life and God are interchangeable. If the process you are observing is the process of life in formation, then it is as I have said to you before: you are all Gods in formation. That is, you are *God's Information.*

Okay, I suppose . . . but what does this have to do with anything—least of all, politics?

If spirituality is really another word for life, then that which is spiritual is life affirming. To inject spirituality into your politics, therefore, would be to make all political activities and all political decisions life affirming.

Indeed, this is what you are trying to do with your politics. That is why I have said that your political viewpoint is your spirituality, *demonstrated.* The only reason you have created politics is to produce a system by which life may be lived harmoniously, happily, peacefully. That is, a system by which life itself may be affirmed.

I have never thought of it quite that way.

Those who founded your country have. The United States has a Declaration of Independence which says that all of you are created equal, with certain unalienable rights, among them, Life, Liberty, and the Pursuit of Happiness. Your government was *based* on the notion that human beings could construct a system of self-governance that guaranteed these rights. All governments everywhere were created for basically the same reason. You may differ on the *form,* but never the *purpose,* of government. Different cultures and societies may spell out differently their ideas, and how to achieve them, but their desires are basically the same.

You see, then, that governments and politics were *created* in order to guarantee the experience of what spirituality *is*—which is life itself.

Still, most people don't want to hear God talking about politics, or political issues. Whenever I write in our foundation newsletter about political issues as they are affected by the message in *Conversations with God,* I begin receiving negative letters. "Cancel my subscription!" they say. "This is not God's work! These are political views, and I did not subscribe to this newsletter to hear political views!"

When Marianne Williamson, James Redfield, and I sponsored a Peace Prayer Vigil in Washington, D.C., a few years ago, everyone thought it was marvelous. We were calling upon all people everywhere to use the power of prayer to bring peace to the world, and we received wide support. Yet as soon as any of us starts talking about *how* to produce peace—the spiritual principles which underlie it—the mail starts pouring in. People are infuriated.

Yes. People want you to *pray* for peace, but not to do anything about it. They want *God* to find a solution—but they eliminate the possibility that God's solution might just be *You Doing Something About It.*

In fact, that is the only solution there will ever be, because God works in the world through the people who are in it.

Oh, I don't think people mind other people doing something about it. What they do mind is God telling them *what* must be done.

Yet I have never told you what you must do about it, and I never will. I have never given orders, barked commands, or issued ultimatums. I have merely listened to you tell Me where you want to go, and offered you suggestions on how to get there.

You say you want a world that can live in peace and harmony and joy, and I tell you this: joy is freedom. Those words, too, are interchangeable. Any curtailing of freedom is a curtailing of joy. Any curtailing of joy is a curtailing of harmony. Any curtailing of harmony is a curtailing of peace.

You tell Me that you wish to live in a world without conflict, without violence, without bloodshed, without hatred. And I tell you this: a way to have such a world, a way to create it virtually overnight, is to preach and live *The New Gospel.*

WE ARE ALL ONE.

OURS IS NOT A BETTER WAY, OURS IS MERELY ANOTHER WAY.

Speak it not only from your pulpits, but from the halls of your governments as well; not only in your churches, but in your schools; not only through your collective conscience, but through your collective economies.

You keep repeating Yourself.

You keep repeating *your*self. Your whole history has been a repeating of your own failures—in your personal life, and in the collective experience of your planet. The definition of insanity is repeating, over and over again, the same behaviors, and expecting different results.

All that those who are seeking to overlay spirituality on politics are trying to do is to say: "There is another way."

These efforts should be blessed, not criticized.

Well, it doesn't work that way. You addressed social issues in book 2 of *Conversations with God,* and it was lambasted by many for being too political. Marianne Williamson wrote an absolutely wonderful book called *Healing the Soul of America,* and has preached about "social spirituality" from her pulpit at the Church of Today near Detroit, and she was lambasted by some people within her own congregation for being too political.

They said the same thing about Jesus.

"Too political," they said.

"When he was just teaching spirituality, he was safe. But now he's suggesting that people actually *apply* the spiritual truths they've learned. Now he's becoming dangerous. We've got to stop him."

Yet if there is no "better" way, what is the point of spiritual activism? What is the point of politics? Or of *anything?* Why should I get involved, if it's all just a toss-up? If it doesn't matter one way or the other, how am I to be inspired to participate?

Out of your desire to make a statement of Who You Are. It may be a "toss-up" whether you comb your hair this way or that, yet notice that you've been combing it the same way for years. Why do you not comb it another way? Could it be because that is not Who You Are? Why do you buy the car that you buy, wear the clothes that you wear?

Everything you do makes a statement, produces an expression, of Who You Are. Every act is an act of self-definition.

Does this matter? Is defining the Self a thing that matters to you? Of course it is. It is the very reason you *came* here!

Who You Are is not a "toss-up." Who You Are is the most important decision you will ever make.

The point of *The New Gospel* is not that Who You Are doesn't matter, but just the opposite. Who You Are matters *so* much that each of you is utterly magnificent. The new teaching is that each of you is *so* magnificent, that not one of you is more magnificent than the other—not in the eyes of God, and not in your eyes, either, if you *look* with the eyes of God.

Because it is impossible for you to "better" someone, does that take away your reason for living?

Because you can't have a "better" religion, or a "better" political party, or a "better" economic system, does not mean you should not have any at all?

Must you know that yours will be the "better" picture before you pick up a brush and paint? Can it not be simply *another* picture? *Another* expression of beauty?

Must a rose be "better" than an iris in order to justify its existence?

I tell you this: you are all flowers in the Garden of the Gods. Shall we turn the garden under because one is no more beautiful than another? You have done exactly that. And then you lament, "Where have all the flowers gone?"

You are all notes in the Celestial Symphony. Shall we decline to play the music because one note is no more crucial than another?

But what if one note is a sour note? Does the sour note not spoil the symphony?

That depends on who is doing the listening.

I don't understand.

Have you ever heard children sing and experienced the song as beautiful, even though half the notes were off-key?

Yes. I have had exactly that experience.

And do you imagine that you are capable of an experience of which I am not?

I never thought of it that way.

And tell Me this. If a child is singing off-key, do you tell her to shut up? Is that how you imagine you will encourage her to love music, or to love herself? Or do you inspire her to even greater heights by telling her to *keep singing?*

Of course.

I have been listening to your songs for centuries. Your singing is music to My ears. Yet do you imagine that none of you has ever sung off-key?

I'm sure one or two of us has.

Here, then, is your answer.

You are My children. I listen to you sing, and I call it beautiful.

There are no "sour notes" when you sing. There is only you, My child, singing your heart out.

You are God's orchestra. It is through you that God orchestrates life itself. There are no "sour notes" when you play. There is only you, My child, playing your heart out, trying to get it right.

If I failed to see the beauty in that, I would have no soul at all.

Remember this, always:

> *The soul is that which beholds beauty even when the mind denies it.*

Oh, that's an extraordinary teaching. Oh, my gosh, what a wonderful insight.

> Therefore, in life, always see with your soul. Listen with your soul.
>
> Even now, concerning the words on the paper right before you, see them with your soul, hear them in your soul. Only then can you begin to understand them.
>
> It is your soul which sees the beauty and the wonder and the truth of My words. Your mind will deny it forever. It is as I have told you: to understand God, you must be *out of your mind.*
>
> Do not stop the symphony in which you are playing because you think you hear a sour note. Simply *change your tune.*
>
> Effective political activism does not come from anger or hatred—and *spiritual* activism never does—but rather from love. It is not a question of making someone or something wrong; it is simply a decision to exchange the present reality for a new one, out of a new thought about Who You Are, and Who You Choose to Be.

Yes, this is what I have called the New Thought Movement. Yet I still must ask my question—I guess I'm still "in my mind" about this—but does this "we are all One" New Gospel mean we may not harm a thing: may not swat a mosquito, may not trap a mouse, may not pick a weed (much less a flower)? Does it mean that we may not lead a lamb to slaughter for those delicious, tender chops?

> Is it okay to cut off your hair?
> Is it okay to cut out your heart?
> Is there any difference?

You're not answering my question. Why will You not make Your will known to me? Just tell me Your will, and it all becomes very simple for me.

> I have no will separate from your own, on this or any other matter. I have no preference other than yours.
>
> This is what so many of you cannot understand. This is what so many of you cannot abide. For if I have no separate will or preference, what should you do? How can you know what is right and what is wrong? In this, or any other, matter?
>
> And now I've gone even further. Now I've even taken away your idea of better. So now what are you to do? What now is the basis of any choice or decision?
>
> I tell you, the purpose of life is for you to decide and declare, express and fulfill, Who You Really Are. It is not for Me to tell you what is right and wrong, what is better or worse, what to do and what not to do, and for you, then, to simply decide whether or not to obey Me—and for Me, then, to reward or punish.
>
> You have tried this system, and *it does not work.* You have announced over and over again what *you* think My

will to be, but this has not helped you. You have not obeyed it.

Behold, you have declared that I am against killing, yet you continue to kill—some of you even do it *in My name!*

You have said I am against mistreatment and suppression of people, of any classes, races, or genders, yet you continue to allow it.

You have said that I am against the dishonoring of your parents, abuse of your children, ill treatment of your very Selves, yet you continue to commit it.

You have said that I am against all manner of things that you continue to do. You have not managed to change your behaviors no matter *what* you claim that I prefer or command.

You have said that I am against lying, yet you lie all the time. You have said that I am against stealing, yet you steal right and left. You have said that I am against adultery, yet you take each other's husbands and wives every day and every night.

Even your governments—those institutions you have created to protect you and care for your needs—lie to you. Indeed, you have created an entire society based on lies.

You call some of these lies "secrets," yet they are lies nonetheless, for a withholding is a lie, plain and simple. It is a failure to reveal the whole truth, to let others know all that there is to know on a subject, so that everyone can make choices based on all the data.

You have said that I am against the breaking of promises and pledges, yet you break your promises and pledges all the time, and you seek to do so with impunity, using whatever rationale allows you to justify yourself in the moment.

No, the human race has demonstrated quite clearly that My will, as you have understood and enunciated it, means nothing.

The interesting thing is that, in the end, this is perfect. Because there are so many disagreements over what My will is, you would probably do even more killing in My name if you suddenly became *fervent* in your beliefs.

I am reminded of that bumper sticker: GOD, SAVE ME FROM YOUR PEOPLE.

Yes, there is some irony in that.

And so, to your question. Is it okay to swat a mosquito? Trap a mouse? Pull a weed? Slaughter a lamb and eat it? That is for you to decide. *All* is for you to decide. And there are larger questions, of course.

Is it okay to kill a person as punishment for killing? Abort a birth? Beat a homosexual? *Be* a homosexual? Have sex before marriage? Have sex at all, if you want to be "enlightened"? And on and on and on . . .

Each day you must make your decisions. Know only that, in deciding, you are announcing and demonstrating Who You Are.

Every act is an act of self-definition.

You are getting it. You are understanding.

Because You are repeating it so much.

Repetition is good. It allows integration. So now I will repeat something else I have said before. In your daily actions and choices, you are not only announcing Who *You* Are, you are also deciding Who *I Am,* because you and I are One.

Thus, in the largest sense, I *am* answering the question. I am doing it *through you.* And that is the only way the question *can* be answered.

Out of your answer will come your truth. This is the truth of your being. It is what you are *being,* in truth.

Remember that you are a human *being. What* you are being is up to you. Although I have told this to you now many times, this is something you may not have previously seriously considered.

Okay, okay, but "Oneness" does not mean "equality," right? Can I at least get that out of You?

Oneness does not mean sameness, that is correct.

Then what *does* Oneness mean?

The question is not, What does Oneness mean? The question is, What does Oneness mean to *you?*

This is a decision that must be made within each human heart. And out of your decision will you create your future—or end it.

Yet even as you ponder this, there is guidance, there is insight, there is wisdom that has been given to you to help you—not to do what is right, because "right" is a relative term, but to get to where you say you want to go; to do what you say you want to do.

As I have noted before, as a human race, as a species, you say that you want to live together in peace and harmony; you want to create a better life for your children; you want to be happy. If on nothing else, on this all of you can agree.

And so, this guidance has been given you, and it comes in the form of The Three Points. These are, again: (1) We are all One; (2) There's enough; and (3) There's nothing we have to do.

The First Point, which we have been discussing at length here, may be more readily and easily applied when the Second and Third are understood.

And I want to keep looking at the *application* of this wisdom, at how to make it practical in everyday life, so let's get to those other points.

Nineteen

At the end of the *Conversations with God* trilogy, You made those same Three Points.

Yes, and if you understand the Second Point, *There's Enough,* you will have given yourself a big clue on how you may apply the First Point, *We are all One,* if you choose.

What does *there's enough* mean?

Exactly what it says. *There's Enough.* There's enough of everything you think you need to be happy. There's enough time, there's enough money, there's enough food, there's enough love . . . all you have to do is share it. I have given you plenty. There's enough for all of you.

When you live this truth, when you make it a functional part of your reality, there is nothing you are unwilling to share, nothing you seek to hoard—certainly not love, or food, or money.

Does that mean we ought not to gather wealth?

There is a difference between choosing to *have* something and choosing to *hoard* it. In fact, only when you know the truth that "there's enough" can you easily have any of the good things in life that you, yourself, would choose.

That's true! It was only when I finally got that there is enough for everybody that I could give myself permission to believe that there was *enough for me.* Still, I had to go on faith, because it doesn't look like there's enough for everybody.

Judge not by appearances. The reason it does not look as though there is enough for everybody is that so many people who have *more* than enough are sharing only the smallest part of what they have with those who have less.

A tiny percentage of your world's people holds a massive share of your world's wealth, and uses a colossal share of your world's resources. These holdings are wildly disproportionate—and the disproportion is growing *larger,* not smaller, every day.

"Yes, yes, yes," I can just hear some people now impatiently saying, *"you've made this point before."*

And they would be right, of course, because, as always, this dialogue is circular, curling back in upon itself. But if they are impatient, it may be because something is being said here, over and over, which they do not want to hear. Something is being observed which they do not want to see.

We are venturing again near that domain that you call "social spirituality," and many people do not want to go there. It forces them to look at things they do not want to look at.

Yet you have just made My larger point. Only you can decide how to apply the truth of Oneness. All the preaching and all the teaching in the world will not change a thing. Only when there is a change in the human heart will there be a change in the human condition.

What can cause such a change?

The question is not, "What"? The question is, "Who"? And the answer is, "You." *You can.* Right now.

Me? Now?

If not you, who? If not now, when?

An ancient question from Jewish wisdom literature.

Yes, I have been asking it for a very long time. So what is your answer?

Okay, my answer is: me, now.

From your mouth to My ears.

Remember, My child, one of the Seven Steps in creating a friendship with God is to *help God.* You have just decided to do that. Good for you. That's exactly what it will produce. Good, for you.

When you agree to spread the word, to carry the message that can change the human heart, you play an important role in changing the human condition.

This is why all spirituality is ultimately political.

But—may I argue with You a bit here?—I thought You said that there was "nothing we have to do."

I did say that, and there isn't.

So what are we talking about here? Isn't "carrying the message" something that I am doing?

No. It is something you are "being." You cannot *do* the message, but only *be* the message, for you are not a human doing, you are a human being.

You carry the message *as* you, not *with* you. You *are* the message! This is your spirituality in action. Do you not see that?

Your message is your life, *lived.* You spread the word that you *are.*

Is it not written: *And the Word was made flesh?*

Yes, but is this what that meant?

Yes.

How can I know that? I mean, for sure.

You have My word. You have My word, *in you.* You are, quite literally, the Word of God, made flesh. Now, say but the word, and your soul shall be healed. Speak the word, live the word, *be* the word.

In a word, be *God.*

Oh, my word.

Exactly. That is exactly right.

Is that where this is going? I'm supposed to be You?

You are not "supposed to be," you *are.* I'm not asking you to do anything, I'm telling you Who You Really Are.

You are already what you seek to be. *There is nothing that you have to do.* And that is the Third Point in the Holy Wisdom Trinity.

But if I go out and try to act like God, people will think that I'm crazy.

They'll think you're crazy for being totally joyful, totally loving, totally accepting, totally blessing, and totally grateful?

No. I mean, if I go out and try to *act like God.*

But that is how God acts! What *you* mean is that people will think that you're crazy if you go out and try to act the way *you think God acts.* Namely, all powerful, controlling, demanding, vengeful, and punishing.

But vengeance is Yours, sayeth You.

No, *you* sayeth that. I never sayeth that.

And so, one "acts like God" by adopting the Five Attitudes of God—not the God we imagine in our nightmares, but the God who really is—is that it?

Yes. And remember, this is not about doing, but about being. These attitudes are things you are being. And as you make these statements of being *consciously,* rather than unconsciously, you begin to live from intention; you begin to live deliberately. Remember, I have suggested that you live deliberately, harmoniously, and beneficially, and I have explained to you what it means to do so. Do you need more examples of that?

No, I think I understood that when we explored it before.

Good. But now let Me tell you a secret. Do the third, and the first two will come automatically.

Determine to live beneficially—decide that your life and work will benefit others—and you will find yourself living deliberately and harmoniously. This will be true because to live beneficially will cause you to live from intention, doing things deliberately and consciously, rather than unconsciously, and will result in your living harmoniously, because that which benefits others cannot be in disharmony with them.

Now I will give you a trio of tools with which you may be sure that your life will be lived beneficially. These are the Core Concepts of Wholistic Living:

Awareness
Honesty
Responsibility

You are giving me a lot of meat here; a lot of material. How much longer is this teaching going to go on?

All of your life, My friend. All of your life.

It's never going to be over, is it? There's never going to be a time when I can say, "I've got it," and be done with it.

There may very well be a time when you can say, "I've got it." But the moment that time arrives, you will notice that there is more to "get." This is because the more you see, the more you see that there is more to see.

Do you see?

And so, you will never stop the process of growing and getting. You cannot grow too big, you cannot grow too fast, you cannot grow too much. That is not possible. You cannot finish growing. There is no end to how big you can be.

And you do not have to worry about "getting it while the getting's good," because the getting is *always* good. All you are getting through these teachings about Life is good for you.

And yet You have said that I have nothing to learn.

True teaching is not a process by which you learn, but by which you are caused to remember.

There is nothing here that is new to you. Your soul is being startled by none of this. True teaching is never a process of putting knowledge in, but of drawing knowledge out. The real Master knows he has no greater knowledge than the student, only greater memory.

You said you wanted to know how to apply—in the real world, in everyday life, as practical, functioning truth—what you have found in our conversations to be of value. I am suggesting ways in which you may accomplish that. I am helping you get what you want. This is what it means to have a friendship with God.

Thank you. Tell me, then, about the Core Concepts.

Awareness is a state of being in which you may choose to live. It means to be awake to the moment. It is about being keenly observant about what is so, and why; about what is occurring, and why; about what can cause it not to occur, and why; about all the possible—and the most probable—outcomes of any choice or action, and what *makes* them possible and probable.

To live in awareness is to not pretend that you do not know.

Remember, I told you that there appear to be those who know, but who pretend that they do not know. Awareness is about being aware, and being aware that you are aware. It is about being aware that you are aware that you are aware, and about being aware that you are aware that you are aware that you are aware.

Awareness has many levels.

Awareness is about being aware of the level of awareness of which you are aware, and it is about being aware that there is no level of awareness of which you cannot be aware, if you are aware of that.

When you live a life of awareness, you no longer do things unconsciously. You cannot, because you are aware that you are doing something unconsciously, and that, of course, means you are doing it consciously.

It is not difficult living a life of awareness when you are aware that it is not difficult. Awareness feeds on itself.

When you are unaware of awareness, then you cannot know what it is like. You do not even know that you do not know. You have forgotten. You really do know, but you have forgotten that you know, and so you might as well not know at all. That is why remembering is so important.

This is what I am here to do. I am here to help you remember. That is what friends are for.

It is what you are doing, too, in the life of another. In the life of all others. You are here to help others remember. This is something you may have forgotten.

Once you have been made to remember, you are brought back to awareness. Once you come back to awareness, you begin to become aware of your awareness, and you are aware that you are aware.

Awareness is about noticing the moment. It is about stopping, looking, listening, feeling, experiencing fully what is happening. It is a meditation. Awareness turns everything into a meditation. Washing dishes. Making love. Cutting the grass. Saying a word out loud to another. All becomes a meditation.

What am I doing? How am I doing this? Why am I doing this? What am I being while I am doing this? Why am I being this while I am doing this?

What am I experiencing right now? How am I experiencing it? Why am I experiencing it the way I am experiencing it? What am I being while I am experiencing it? Why am I being this while I am experiencing it? What does any of this have to do with what I am experiencing? What does any of this have to do with what other people are experiencing of me?

Awareness is moving to the level of the Unobserved Observer. You are watching yourself. And then you are watching yourself watch yourself. And then you are watching yourself watch yourself watching yourself. Finally, there is no one watching you watch yourself. You have become the Unobserved Observer.

That is Full Awareness.

It is easy. It is not as difficult or as complicated as it sounds. It is about stopping, looking, listening, feeling. It is about knowing, and knowing that you know. It is about ending the pretending.

Now you are really tending to business. You are tending

to yourself. In the past, you were doing what you did *before* you were tending. You could call that pretending.

This is remarkable. I have never heard anything like this.

Yes, you have. This is what The Buddha taught. This is what Krishna taught. This is what Jesus taught. This is what every Master who ever lived, and who lives now, has taught. There is nothing new here, there is nothing that is startling your soul.

When you stop pre-tending, you become totally honest. Honesty is the second tool. Honesty is about saying, first to yourself, then to others, what it is of which you are aware.

Honesty is what you stand for. You are no longer taking things lying down, but standing for something. You may have noticed that you cannot stand for something until you stop lying all around. This is why it said that when you are totally honest, you are truly upstanding.

In *Conversations with God, book 2,* the Five Levels of Truth Telling are listed, and it is explained how those five levels can result in a life of total visibility, or what is also called transparency. These two words stand in interesting juxtaposition to each other. To be totally visible is to be utterly transparent. That is, people can see right through you. There are no hidden agendas. The more visible you become, the more transparent you are.

Use the tool of honesty consistently, and watch your life change. Use it in relationships. Use it in business interactions. Use it in your politics. Use it in school. Use it everywhere, all the time.

> Be aware of what you have done, and then be honest about it. Be honest about the outcomes you know very well that you have produced. Then choose to take responsibility for them. This is the third tool. It is a sign of great maturity, great spiritual growth.
>
> You will never want to do this, however, as long as your society equates responsibility with punishment. Too often in the past, taking responsibility has meant "taking a fall." But responsibility does not mean guilt. Rather, it means a willingness to do whatever you can to make the outcomes you produce the best they can possibly be, and to do what it takes to remedy whatever can be remedied, should others choose to experience the outcomes as damaging in any way.

Some people have chosen to walk a path that says, "Each person is responsible for his own outcomes, since we are all creating our own reality, therefore, I am not responsible for what happens to you, even though I may have caused it." This is what I call a *New Age bypass.* It is an attempt to twist the logic of the New Thought Movement, which proclaims that every human being is a creator.

> Yet I tell you this: you are each responsible for each other. You are, truly, your brother's keeper. And when you understand this, all the misery, all the sorrow, all the pain of the human experience will disappear.
>
> You will then create a New Society, based on The New Gospel, WE ARE ALL ONE, and supported by the Core Concepts: awareness, honesty, responsibility.

There will be no other laws, no other rules or regulations. There will be no legislation, and no need for legislation. For you will have learned at last that *you cannot legislate morality.*

Your schools will teach these Core Concepts. The entire curriculum will be built around them. Subjects such as reading, writing and arithmetic will be taught through them.

Your worldwide economy will reflect these Core Concepts. The entire infrastructure will be built around them. Activities such as buying, trading, and selling will be guided by them.

Your self-governance will support these Core Concepts. The entire bureaucracy will be built around them. Departments such as public service, justice, and resource management and distribution will be administered according to them.

Your religions will support these Core Concepts. The entire spiritual belief system will be built around them. Experiences such as unconditional love, unlimited sharing, and emotional and physical healing will be possible because of them.

You will have come to know, at last, that it is impossible to avoid responsibility for the experience of another, for there *is* no "other." There is only You, expressing in a multiplicity of forms.

Because of this knowingness, everything will change. The shift will be so dramatic, so pervasive, and so complete that the world as you now experience it will seem like a nightmare that has finally ended. And, indeed, you will have truly awakened.

The time of your awakening is at hand. The moment of your renewal, of your re-creation, is upon you. You are about to re-create yourself anew in the next grandest version of the greatest vision ever you held about Who You Are.

This is the agenda of your worldwide society in the new millennium. You, yourself, have set this agenda. You have called it forth. You have already set it into motion. Human beings everywhere are moving into alignment with it. They are joining hands in this re-creation. East is meeting west. Whites are embracing people of color. Religions are merging, governments are adapting, economies are expanding. In everything, you are moving to a global approach, adopting a global perspective, creating a global system.

There will be chaos before the shift. This is natural in advance of any shift of this proportion. For you are not merely changing your way of doing things, you are shifting your whole idea of Who You Are, as a person, as a collection of nations, as a species. And so, there will be chaos, created largely by those who do not want to make the shift, who cannot accept the end of "better" and The New Gospel of Oneness. There will also be those who are simply afraid that such a change will produce a loss of control over one's whole life, a surrendering of personal and national identity. None of these outcomes will occur.

The shift will not mean the disappearance of ethnic or national or cultural distinctions. It will not mean the dishonoring of traditions, or the disowning of heritage, or the disassembling of families, tribes, or communities. On the contrary, the shift will produce a strengthening of those ties as you come to realize that you can experience them without having to do so at the expense of another.

The shift will not mean the end of that which makes you different, but only the end of that which makes you divided. Differences and divisions are not the same thing.

Differences confirm, and make possible, your experience of Who You Are. Divisions confuse, and render impossible that experience. Without the differences between here and there, up and down, fast and slow, hot and cold, none of these things could be experienced. Yet there is no *division* between here and there, up and down, fast and slow, hot and cold. These are merely different versions of the same thing. Similarly, there are no *divisions* between black and white, male and female, Christian and Muslim. These are merely different versions of the same thing.

When you see this, then you, too, will have made the shift. You will have become part of the New Society, in which you honor diversity, but not division.

You do not have to disappear as an individual in order to experience Oneness. That is the great fear, of course. The great fear is that Oneness will mean sameness, and that that which separates you from The Whole will disappear. Thus, *you* will disappear. And so, the struggle against Oneness is a struggle for survival.

Yet Oneness will not put an end to your survival as an individual expression of The Whole. Rather, it will allow it.

Right now, you are killing each other out of your love for yourself and your beliefs, and your hatred of others and theirs. You have it constructed that in order to survive as an individual person, race, religion or nation, you have to make sure that no one else survives. This is your myth, called Survival of the Fittest.

Living The New Gospel of Oneness, you will not have to fight for survival, but will guarantee it by *not* fighting for it. This simple solution, which has so long evaded you, will change everything.

You will stop fighting for survival the day you realize that you cannot *fail* to survive. You will stop killing each other the day you realize that there *is* no "other."

Life is eternal, and there is only One of Us.

These two truths render pointless virtually everything you have done in your life. When understood, they will transform your life, turning it into a glorious expression of the grandest version of the greatest vision ever you held about Who You Are.

Life is eternal, and there is only One of Us.

These two truths summarize everything, and change everything.

Life is eternal, and there is only One of Us.

These two truths are all you will ever need to know.

Twenty

What does it mean to have a friendship with God? It means having wisdom such as this at your fingertips. Any time, anyplace, anywhere.

It means never wondering, ever again, what to do, how to be, where to go, when to act, or why to love. All the questions disappear when you have a friendship with God, because I will bring you all the answers.

In truth, I will not bring you any answers at all, but simply show you that you have brought them with *you* when you came into this life; that you have had them all along. I will show you how to call them forth, how to have them radiate from your being in the space of any problem, any challenge, any difficulty, so that, in fact, problems, challenges, and difficulties are no longer part of your life, but will be replaced by simple experiences.

To the outer world it may very well appear as if nothing, in fact, has changed. And, in actual fact, nothing *may* have changed. You may continue to be confronted with the same conditions. Only you will sense the difference. Only you will notice the shift. It will be an experience of your inner world—yet it will begin to affect your outer world as well. And while others may not see a change in your conditions, they will see a change in *you*. They will wonder about this change. They will marvel at it. And eventually, they will inquire about it.

What will I tell them?

Tell them the truth. The truth shall set them free. Tell them that nothing has changed in your outer world. You still have toothaches. You still have bills to pay. You still put your pants on one leg at a time.

Tell them that you still face conditions you once described as less than perfect, you still confront all the rough and tumble encounters of life. Tell them that nothing has changed but your experience.

What does that mean? I don't know what that means.

What do you understand the word "experience" to mean?

Well, the Random House Dictionary of the English Language defines "experience" as "the totality of the cognitions given by perception; all that is perceived, understood, and remembered."

Good. And so, when you know life's great truths, what changes is the totality of your cognitions. Your experience includes all that is "perceived, understood, and remembered." That is the important word: *"remembered."*

In short, your experience changes when you *remember, totally,* Who You Really Are.

I am here to help you remember. You are here to help others remember. As you remember, you re-*member*—that is, become a Member Once Again of the Body of God. You become One with All That Is, though the part of you that expresses the Whole in a specific individuation does not disappear, but, quite to the contrary, appears more gloriously than ever before.

When your individual expression is that glorious, others may call you God, or the Son of God, or The Buddha, the Enlightened One, the Master, the Holy One—or, even, the Savior.

And you *will* be a savior, come to save everyone else from forgetfulness, from not remembering their Oneness, from acting as if they were separate from one another.

You will spend your life working to end this illusion of separateness. And you will join with others who are doing so also.

You have been waiting for these others. You have been waiting for them to show up in your life, to make themselves known to you. Now you have found each other, and you are no longer alone in this work.

This is what it means to have a friendship with God. It means to no longer be alone.

So now, as you go about your day-to-day life, know and understand that nothing is ever going to be the same. Your friendship with Me has changed everything. It has brought you My partnership and My love, My wisdom and My awareness.

You will now be aware, and you will be aware that you are aware. You will walk in wakefulness. You will grok in fullness.

Except when you do not.

There may be times when you will slip back into forgetfulness; when you imagine your Self to be other than Who You Really Are. At those times, in particular, use our new friendship. Call on My name, and I will be there. I will show you to your answers, I will lead you to your wisdom, *I will give you back to yourself.*

This, then, do for all others. Give people back to themselves. This is your assignment, this is your mission, this is your purpose.

And through their friendship with you will they come to know that they have a friendship with God.

Twenty-One

My story ends here, for now. It is June 29, 1999, at 6:25 in the morning. I have been up since 2:30 A.M., in my cozy office in my wonderful home in the rolling hills outside of Ashland, Oregon, finishing this book. I have been looking to see what would come through to bring it to an end. That last chapter did it for me. There is nothing more to say. All of it is here. All of it is clear. When you are aware, and when you are aware that you are aware, there is nothing more to ask.

I'll leave my personal narrative where I began it in *Conversations with God, book 1.* From the campground near Ashland, I went back to "real life." But I wanted to make a *life* this time, rather than just a *living.* This was the source of much of my sadness during the years before writing the first *Conversations with God* book, before writing my angry letter to God. This was the source of much of my unhappiness in relationships. I have since learned two important questions to ask in life: Where am I going? Who is going with me? I have also learned never to transpose those questions again; never to ask the second one first, and then change the first to suit the second.

Now I have a wonderful life, I am blessed with my wonderful wife, Nancy, and with wonderful friends. And my most wonderful friend of all is God.

I do have a friendship with God, and I use it every day. That's what friends are for—to be used. That's what God loves us to do. God says, "Use Me." Those are the two magic words. Those are the words that will change your life. When you hear God say those words, your life will change. And when others hear *you* say those words, your life will change.

Those words are even more powerful than "I love you." Because when you say "Use me," you are saying "I love you"—and a great deal more. You're saying "I love you," and "I'm going to show you right now."

This is what God says. This is what God says all the time.

I am sure that this statement is difficult to accept for people who have suffered trauma and injury and deep wounds in their lives. Yet I promise you, it's true. Even our darkest moments are gifts. That is what every Master has taught us, and either it is so, or every Master has been lying to us. I don't think The Buddha was a liar. I don't think Jesus was into fibbing. I don't think Mohammed was pulling our leg.

I think that salvation from the slings and arrows of outrageous fortune lies in our beingness. To be, or not to be, that is the question. To be Who We Really Are, or to be something less than that. That is the choice.

What God has given us in this dialogue will change our lives, and can change the world. This is powerful stuff. So share it. Give it away. Go out and preach The New Gospel.

Do not ignore the opportunities that present themselves every day to share this message. Yet remember that the most effective way to share it is to *be* it. I choose now to dedicate the rest of my life to that *being*. I invite you to do the same.

My wonderful and glorious children, My new friends, all . . .

Yours has been a difficult and challenging path. Yet now you have found your way home. You have overcome obstacles, met challenges, healed injuries, resolved conflicts, removed blockages, asked questions, and heard your own answers, in your efforts to return to Me. Your work is now over. Your joy has just begun.

Let it be your joy now to return others to Me, to show others the way home, to give others back to themselves. For that is where home is, and that is where I am—living in the hearts, and as the souls, of every member of the Body of God.

Go home to your own heart, and you will find Me there. Unite again with your own soul, and you will unite again with Me.

Have faith, for I tell you that you and I can be different, but we cannot be divided. Go, then, and end the division among *you*. Celebrate your differences, yet end your divisions, and join in the unified expression of the one truth: I Am All There Is.

Have hope, for My love for you will never end, nor will it ever know a limitation, or a condition of any kind.

Have love, then, for each other, as an expression of Me.

In your decision to be an expression of God will you

be glorified. In your choice to experience your unity with God and with all things will you be Self-realized. In your determination to know the truth will you show the truth, indeed. Not merely in thought, not merely in word, but indeed.

You have been deeded a place in the Kingdom of Heaven, and in the heart of God. These are your deeds. And when they are reflected in your deeds, you will have become a Master, indeed.

And know this: mastery is where you are headed. It is where you have said that you've wished to go, and it is therefore, where I am leading you, and where I invite you to lead each other.

Have now a friendship with God, and cause others to know that in their friendship with you, *they* have a friendship with God, for you and I are One, and thus, you are the God they would befriend.

They, too, are the God *you* would befriend. You cannot experience having a friendship with God if you do not have a friendship with each other—because I *am* the "other." There is no "other," other than Me. When you know this, you know the greatest secret. It is time now to go out and live that secret. Live it with faith, share it with hope, demonstrate it with love.

Especially, go now and live your love, and do not merely speak of it. For if you speak in the tongues of men and of angels, but have not love, you are but a clanging cymbal. And if you have prophetic powers, and understand all mysteries and all knowledge, and if you have all faith, so as to remove mountains, but have not love, you are not expressing the grandest version of the greatest vision ever you held about Who You Are.

Love is patient and kind; love is not jealous or boastful; it is not arrogant or rude. Love does not insist on its own way; it is not irritable or resentful; it does not rejoice at wrong, for it knows that there is no such thing as right and wrong. Love bears all things, knows all things, endures all things, embraces all things, yet forgives nothing, for love knows that nothing and no one needs to be forgiven.

Love never ends. As for your prophecies, they will pass away; as for your tongues, they will cease; as for your knowledge, it will grow, and change. For your knowledge now is imperfect, yet when you realize at last that all is perfection, imperfect knowledge will pass away, as will your calling imperfect anything in your life.

When you were a child, you spoke as a child, you thought as a child, you reasoned as a child. But now you have grown in spirit, and have given up childish ways. Then you saw in a mirror dimly, but now, face to face, for we are now friends. Then you knew in part, now you understand fully, even as you are fully understood. That is what it means to have a friendship with God.

I leave these pages now, but not your heart and never your soul. I cannot leave your soul, because I *am* your soul. Your soul is made of what I Am. Go, then, My soul partner, and live in faith, hope, and love, these three; yet know that the greatest of these . . . is love.

Spread it, share it, *be* it, wherever you are, and yours will be a light that can truly light the world.

I love you, you know that?

I know you do. And I love you.

In Closing . . .

As always when finishing one of these dialogues, I am struck now by the wealth of wisdom with which the human race has been gifted. Not just here, but in many other books and through many other sources, God is talking with us all the time. It is clear to me that all of our problems on this planet could be solved *if we only listened.*

I want to put into action the wisdom that we are all being given. That is why I have taken the liberty, in the final words of each of my books, to recommend ways in which we can all become more involved, in which we can all participate at the next level, in putting our spirituality into action.

The first step in putting your own spirituality into action is to get in touch with it. For many people this is not only the first step, but the biggest one—because for many people, the question is, "How do I do that?" I asked that question here, in this book. Perhaps you recall God's response:

> Spend a few moments each day embracing your experience of Me. Do this now, when you do not have to, when

> life circumstances do not seem to require you to. Now, when it seems that you do not even have time to. Now, when you are not feeling alone. So that when you are "alone," you will know that you are not. Cultivate the habit of joining Me in Divine Connection once each day. Once you have made that connection, you will never want to lose it, for it will bring you the greatest joy you ever had.

There are many ways to do this, and, as is pointed out repeatedly in this dialogue, there is no one way that is the right way, or the best way. One method that I have found to be effective for many people, myself included, and that I have personally investigated, is *Dahnhak*. It is a disciplined, scientific approach to connecting with the Creator Within, devised and taught by Grand Master Seung Heun Lee through his 230 Dahn Centers in Korea, the United States, and elsewhere.

Throughout the history of humankind many wise men and women have taught us that we are indeed One, that we are inseparable from one another, and that something that affects a part of us affects us all. Although we have received this message repeatedly, the question remains, How do we make this wisdom truly ours? How can we "feel" the truth of this Oneness, instead of just "knowing" it on a superficial level? *Dahn* is one answer.

Dahn is a comprehensive, holistic exercise that involves calisthenics, deep stretching, meditation, breathing techniques, and other processes that sensitize oneself to the *Ki,* also known in some cultures as *Chi,* or Life Energy that permeates us all. Once you feel this energy, you can use it to not only attain physical health, but to connect yourself to the universal energy and achieve a spiritual awakening in which this sense of Oneness is imprinted into every single cell of your being.

Dahn is simple, easy, and profound. If you are interested in learning more about this practice, you may find the Dahn Center nearest you by calling 1-877-DAHNHAK.

There are many other forms of physical and mental practice that are worthy of your investigation as well, and it is really not possible to go astray with any one of them—as long as you are serious about using them, and committed at a deep level to now becoming not only a seeker, but a bringer of the light to our world. For we must do more now than merely concern ourselves with our own lives. These practices and disciplines are about connecting your body to your consciousness, they are about connecting "doingness" to "beingness," and raising individual and group awareness.

In the past we have tried to alter our collective experience solely by encouraging a change in the things we are doing, and that has not worked. Our species is still acting pretty much the way it was acting a thousand years ago. I believe that this is because we have been seeking to change behaviors, rather than the consciousness which creates them.

My ongoing dialogue with God repeatedly makes the point that there is nothing we have to do; that "doingness" is not where the solution lies. It lies, rather, in *beingness.*

What is the difference between "beingness" and "doingness," and how can we translate that to our work-a-day world? That is the subject of an extraordinary booklet that came through me as a result of my confronting this very issue. I wanted to find a way to live in the real world as God was inviting me to. I wanted to turn God's wonderful wisdom about being into some practical application. I knew "beingness" was an idea that could change the world, yet I didn't know how to apply it.

Then it came through me, in one weekend, during which I felt nearly obsessed. All I could do was write, and out came a booklet called *Bringers of the Light.* It provides real-world answers to one of modern life's most important questions—how to find right livelihood, how to make a *life,* rather than a living. We all have to spring ourselves free from the day-to-day "doingness" trap if we are ever to become, as God invites us to become, "a light that can truly light the world."

ReCreation, the non-profit foundation that Nancy and I formed to continue spreading the message of this dialogue, has published this little booklet, and I hope that every person who has ever wondered how to move from doingness to beingness in their life will read it. We named the foundation ReCreation out of our understanding of the purpose of life: to re-create yourself anew in the grandest version of the greatest vision ever you held about Who You Are.

Once you engage this process, you will find yourself wanting to do something for the rest of humanity. It's only natural. It's what follows. And one way we can be of service is by bringing our spirituality to the political arena. Now, I know there are some people who believe that spirituality and politics do not mix. Yet God says in this book, "Your political viewpoint *is* your spirituality, demonstrated."

I am very clear that this is true. That is why I've searched for years to find a political party or movement based soundly on spiritual, life-affirming principles. To put it bluntly, I needed a reason to vote. I could not find much of what I was looking for in our traditional political parties. Then I read a paradigm-shifting book by Robert Roth. If you are in the place that I have been—a place of searching and of losing hope—I promise you that this book will show you an exciting way to turn your spiritual truth into practical political action.

Mr. Roth's book is titled *A Reason to Vote.* It is a must-read, even if you are not "interested in politics." *Especially* if you are not interested in politics. The reason you haven't been is probably that you haven't resonated with what politicians are doing. Politics have not provided you with any real way to express who *you* are. You have not had *a reason to vote.*

Now you will.

Marianne Williamson says, "As the power of the spirit rises within us, so does our desire to be of service to the world." Her stunning book, *Healing the Soul of America,* shows us what needs to be done, and how we can do it. Its insights apply not only here, but everywhere on Earth.

Marianne and I have cofounded the Global Renaissance Alliance, linking people around the globe in Citizen Circles committed to using spiritual principles and social action to change the world. This is the most exciting transcontinental, spiritual-political movement of which I am aware, and numbers among its board of directors Deepak Chopra, Wayne Dyer, Thom Hartmann, Jean Houston, Barbara Marx Hubbard, Thomas Moore, Carolyn Myss, James Redfield, Gary Zukav, and others. All of us are teaming together, and we hope that you will join our team. To learn more about this truly spectacular initiative, contact:

Global Renaissance Alliance
P.O. Box 15712
Washington, D.C. 20003
Telephone 541-890-4716
e-mail: *office@renaissancealliance.org*
on the web at www.renaissancealliance.org

There are many other ways to put into action the specific messages and wisdom that we have been given in these extraordinary conversations with God. Doing so is a great desire of my life, and I know that many people feel the same way. If you are among them, I invite you contact our foundation, asking for information about *CWG In Action.*

This is a new program that includes a Wisdom Circle (groups throughout the country which help answer the three hundred letters a week we receive with questions about the material), a Crisis Response Team (volunteers who supply us with information from their community, and in some cases act as lay counselors to people who call us when in spiritual crisis), and a Resource Network (connecting people from all over the world who are working on spiritual and human betterment projects and ideas).

Upon request, you'll be sent a one-sheet description of the program, and how you can join with us in this, and our other efforts—not the least of which is the founding of a new school based on my conversations with God, and the invitation I received on page 126.

The curriculum at the Heartlight School will be built around the three Core Concepts given us in this ongoing dialogue: Awareness, Honesty, Responsibility. It will lead children to experience, and further develop, *in a natural way,* the understandings that already reside within them. We intend to give children plenty of knowledge—we'll help each child achieve academic excellence in a loving, caring environment—and also lead them to their own inner wisdom.

Wisdom is knowledge applied.

Heartlight School will teach our children to invent our future, rather than repeat our past. It will provide them with the *information* they need to survive in our world, but not the *direction* historically given them that encourages them—in some cultures *requires* them—to duplicate old ways of living. We anticipate that Heartlight Schools will be opened in cities across the planet when word of what we are doing—and how we are doing it—begins to spread.

Finally, there are many people who, having read the material in the *CWG* series, are deeply touched by this experience and yearn for it to continue. If you wish to "stay connected," an excellent way to do so is through our newsletter, *Conversations.* Each issue contains a lengthy reader's forum, in which we show people how they can apply God's messages to their daily lives, and answer some of the most probing questions I've ever had about the material. The letter also contains information on opportunities to expand their experience of this energy, including God's Pen Pals, our five-day Re-creating Yourself retreats, the Books for Friends program, and other activities of the foundation. Subscriptions to the newsletter may be had by sending $35 for 12 issues ($45 for addresses outside the United States). Scholarship subscriptions are available.

For information on *Bringers of the Light, CWG In Action,* the

Heartlight School, or the *Conversations* newsletter, the address of our foundation is:

The ReCreation Foundation
PMB 1150
1257 Siskiyou Blvd.
Ashland, OR 97520
Telephone 541-482-8806
e-mail: *Recreating@aol.com*
on the web at www.conversationswithgod.org

Whether you read any of these books, or extend the impact of your vision for the world through the work of any of these organizations, I hope that you will join in partnership with me in spreading The New Gospel.

Should you do so, you will be helping to produce a fundamental shift in our collective consciousness. This shift can produce a change in our religious, political, economic, educational, and social values of such proportion that it could herald a golden age. For as all people develop a new consciousness about God, they will develop a new relationship *with* God, abandoning at last the notion of a vengeful, retributive, untouchable, and unknowable deity, and developing a working, functional *friendship with God.*

Powerful as this will be, of even greater importance will be where that new friendship will take us: not only to an experiential awareness of our deep connection with the Creator, but also of our essential Oneness with all living things. That, in turn, will bring an end to the belief that has produced so much misery in our lives: the belief that one of us, or one *group* of us, is somehow better than another.

This book sends a huge message about that. I hope you will join with me now in spreading that message. Join with me in this partnership, so that in the twenty-first century—and earlier, rather than later—we will see religious leaders, political figures, educators, and social scientists of every persuasion accepting God's invitation, and proclaiming:

"Ours is not a better way, ours is merely another way."

This single, startling statement will change the world.

We are talking here about altering our entire cultural story, changing forever our collectively held idea of what is true about human beings, and how things are with us.

Our oldest and most far-reaching story is the story of separation. In this story, we have imagined ourselves to be separate from God, and therefore separate from each other. Out of this story of separation has come our need for competition, for if we are separate from each other, then we are each on our own—each person, each culture, each nation—and must vie with each other for limited resources.

From this misunderstanding we have generated the idea of "better." Because if we are competing with each other, we must have a *reason* to declare that *our* claim on food, land, resources, and rewards of one kind or another is the claim that should be honored. That reason, we tell ourselves, is that we are "better." We *deserve* to win.

This judgment about our relative goodness has allowed us to justify the actions we felt were necessary in order to produce the win. Yet it is what we have done when we have imagined ourselves to be "better" that has set the stage not for victory, but for defeat.

This is the human tragedy. In the name of our "betterness," we have "ethnically cleansed" entire nations. We have claimed prerogatives and hoarded resources. We have dominated those we've labeled as inferior, condemning them to lives of quiet desperation.

All of this has happened because people have believed they have a "better" way of approaching God, a "better" method of governing, a "better" economic system, or a "better" reason for claiming land. Yet the message of the *CWG* books is clear. No one is better. We are *One.* And we cannot have peace on Earth until we learn to speak with one voice. That voice must be the voice of reason, the voice of compassion, the voice of love. It is the voice of divinity within us.

I know that our *Conversations with God* can produce a *Friendship with God* so wonderful that we will ultimately experience *Communion with God,* allowing us to speak with a Single Voice at last.

And that Voice shall be heard across the land—on Earth, as it is in Heaven.

Index